Youth Justice in Context

Drawing on the international literature and original empirical research from Northern Ireland and the Republic of Ireland, *Youth Justice in Context* examines the influence of legislative, organizational, policy and practice issues in shaping what constitutes compliance and how non-compliance is responded to when supervising young offenders in the community. It also addresses the impact of adolescent developmental immaturity and social and personal circumstances in mediating expectations of compliance.

A central concern of the book is to explore the manner in which compliance changes over time through the dynamics that arise in the supervisory relationship between practitioners and young people, and against the backdrop of the social and psychological changes that occur in adolescents' lives as they move towards early adulthood. A detailed examination is provided based on the perspectives of probation and youth justice professionals operating across different organizational contexts, and of young people subject to community supervision. To this end, the book offers in-depth analysis on the strategies employed by practitioners in promoting compliance and responding to non-compliance. It also provides unique insights into young people's perceptions of the supervision process, their motivations to comply, and their perspectives on desistance from offending.

This book offers an alternative perspective to policies and practices that focus primarily on stringent enforcement and control measures in responding to non-compliance. *Youth Justice in Context* is suited to academics, researchers, students, policy makers, social workers, probation officers, youth justice workers, social care workers and other practitioners working with young people in the criminal justice system.

Mairéad Seymour is a senior lecturer at the Dublin Institute of Technology. Her research interests include youth crime and justice, comparative youth justice, offender compliance and community sanctions.

Routledge Frontiers of Criminal Justice

1. **Sex Offenders, Punish, Help, Change or Control?**
   Theory, policy and practice explored
   Edited by Jo Brayford, Francis Cowe and John Deering

2. **Building Justice in Post-Transition Europe**
   Processes of criminalisation within Central and Eastern European societies
   Edited by Kay Goodall, Margaret Malloch and Bill Munro

3. **Technocrime, Policing and Surveillance**
   Edited by Stéphane Leman-Langlois

4. **Youth Justice in Context**
   Community, compliance and young people
   Mairéad Seymour

Youth Justice in Context

Community, compliance and young people

Mairéad Seymour

Routledge
Taylor & Francis Group
LONDON AND NEW YORK

First published 2013
by Routledge
2 Park Square, Milton Park, Abingdon, Oxfordshire OX14 4RN

Simultaneously published in the USA and Canada
by Routledge
711 Third Avenue, New York, NY 10017

First issued in paperback 2014

Routledge is an imprint of the Taylor & Francis Group, an informa company

British Library Cataloguing in Publication Data
A catalogue record for this book is available from the British Library

Library of Congress Cataloging in Publication Data
Seymour, Mairéad.
Youth justice in context : community, compliance and young people /
by Mairéad Seymour.
p. cm. – (Routledge frontiers of criminal justice)
1. Juvenile justice, Administration of–Ireland. 2. Juvenile justice, Administration
of–Northern Ireland. 3. Juvenile delinquency–Ireland. 4. Juvenile delinquency–Northern
Ireland. I. Title.
HV9148.A5S493 2012
364.3609415–dc23 2012008336

ISBN 13: 978-0-415-66792-0 (hbk)
ISBN 13: 978-0-415-62842-6 (pbk)

Typeset in Times New Roman
by Cenveo Publisher Services

Contents

Acknowledgements

The research on which this book is based was made possible through funding provided by the Supporting Academic Research Achievement (SARA) fund at the Dublin Institute of Technology (DIT). I am very thankful to the external reviewers who saw potential in this project and to the Directorate of Research and Enterprise for providing the opportunity. Most sincere thanks to staff and management at the Probation Service in the Republic of Ireland, the Irish Youth Justice Service, the Probation Board for Northern Ireland, and the Youth Justice Agency for so generously sharing their time and expertise with me. In particular, I would like to acknowledge the role of Young Persons' Probation officers, and senior officers, who went over and above the call of duty in facilitating the research with young people. Additional information and statistics were provided by the Probation Service, the Probation Board and the Youth Justice Agency and I am thankful to the staff who collated this data. My thanks are also due to An Garda Síochána, the Police Service for Northern Ireland, and to a number of youth justice policy and academic experts who informed the research in a variety of ways. A special word of thanks is reserved for the young people whose perspectives were so central to this book.

I am very grateful to Ben Meehan, Nvivo trainer and consultant, who provided superb instruction and advice at each stage of the data analysis phases. I am indebted to Matt Bowden, Michelle Butler, Brian Dack, Laura Duncan, Ruairí Gogan, Ann-Marie Halpenny, Sylda Langford, Aideen McLaughlin, David O'Mahony, Roisin Muldoon, and Suzanne Shaw who gave invaluable advice and feedback on various chapters. Any mistakes that remain are the author's responsibility. The excellent work completed by Toni Owens in transcribing the interviews and focus groups made the process of interpreting the data a far more manageable task. My deepest gratitude is due to Toni for her remarkable commitment to this project, for providing detailed comment and recommendations on the entire manuscript, and for being a constant source of support and encouragement to me throughout the writing process. I would also like to acknowledge Sinéad Freeman whose editorial input at the final stages helped enormously in getting this book to the finishing line. To my colleagues at the Department of Social Sciences, thank you for providing a supportive environment, and for the welcome distraction of some good-natured banter. I wish to pay tribute to the library staff at DIT Mountjoy Square for their exceptional assistance and to the technical team, especially Geraldine Donohoe, for keeping the wheels oiled. Thanks also to Nicola Hartley at Routledge for her advice and assistance along the way.

At the early stages of this current project, I was fortunate to have been selected to participate in a programme that explored the theme of marginalized youth with colleagues working in the youth justice area in Ireland and Northern Ireland. I am very grateful to the programme sponsors, the Irish Institute at the Center for Irish Programs, Boston College, and the U.S. Department of State, Bureau of Educational and Cultural Affairs for the opportunities afforded through this programme, and to my fellow programme participants whose points of view were so helpful in challenging and developing my thinking in the area. Last and by no means least, I would like to express my heartfelt thanks to my family and friends for their unfailing support throughout this process, most especially to my husband Con who kept it all in perspective.

List of abbreviations

AA	Alcoholics Anonymous
ACE	Assessment, Case Management and Evaluation
ADAS	American Drugs and Alcohol Survey
ADHD	Attention Deficit Hyperactivity Disorder
ASBO	Anti-Social Behaviour Order
CAQDAS	Computer Aided Qualitative Data Analysis System
CCTS	Criminal Case Tracking System
CHS	Children's Hearing System
CPT	European Committee for the Prevention of Torture and Inhuman or Degrading Treatment or Punishment
CYPU	Children and Young People's Unit
DCYA	Department of Children and Youth Affairs
DOJ	Department of Justice (in Northern Ireland)
DPP	Director of Public Prosecution
ECS	Extended Custodial Sentence
ICS	Indeterminate Custodial Sentence
IEP	Incentives and Earned Privileges
ISSP	Intensive Supervision and Surveillance Programmes
JJCO	Juvenile Justice Centre Order
MacCAT-CA	MacArthur Competence Assessment Tool-Criminal Adjudication
MacJEN	MacArthur Judgment Evaluation
NAPO	National Association of Probation Officers
NDPB	Non Departmental Public Body
NIO	Northern Ireland Office
NIPS	Northern Ireland Prison Service
OMCYA	Office of the Minister for Children and Youth Affairs
PBNI	Probation Board for Northern Ireland
PPS	Public Prosecution Service
PSNI	Police Service for Northern Ireland
RYDS	Rochester Youth Development Study
UNCRC	United Nations Convention on the Rights of the Child
YCJA	Youth Criminal Justice Act

YJA	Youth Justice Agency
YLS/CMI	Youth Level of Service / Case Management Inventory
YOC	Young Offenders Centre
YOT	Youth Offending Team
YPP	Young Persons' Probation

To Seán

1 Introduction

In the opening sections of his influential work on theorizing compliance, Bottoms (2001: 89) differentiates between what is termed 'short-term requirement compliance' and 'longer-term legal compliance'. The former describes offenders' compliance with the legal requirements of community penalties, while the latter refers to compliance with the criminal law by not reoffending within a specific time period. The book adopts this definition in locating contemporary theoretical perspectives on compliance in the social and developmental context of young people's lives. Drawing on the perspectives of young people and professionals, an in-depth analysis of the processes underpinning compliance for young offenders on supervised community disposals is presented. To this end, the book explores change in young people's attitudes to compliance over time through the dynamics that occur in the supervisory relationship, as well as the social and psychological changes that occur in adolescents' lives as they move towards early adulthood. It also examines how professionals' perceptions of what constitutes compliance, and the strategies employed to promote compliance and respond to non-compliance, are shaped by the interactions that take place with young people during the supervision process, as well as by the broader legal, organizational, policy and practice settings within which they operate. Adopting a broader lens, the book demonstrates that compliance is socially and legally constructed within the parameters that govern the operation and implementation of community supervision within and between jurisdictions, leading to different outcomes and criminal justice responses to non-compliance, for young people in conflict with the law.

Setting the context

The empirical foundation of this book is informed by three main sources: (1) practitioners involved in supervising young people in the community; (2) youth justice managers and policy makers; and (3) young people supervised on community disposals (see Table 1.1). As the purpose of the enquiry was also to explore how offender (non)compliance on community supervision is interpreted and addressed in different contexts, the research was based in Northern Ireland and the Republic of Ireland and took place between June 2010 and

February 2011. The youth justice systems in Northern Ireland and the Republic of Ireland have embarked, to varying degrees, on processes of review and reform in recent years and while some similarities are shared, key differences exist in the ethos, laws, policies and approaches underpinning practice in the two jurisdictions. Each of the three organizations tasked with supervising young offenders on statutory orders in the two locations participated in the study. These consisted of Young Persons' Probation (YPP), a specialist division of the Probation Service in the Republic of Ireland, the Probation Board for Northern Ireland (PBNI) and the Youth Justice Agency (YJA) in Northern Ireland. Focus groups were facilitated with practitioners in each organization in a number of cities and towns across both jurisdictions to ensure sufficient urban/rural diversity in the sample.[1] Typically, groups consisted of five to six participants and lasted 90–120 minutes. The discussion centred on practitioners' perspectives on young people's compliance with community supervision and the role of the supervisory relationship in supporting compliance and responding to non-compliance. In all, 33 practitioners took part and there was an even representation from each of the three organizations. The 'newness' of youth justice as a specialism in both jurisdictions meant that with some exceptions, the majority of participants had been recruited into youth justice work in the previous 5–10 years or less in some cases, and all were qualified in the areas of social work, youth and community work or education (see also Chapter 5). Perhaps reflecting the gendered nature of youth justice work, females accounted for just under three-quarters of the sample group. The dearth of criminological investigation in the Irish context has been previously documented (Kilcommins *et al.* 2004) and a lack of empirical enquiry extends to the area of youth justice research. In an effort to illuminate the context within which youth justice has evolved in both jurisdictions, and more specifically to ascertain the extent to which differences exist in the approaches and policies adopted in responding to young people on community supervision, a number of interviews were conducted with individuals who held managerial responsibility within YPP, PBNI and the YJA, and with others who had current or previous involvement in youth justice policy making.

The other main dimension of the study – based in the Republic of Ireland only – consisted of an in-depth exploration of young people's perceptions of the events and processes that occurred within, and beyond the supervisory relationship, which may have influenced their perspectives on compliance over time. For this reason, one of the main criterion for inclusion in the study was that young people had been supervised in the community for a minimum period of six months. Although no prior assumptions were made about their level of maturity, it was expected that older adolescents would be better equipped in cognitive terms to reflect on and discuss changes in their participation with the supervision process and their perspectives on offending behaviour over time (Grisso *et al.* 2003). Based on this premise, the age criterion for the sample was pitched at 18–19 years. Eighteen is the normal age of transition to the adult criminal justice system in the Republic of Ireland however, where individuals are sentenced before their 18th birthday, they may continue under YPP supervision if it is deemed to be in

Table 1.1 Number of research participants

Practitioners/supervisors	33
Key informants	8
Young people	20
Young people's supervisors	20

the interests of completing the order. It was these cases – that had not been transferred to the adult supervision teams – that were approached to partake in the study. Young people who met the criteria were recruited from five YPP teams within the same geographical sites selected for the focus group research with practitioners. Overall, 20 agreed to participate, three refused and one consented, but was subsequently remanded in custody and deemed unfit to participate on medical grounds. Interviews were scheduled at the probation offices or community facilities where young people reported for appointments or at the young person's home in a small number of cases. The final aspect of the empirical investigation involved the completion of validation interviews with each young person's supervising officer. These were conducted to ascertain standard profile data on each case but also to minimize the potential impact of 'cognitive rationalisation' (Bottoms *et al.* 2004: 376) on the data, given that young people had been asked during the interview to provide present as well as retrospective perspectives on compliance.

Profile of the young people

The average age of participants was 18.5 years (SD = 5.47 months) and 17 of the 20 were young males. With the exception of one immigrant youth, most described their nationality as Irish (within that, four young people were identified as members of the Traveller community, an ethnic minority group in Irish society). Three-quarters of participants resided in areas adjacent to the city centre or in suburban housing estates typically characterized by high unemployment rates, poor housing, social disadvantage, criminality and limited service provision. Others lived in small- to medium-sized rural towns where the concentration and visibility of poverty and disadvantage was less apparent. Over two-thirds of the young people resided in the family home with at least one of their parents and the remainder either stayed with a sibling (two cases), or lived in supported lodgings (two cases), independently (one case), or with a partner (one case). Four had recently become parents and two were due to become parents. They were similar to other young people before the courts in that many, though not all, had left school before the legal age of 16 years or following three years of post-primary education (15.4 years, SD = 1.47) (Carroll and Meehan 2007). More than half of participants were engaged in education or training programmes at the time of interview, which is not unexpected given the emphasis placed on engaging young people in such activities as part of YPP supervision (see Chapter 8). In addition, one was employed in his family business and another, a Traveller youth, described his occupation as taking care of horses.[2]

Involvement in offending behaviour and the criminal justice system

Self-report data suggest that the average age at which young people committed their first offence was 13.5 years (SD = 1.54, with a range of 11 to 16 years). A detailed account of the youth justice system in the Republic of Ireland is provided in Chapter 5; however, at this juncture, it is worth noting that the majority of young people who come to police attention are diverted out of the criminal justice system through a statutory system of informal and formal police cautioning (An Garda Síochána 2011). Cautions are not restricted to first-time offending, and young people who come into contact with the law may be in receipt of a number of cautions before a decision is taken to prosecute them. What this means is that young people will frequently have been involved in offending behaviour for a considerable period of time, and will have accumulated a number of charges, before appearing in the Children Court. For young people in this study, the average number of previous convictions was 2.8 (SD = 1.5) with a range of one to six. Data on previous convictions were drawn from official criminal records and were calculated on the basis of the number of court appearances, in accordance with the standard method adopted in criminological research. Given that most young people were convicted of more than one offence at each court appearance, this approach is likely to have underestimated the full extent of their previous convictions. Young people were convicted of a wide range of offences with the most common being theft and public order offences, echoing previous research on young people before the courts in the Republic of Ireland (Carroll and Meehan 2007). In addition, convictions were recorded for more serious offences including burglary and aggravated burglary, causing serious harm, and violent disorder. That more than one-third of the young people had been, or were waiting to be, sentenced on indictable matters in the Circuit Court provides a further indication of the level of offending seriousness in some cases.

According to their supervisors, young people were known to YPP for an average time period of 22.7 months (SD = 12.2) ranging from one to four years. At the time of referral, young people had been assessed as at moderate or high risk of reoffending (see Chapter 5 for further detail on assessing risk with young people under YPP supervision). Three-quarters of participants were under the supervision of YPP arising from a probation order imposed by the Children Court, while the remainder were subject to supervision as part of the terms of a suspended sentence, voluntary supervision or adjourned supervision. Adjourned supervision is a common judicial practice despite having no statutory basis in Irish law (Seymour 2006). The court adjourns sentencing until a later date, usually not more than one year, to assess the young person's motivation to stop offending and their willingness to engage with YPP (Seymour 2012). Young people are normally required to attend regular supervision appointments during this period and the probation officer is obliged to furnish progress reports to the court. In the cases outlined above, it was not uncommon for young people to be simultaneously supervised as part of a probation order while also subject to adjourned supervision. The probation order tends to be the default community disposal used by the courts for young people under 18 years in the Republic of Ireland and few participants had had exposure to other types of supervised community orders. With one exception, most had not served a custodial sentence, a finding that resonates in the Irish youth justice ethos of retaining custody as a sentence of last resort. The pattern was not reflected in relation to remand cases in that 40 per cent of young people had previously spent time in custody on remand (see further Chapter 5).

Structure of the book

This book consists of three main parts. Chapters 2–4 are contained within Part I and provide the theoretical and conceptual backdrop to the book. In Part II, the context of the empirical study is presented in Chapter 5, and Chapters 6 and 7 offers an account of practitioners' perspectives on compliance and the strategies employed to manage compliance with young offenders under supervision in Northern Ireland and the Republic of Ireland. Part III is made up of Chapters 8 and 9 and is concerned with young people's perspectives and changing attitudes to compliance with supervision requirements and in relation to desistance from offending.

Part I

Chapter 2 commences with an overview of some of the key youth justice developments of recent decades that have resonance in terms of influencing the scope and purpose of community disposals across the world. It addresses the rationale for focusing on compliance as an aspect of effective supervision practice and explores the evidence relating to young people and compliance with supervision requirements. The chapter draws on examples from England and Wales, Canada, Scotland, New Zealand and the United States in exploring how non-compliance with the terms of community supervision is addressed within different youth justice contexts. In so doing, it highlights that considerable differences exist between jurisdictions in the approaches and responses adopted when young people fail to abide with the legal conditions imposed on them while under supervision in the community. Chapter 3 expands on the definition of compliance introduced earlier in this chapter and presents the main theoretical perspectives that are relevant to explaining compliance with community disposals. Drawing on the work of Bottoms (2001) and Tyler (1990) respectively, the chapter examines the mechanisms that underpin compliant behaviour, and focuses on the role of legitimacy and procedural justice in encouraging compliance. Evidence of diversity in offenders' perceptions of community supervision is used to demonstrate how differing stances mediate decisions to comply. The complexity of compliance as a construct central to offender supervision is further highlighted by identifying that motivation to comply changes over time and may be influenced by social and psychological factors within and beyond the supervision process. Chapter 4 addresses the influence of cognitive and psychosocial immaturity on young people's decision making in the criminal justice system. It relates the psychological evidence to the context of community supervision and outlines the manner in which cognitive and psychosocial factors are likely to shape young people's decisions to comply with the requirements of supervision. In recognizing that individual decision making takes place within the broader social environment, the second part of the chapter explores the family, school and community context of young people's lives and by implication the typical settings within which decision making occurs. It suggests that decision making by young people on community supervision is often executed within social contexts where few pro-social outlets exist and criminal commodities are easily accessible.

Part II

Chapter 5 provides the background for the remaining chapters of the book. It describes the factors and events that have influenced the direction of youth justice in Northern Ireland and the Republic of Ireland in recent decades. Detailed analysis is provided on the historical and contemporary influences that have shaped the organizations responsible for supervising young people in the community in both jurisdictions. By bringing together these macro-level influences, the chapter provides the foundation from which practitioners' responses to offenders' non-compliance is explored in subsequent chapters. Chapter 6 investigates how compliance is interpreted in practice, drawing on the perspectives of probation officers, probation service officers and youth justice workers involved in the supervision of young offenders in Northern Ireland and the Republic of Ireland. It identifies that making a distinction between adolescent-related behaviour and genuine resistance to change is an important aspect of conceptualizing compliance when supervising young people. Decision making about what constitutes non-compliance emerges as a negotiated process influenced by organizational policy, young people's age, maturity, social circumstances and level of risk, as well as practitioners' perceptions of their clients' overall commitment to the supervision process and to behavioural change. Chapter 7 commences with an overview of practitioners' perspectives on the challenges of engaging young people in the supervision process. It is followed by a detailed account of the dynamics that evolve over time within the supervisory relationship which are attributed to encouraging young people to comply. A central argument of the chapter is that when working with young people where enforcement action and the threat of custody often have limited deterrent impact, the possibilities for change and compliance are firmly located within a relational approach, based on the principles of 'front-end compliance', and centred on building capacity and strengths with young people and their families.

Part III

Chapter 8 documents young people's perspectives on their experiences of community supervision. Attention focuses on the changes that occur in their attitudes towards compliance with supervision requirements and the reasons underpinning such changes. Specifically, the chapter examines their views on the role of the supervisory relationship in influencing change over time. It identifies that the development of a positive supervisory relationship is an important aspect of improving motivation to comply and in providing the basis from which directive guidance from supervisors is accepted. The chapter also explores young people's perceptions of power within the supervisory relationship and suggests that their legal obligations to comply are reinforced when combined with a social and psychological investment in the process. Chapter 9 explores young people's perspectives on the process of desistance from offending. It provides in-depth analysis on young people's changing motivations to stop offending and to this end is contextualized within the transition period of early adulthood and the social and psychological changes linked to this life stage. The chapter highlights that the process of change unfolds over time, and while maturity is associated with facilitating desistance insofar as it contributes to changing subjective perspectives, the actual decision to stop offending is one that has to be actively chosen by participants. Nevertheless, desistance is identified as a challenging process that requires a strong sense of personal agency and high levels of social support from significant others. It also points to the potential for community supervision to support offenders in maintaining 'longer-term legal compliance' with the criminal law (Bottoms 2001). Chapter 10 concludes with a discussion of the implications of the findings for youth justice policy and practice.

A note on the data analysis process

All interviews and focus groups with young people, practitioners and key informants were digitally recorded, fully transcribed and reviewed before the analysis process commenced. A number of phases were involved in the data analysis process. In Phase 1, each transcript was examined chronologically and segments of meaning were coded into broad themes. At this descriptive phase, themes were broad in the sense that they contained divergent views and perspectives on a stated topic. Each code generated was given a clear label and definition or 'rule for inclusion' so as to ensure consistency in the coding process. By the end of Phase 1, the data had been deconstructed into a non-hierarchical structure made up of broad themes. Phase 2 was concerned with reordering, renaming, merging, distilling and clustering related codes into categories of themes so as to reconstruct the data into a framework that made sense to the analyst and brought clarity and focus to the enquiry. Phase 3 involved breaking down the now reorganized themes into sub-themes so as to better understand the meanings embedded therein. This process moved the data from the first-level codes generated in Phase 1 into second, third and fourth level codes until the data were saturated and no new lower generational codes emerged. In Phase 4, the task involved generating analytical memos using writing as a tool to prompt deeper thinking of the data (Bazeley 2009). Memos were written against sets of coding starting with the lower-order codes and synthesized up the coding tree to the top-level codes and categories of codes. This process ensured that findings were borne of a systematic review of the coded content and were built up step-by-step out of the data. Although the memos varied in content, they broadly incorporated: the content of the code; the processes included within the code; its importance in sequencing events and outcomes that influenced the overall findings; the relevance of background factors; how the code related to other codes and how it differed; and consideration of the broader literature in locating the study findings in context (Bazeley 2009; Charmaz 2006). Phase 5 involved a process of validating the analytical memos through critical reflection and by running queries and reports on the data to confirm the key findings, while in the final instance, at Phase 6, the analytical memos were synthesized into a cohesive set of findings. NVivo, a specialist package developed as a computer-aided qualitative data analysis system (CAQDAS), was used to manage and support the analytical work.

Terminology in the book

The term 'community disposals' is used throughout to refer to measures, sanctions, orders, penalties and sentences where young people are supervised in the community. Teenagers and their younger contemporaries in the criminal justice system are referred to as 'young people' in this book.

2 Responding to non-compliance with the requirements of community disposals

Most contemporary youth justice systems are neither characterized nor polarized by one dominant philosophical influence. While law, policy and practice within individual youth justice systems may be grounded in a core value-base, in practice, responses to young people in conflict with the law are likely to draw upon a more eclectic mix based on prevention, punishment, rehabilitation, reparation, restorative justice and risk-based actuarial measures. Considerable expansion in the scope and diversity of community disposals has taken place in recent decades, in many cases, drawing increasing numbers of young people into the criminal justice system. The broadening out of the range and intensity of community disposals, while rooted in the unique exigencies and circumstances of each jurisdiction, is reflective of the increasing and competing demands within youth justice systems to protect the status and rights of children and young people, to prevent reoffending, to protect communities, to be responsive to the needs of the victim, and to address public, political and judicial perceptions about youth crime and disorder. Factors that influence the shape of respective youth justice systems emanate from a wide variety of sources; however, those that have broader international resonance and applicability are considered here.

The United Nations Convention on the Rights of the Child (UNCRC), which sets out the civil, cultural, economic, health, political and social rights for all children (defined as persons under 18 years) including those who come into conflict with the law, has been ratified by over 190 countries and as a result has the most widespread and important influence on youth justice developments at an international level. Goldson and Hughes (2010: 212) have described the convention as well as a number of other important international human rights instruments – such as the United Nations Standard Minimum Rules on the Administration of Juvenile Justice 1985 (Beijing Rules), the United Nations Guidelines for the Prevention of Juvenile Delinquency 1990 (Riyadh Guidelines) and the United Nations Rules for the Protection of Juveniles Deprived of their Liberty 1990 (Havana Rules) – as providing 'a unifying framework for youth justice policy on a global scale'. A number of provisions within international human rights instruments have direct relevance for the treatment of, and responses to, young people who come into contact with the criminal justice system. In particular, Article 37(b) of the UNCRC outlines that the arrest, detention and imprisonment of a child should be a measure of last resort and for the minimum period of time required. Article 40(4) promotes the use of community-based responses including care, guidance and supervision orders; foster care; education and training programmes; counselling; probation measures and other alternatives to institutional detention for children found to be in breach of the criminal law. The extent to which countries embrace the UNCRC is monitored by the United Nations Committee on the Rights of the Child who require government representatives to appear before it periodically and to report on their level of compliance with the substance and spirit of the convention in advancing children's rights. Although the degree to which signatories to the convention adhere to their commitments has been the subject of criticism in reports published by the monitoring committee (United Nations Committee on the Rights of the Child 2007), the evidence suggests that the convention has been influential in improving the quality and provision of non-custodial sanctions for children in conflict with the law. By way of example, Smandych (2006) argues that a key agenda reflected in the Youth Criminal Justice Act (YCJA) 2003 was a concern to ensure that the Canadian youth justice system was sufficiently aligned with the principles of the UNCRC. To this end, requirements that placed strict limitations on the use of custody, and provisions to increase the scope for using extra-judicial measures for lower risk offenders, were just some of the measures introduced. Against this, other commentators such as Denov (2004) have argued that Canada has some way to go in achieving full compliance with the UNCRC, particularly in relation to administering adult sentences to young people and detaining them in adult facilities.

Restorative justice has been described as 'possibly … the most influential development in "crime control" in the past decade' (Crawford and Newburn 2003: 38). There exists no agreed definition of restorative justice and it is often described in terms of what it is not, emphasizing its non-punitive and non-authoritarian status (Bazemore and Schiff 2005). Crime, in restorative justice terms, is seen as a violation of social relationships between the offender, the victim and the community and a form of interpersonal conflict involving concrete harm (Zehr 1990). How restorative justice is utilized in practice varies considerably, but for young offenders some of the most common practices involve family group conferencing, restorative justice panels, restorative justice circles and victim–offender mediation (Galaway 1988; Maxwell and Morris 2006). Many restorative justice practices bring together a wider group of participants beyond the offender and the victim, including family members and other supportive advocates who are perceived to be beneficial to the process of seeking a collective solution to the harm associated with offending behaviour (Marshall 1996; Bazemore and Schiff 1996). Originating primarily from practices developed in Australia, Canada and New Zealand, one of the most notable aspects of restorative justice is the manner in which it has spread globally and become woven into the youth justice systems of many countries across the world over the last two decades. Goldson (2011: 15) argues that restorative justice 'has induced a paradigm shift in global criminal justice (in general) and transnational youth justice (in particular)'. Restorative justice has become an integral part of the operation of some youth justice systems, while in others, restorative justice practices are used as additional measures either to divert lower risk young offenders from prosecution or conviction, or as an additional requirement for those deemed to be higher risk.

A hardening of attitudes towards young people in conflict with the law is evidenced in practices that make provision for them to be transferred and tried in adult courts, to receive adult sentences or to be locked up from a young age (Hammarberg 2008; Krisberg 2006). The provision of intensive forms of supervision in the community with stringent reporting and monitoring conditions attached has evolved in tandem with broader punitive shifts in youth justice responses to offending behaviour. Although punitive shifts emerged from the early 1990s in England and Wales, the introduction of the Crime and Disorder Act 1998 signalled a new era in youth justice where the focus came to rest 'on legal priorities, such as establishing intent, proving guilt, and applying punishment, at the expense of the child's welfare' (Haydon and Scraton 2000: 444). Reflecting on governmental policy since this period, Goldson (2010: 167) suggests that 'the intensification of community-based supervision and surveillance accompanies, rather than substitutes, processes of re-penalization and the significant escalation of custodial detention'. Public concern about the 'problem' of out-of-control or persistent offenders coupled with media and political propagation in many cases has acted as the stimulus for increasingly punitive responses to young offenders across Europe, Canada, Australia, New Zealand, the United States and beyond. Muncie (2009: 369) explains that 'governments of many (but not all) persuasions appear to be increasingly turning to law and order as a means of providing symbols of security and to enhance their own chances of electoral support'. In this regard, punitive responses provide political actors with the ammunition to demonstrate their capacity to deliver tough responses to crime and anti-social behaviour by young people.

Young people perceived to be engaged in anti-social behaviour or to be at risk of offending have increasingly come under the radar of the criminal justice system. A proliferation in early intervention measures to target children and young people deemed to be 'at risk' of future offending has been a key feature of youth justice policy in England and Wales (see Muncie 2009: 313–14), but it has also manifested in other jurisdictions in the form of diversionary activities centred on assessing and addressing risk behaviour. The risk factor prevention paradigm is linked to policy support for such measures (McAra and McVie 2010). Termed 'the jewel in the actuarialist crown' by Case (2007: 92), the paradigm refers to an approach that involves identifying individual, family, school and neighbourhood factors associated with increasing the likelihood of offending, and using the findings as the basis for deciding the level of criminal justice intervention in the young person's life. The value of early intervention in supporting quality of life outputs is undisputed; however, early intervention measures delivered through the criminal justice process risk stigmatizing children and young people before criminal activity occurs. Furthermore, it individualizes risk to the level of the individual and the family while at the same time neglecting the potential negative influence of socio-political and structural factors such as social exclusion, marginalization and poverty (Case 2006; Kemshall 2008). A number of commentators also point out that in the context of an increasing preoccupation with risk, the principle of universality and support for all children under 18 years has been replaced with an emphasis on categorizing and targeting those who are considered to be 'at risk' or potentially at risk (Case 2006; Goldson 2010; Muncie 2011). Broadening out criminal justice in the community in the form of early intervention increases the likelihood that the most disadvantaged children become enmeshed and recycled through the system (McAra and McVie 2011).

The outcome of the developments outlined above is that the more deeply young people are drawn into the system, the greater the challenge becomes to avoid criminalizing and penalizing them. Bearing this in mind, the remainder of the chapter focuses on the context of supervising young people in the community and the responses employed in addressing non-compliance with the requirements of community disposals.

Young people and non-compliance

Public and judicial confidence is central to the operation of community disposals (Hedderman and Hough 2004). That punishment is primarily associated with imprisonment can leave community disposals consigned to the category of 'poor substitutes' (Worrall and Hoy 2005: 11) and their credibility as legitimate responses to offending behaviour open to question. This perspective is strengthened in contexts where punitive attitudes prevail and crime and punishment are highly politicized issues. Here, 'punitiveness squeezes the "space" for community sanctions and measures … and strikes at the heart of their credibility' (McNeill 2011: 19). Maintaining the credibility of community disposals is reliant on offenders' compliance and cooperation, none more so than when it involves young people who by virtue of their lifestyle occupy a prominent visible presence in public space. Youths loitering in groups on the street, in parks and in other public places infringe community expectations of what constitutes appropriate social behaviour and can be perceived as an outward manifestation of defiance and resistance even where no law-breaking has occurred (Crawford 2009). Worrall (1997:138) suggests that juvenile offenders share similar experiences of exclusion as sex offenders in the community where 'respectable citizens and figures of authority are less and less willing to communicate with either group and are increasingly demanding that they be known about, watched and moved on'. She argues that while the term 'community' may imply a sense of belonging to law-abiding citizens, 'its promise of inclusivity can be interpreted in contradictory ways when applied to those who break the law and are criminalized' (ibid.: 46). That young people are often responsible for perpetrating 'those quality of life offences which form the proverbial last straw for people who already have nothing' (Brown 1998: 94) further consolidates perceptions of them 'as criminals deserving of punishment, rather than as citizens entitled to justice' (ibid.: 82).

The potential for supervised community disposals to be effective can only be realized if offenders attend in the first instance (Hopkinson and Rex 2003).

Where disposals are intended to restrict liberty, this does not occur when offenders fail to maintain contact with their supervising officer (Robinson and McNeill 2010). High-tariff disposals are frequently held out as the frontline defence against criticisms about the perceived leniency of community-based responses to crime. As a result, non-compliance not only has implications for the credibility of these disposals but also speaks to wider criminal justice concerns about risk management in a risk-focused environment. Non-compliance also impacts on the integrity of disposals based on restorative justice principles of repairing harm and restoring relationships between the victim, the offender and the community. Undertakings given by offenders to make amends to their victims through reparative or other activities, when not honoured, potentially compromise the ethos of the restorative process. Finally, some evidence suggests that reconviction rates are lower than predicted for those who complete offending-related programmes but higher than predicted for non-completers and non-starters (Raynor and Vanstone 1997). The implication is that the potential for community disposals to have any positive influence on reoffending rates may be reduced where offenders do not engage with the supervision process.

Low social bonds and high-tariff disposals

Failing to abide by curfew requirements and breaching association conditions such as frequenting locations that are out of bounds within the terms of their order are particularly common among young offenders (Wong, Bailey and Kenny 2010). A number of studies report that technical infringements, like failing to inform the authorities of a change of address for instance, and non-attendance at scheduled appointments without providing an acceptable reason are typical violations committed by offenders on supervised community disposals (Farrall 2002a; Fulton *et al.* 1997; Lowe *et al.* 2008; May and Wadwell 2001; McIvor 1992). Non-compliance is more likely to occur among frequent offenders with an above average number of convictions and those with substantive criminal histories and offending experiences (May and Wadwell 2001; McIvor 1992; Roberts 2004). Roberts (2004) sheds light on some of the profile differences between programme 'completers' and 'non-completers', drawing on a prospective study of 490 adult offenders required to attend 'Think First' – an accredited cognitive programme – between September 2000 and March 2002. Of the total sample, 208 individuals were characterized as non-starters (non-attendance at mandatory sessions), and 141 were described as completers or non-completers respectively. Completers were found to be older, to have stronger personal capacity including social, communication and problem solving skills. They also had fewer practical barriers to completion, were more likely to have social capital in the form of employment and supportive influences, to be motivated to tackle their problems, and more willing to think about stopping offending. Overall, completers were less ensconced in criminal lifestyles, and were less likely to have been breached or to have served a custodial sentence in the preceding two years.

Levels of non-compliance with the requirements of community disposals tend to be higher for young offenders than for adults as the former grapple their way through adolescence, seeking greater autonomy and independence while attempting to carve out a sense of identity for themselves (Moore *et al.* 2006; Seymour and Butler 2008; Boyle 2008; Wong *et al.* 2010). Existing research also suggests that young people who are most enmeshed in the criminal justice system are often those who present the greatest challenge in terms of compliance and completion of court-imposed disposals and programmes (Tollett and Benda 1999; Morgan 1995). Hart's (2011) study of the enforcement of statutory youth justice orders in six local areas of England and Wales found that the participants who experienced the greatest difficulty in complying were not the most serious offenders, but were persistent offenders who encountered considerable cognitive and social disadvantage in their life circumstances. Similarly, it emerged that in 10 of 14 cases where orders were revoked as a result of non-compliance with the requirements imposed as part of an intensive probation supervision programme for young people in Northern Ireland, non-completers had a previous history of residential care or detention, in comparison with just one-fifth of those who went on to complete the programme (Seymour 2003). On the basis of the above findings, it appears that young people with the highest levels of system contact and the lowest levels of external attachments to family or significant others are likely to experience the greatest difficulty in complying with the requirements of community disposals.

Given that higher-tariff responses in the main are targeted at offenders with a number of previous convictions or contacts with the criminal justice system (McNeill 2010), it is not unexpected that the likelihood of non-compliance increases with the severity of the disposal imposed. The potential for violations to be detected on high-end disposals is also greater given that they involve more stringent conditions, including more frequent levels of reporting or contact between offenders and their supervisors (Altschuler and Armstrong 2001; Audit Commission 2004). An analysis of breach data for young offenders in England and Wales found that lower-tariff disposals such as referral orders were breached in just 11 per cent of cases compared with over 50 per cent of higher-tariff cases (Hart 2011). The number of conditions attached to disposals may also impact on levels of compliance regardless of their tariff rating. Crawford and Newburn (2003: 140) for example, report that completion rates for action plans or contracts undertaken by young people on referral orders (the main disposal for young people convicted for the first time) in England and Wales decreased according to the number of elements attached. Although the completion rate was 89 per cent for contracts with one element included, it declined to less than 70 per cent where contracts involved four or more elements. Gyateng, McSweeney and Hough's (2010) exploration of the predictors of compliance with community supervision also found evidence to suggest that the likelihood of breach increased in line with the number of requirements imposed on offenders. The danger with forms of supervision in the community that are overly arduous, and enforcement policies that are overly rigorous, is that they risk creating a circuitous route to custody when young people do not meet the anticipated expectations (Moore 2004).

This perspective resonates in Hedderman's (2003: 191) argument that offenders 'most in need of effective supervision' are likely to end up 'being breached and resentenced before they have a chance to be transformed into "completers"'.

Principles and good practice guidance in responding to 'failures to comply'

The European Rules for Juvenile Offenders Subject to Sanctions and Measures were adopted by the EU Committee of Ministers to member states in 2008 (Council of Europe 2008). Although not legally binding, they provide guidance on responding to non-compliance with the requirements of community sanctions in a way that minimizes the risk of further criminalizing young people. They recommend that juveniles and their parents or guardians should be informed in an appropriate manner about the implementation of community sanctions, or measures, their rights and duties in the process, and the consequences of non-compliance. Any intervention in the juvenile's life should be as meaningful as possible, and executed in a way that is conducive to their social and educational needs. The rules recommend that minor incidents of non-compliance are dealt with promptly through discretionary means while significant failures to comply should be reported promptly to the relevant authorities. Where an order is revoked or its terms are modified in response to non-compliance, any new order or conditions should remain proportionate to the offence under consideration. Within the guidance, it is recommended that non-compliance should not automatically culminate in a deprivation of liberty; instead, consideration should be given to imposing an amended or alternative community sanction.

The approach espoused in the European rules resonates with a key principle of responsive regulation, termed the minimal-sufficiency principle which is that 'the less salient and powerful the control technique used to secure compliance, the more likely that internalization will result' (Ayres and Braithwaite 1992: 49). Punishment should be retained as a last resort and the level of sanction used should be the minimum required to secure compliance when other methods of promoting regulation have failed (ibid.). The European rules also allude to the role of discretion when young people do not comply with the terms of community disposals. Referring to England and Wales, Robinson (2011) outlines some of the ways that practitioners exercise discretion when making decisions about non-compliance. These include, though are not limited to, accepting the reasons given by offenders for non-attendance; making judgements about whether an offender's risk level necessitates an immediate return to court for non-compliance; requesting managerial authorization to postpone breach action; seeking to have an order amended rather than breached in light of the offender's personal or other circumstances; and providing professional opinion and advice to the courts on such matters as the offender's motivation, likelihood of future compliance and suitability for the order. The use of discretion lies at the core of responding to offenders on community supervision. Canton and Eadie (2008: 95) contend that because the nature of supervision involves a diverse profile and range of offender circumstances, it requires practitioners to have a high degree of responsible judgement and to exercise professional discretion; at the same time, it is acknowledged that 'unfettered discretion' can lead to unfair and discriminatory practices. To counter this danger, Canton and Eadie (2008) highlight the importance of having management structures and support systems in place to authorize practitioners' discretionary decisions, while at the same time preserving accountability in the process. Eadie and Canton (2002) suggest that an approach that incorporates wide discretion with high accountability offers the most promise in responding to offenders in a fair and consistent manner. In this scenario, practitioners have the flexibility to take relevant factors into account in exercising discretion, but are also required to be accountable for their decision making. In contrast, an approach based on narrow discretion and high accountability is likely to hinder practitioners' responsiveness to offenders in dealing with the diversities in age, gender, race, offending and the social situations that arise in the course of the supervision process. As outlined in the following section, discretion plays a prominent role in practitioners' decision making about young people's non-compliance while under supervision in the community. That said, the extent to which discretion is exercised varies considerably within and between jurisdictions, leading to different outcomes for young people who may have committed the same technical violations or demonstrated similar levels of non-compliance.

Comparative perspectives on responding to non-compliance

Comparing youth justice law, policy and practice across jurisdictions is notoriously difficult not least because of the different age thresholds for entry and exit from the youth justice system, variances in the responses used to deal with young offenders and differences in the nature and extent of data collected within the system (Muncie 2005). Identifying how non-compliance by young people is formally addressed in a comparative context is no exception. Furthermore, few countries publish data on the extent to which young people have their cases reviewed or breached as a result of non-compliance. The absence of data may indicate that a public record of the formal response to incidents of non-compliance is less important in countries that espouse primarily welfare-orientated or restorative justice approaches. Anecdotally, based on informal discussions with academics and policy makers, it seems that in some jurisdictions non-compliance by young people on community disposals is mainly addressed through discretionary measures with limited recourse to formal enforcement action (see also Chapter 7). While it is difficult to comment with certainty in the absence of statistical information, the indications are that formal enforcement procedures – such as breach proceedings – are employed more vigorously in jurisdictions where concerns for public protection or punitive attitudes towards young people in conflict with the law supersede welfare, rehabilitation and reintegration considerations. Eadie and Canton (2002: 14) outline the challenge for youth justice practice as one that has 'to reconcile society's deep cultural ambivalence towards offending by young people'. They suggest that the moral desire to punish sits alongside recognition that rule transgressions are common among young people, developmental maturity impacts on consequential thinking, and social and psychological disadvantage has associated links with offending behaviour. The extent to which this perspective permeates responses to non-compliance relies heavily on the ethos and philosophy underpinning respective youth justice systems. This is discussed in detail with reference to Ireland and Northern Ireland in Chapters 5 to 7 but in this chapter, attention focuses on a number of other jurisdictions.

The family group conference plays a central role in youth justice proceedings for young people under 17 years in New Zealand, where the youth justice system is predominantly grounded in restorative justice and diversionary principles. Maxwell and Morris (2006: 240) highlight the centrality of the family group conference process to the youth justice system in explaining that 'all young people whom the police want to take to court and who have not been arrested and charged have to be referred to a family group conference'. If the conference succeeds in seeking a resolution, the matter involving the young person is pursued no further. Cases appearing in the Youth Court are also referred for a family group conference and judges cannot impose a sentence without taking into account the recommendations of the conference. Recommendations and plans devised at the family group conference are binding where they have been agreed by conference participants or accepted by the courts. Non-compliance with the requirements of conference plans is addressed on a case-by-case basis. In the event that significant issues occur, which compromise completion of the plan, consultation takes place between the youth justice co-ordinator, youth justice supervisor and the social worker where applicable. The purpose is to consider how non-compliance is addressed and how the young person is to be supported prior to reconvening a family group conference or lodging formal proceedings in the youth court. The structures in place in the youth justice system in New Zealand – in particular the family group conference – coupled with a strong policy and practice culture to retain young people within their communities, appears to minimize the use of more stringent enforcement action for young people who do not comply with requirements.

In Scotland, offending behaviour by the majority of young people under 16 years is addressed under the welfare-orientated Children's Hearing System (CHS). Established under the Social Work (Scotland) Act 1968, the system provides for an independent legal or social work official known as a reporter to consider whether sufficient evidence exists to support the referral and to consider if no further action should be taken, if voluntary advice or assistance is required, or if a referral for a hearing is appropriate (Batchelor and Burman 2010). Where a hearing occurs, it is convened by three trained voluntary panel members who take over the decision making role from the reporter and is attended by the child, those with parental responsibility for the child, a social worker, the reporter and a legal representative where appropriate. The purpose of the hearing is to determine if compulsory measures of supervision should be imposed on the child and the nature of the conditions that should be attached, such as who the child should live with, who they should have contact with or what programmes they should take part in (ibid.). Where measures and conditions are imposed, supervision of the young person's case is undertaken by the local authority social work department. In the event of non-compliance, professional discretion and consultation are employed in deciding the outcome, which may include the option to take no further action, to adjust the existing supervision plan or to reconvene the process for the purposes of review.

Few young people aged 16 years or over are referred to the CHS in Scotland (McVie 2011) as 16 is the normal age of transition to the adult criminal justice system and consequently the period when young people are subject to adult criminal justice procedures (Whyte 2004). In practice what this means is that non-compliance with the requirements of community disposals are addressed in accordance with national practice standards for the supervision of community orders (Scottish Government 2011a). The practice guidance suggests that there is some scope for flexibility and professional discretion in the implementation of the standards (ibid.). Nevertheless, in contrast to their younger counterparts, 16 and 17 year olds remain subject to conditions which potentially place them at risk of being returned to court for breach proceedings following three unacceptable failures to comply and the possibility that a more severe sanction including custody will be imposed (Scottish Government 2011a, 2011b). Barry (2011) argues that although data are not available to identify the proportion of young people in secure care or in prison in Scotland as a result of breaching supervision requirements or the terms of community disposals, she reflects the views of other youth justice commentators in expressing concern about the extent to which young people are increasingly drawn further into the system as a result of failing to comply, as opposed to the seriousness of their subsequent offending behaviour. Overall the Scottish experience provides a clear example of how young people under 18 years living in the same jurisdiction are likely to encounter very different outcomes for failing to comply with supervision requirements on the basis of their chronological age.

The punitive shift in youth justice in England and Wales since the early 1990s as described earlier in this chapter provides the backdrop for explaining responses to non-compliance on community disposals in this jurisdiction. The introduction of the first national standards for supervision practice in 1992 – which set out guidelines such that young people would be returned to court for failing to attend appointments on the third occasion without an acceptable reason (Home Office 1992) – coincided with the beginning of a period where increasingly punitive legal and policy stances were adopted towards young people in conflict with the law. Practitioners initially had considerable discretion in the way that they implemented the standards, however as 'the punitive turn kicked in' (Bateman 2011: 122), standards became increasingly prescriptive and practitioners were required to be more rigid in their enforcement actions (Home Office 1995; Youth Justice Board 2004, 2010). In the most recent version for example, requirements stipulate that each 'failure to attend' should be followed up within one working day by telephone, letter or with a home visit and where the reasons given are deemed unacceptable, or where no reasonable excuse is provided within 24 hours, a formal written warning should be immediately issued. After two formal warnings, and another incident of 'failure to attend', breach proceedings should be initiated within five working days, save in exceptional circumstances where youth offending team (YOT) managers have the authority to grant a stay on breach action. In addition to the narrow and regulatory nature of the standards, Bateman (2011) describes that change has occurred within the practitioner culture in England and Wales which has led to a stronger focus on enforcement-orientated practice with less overall emphasis on traditional principles of minimal intervention and diversion from custody. Change is attributed in part to the punitive environment within which practitioners operate and in part to 'a contemporaneous transformation of the workforce' whereby the majority of new staff recruited to work in youth justice are no longer professionally qualified in the areas of welfare, care, probation or education (ibid.: 125). In the context of the changes that have occurred in youth justice in England and Wales over the last two decades, it is perhaps not surprising to find that high numbers of young people are returned to court for breach proceedings. This is borne out in the data, which demonstrate that 6.32 per cent of proven offences resulting in a disposal for young people aged 10–17 years in 2009–10 related to a breach of a statutory order.[1] The figure represents a slight reduction from 2008–09 (6.5 per cent), but a substantive increase from 2002–03, when the proportion was just 3.1 per cent (ibid.). Furthermore, the evidence suggests that breach of a statutory order was the primary offence for 13 per cent of young people serving a custodial sentence in England and Wales in 2009–10 (Ministry of Justice 2011a).

England and Wales is not alone in its reliance on formal enforcement procedures to address non-compliance or indeed in its use of custody as a response. In the USA, technical violations accounted for the most serious offence for 14 per cent of all juveniles placed in residential correctional facilities in 2010.[2] Within the national figure, substantial disparity exists between states, ranging from 2 per cent and 6 per cent respectively in the states of New York and Massachusetts to 25 per cent and 27 per cent in California and South Carolina respectively (Sickmund *et al.* 2011). Administration of justice offences including the offence of failing to comply with an order accounted for a total of 7 per cent of the total youth court caseload in Canada in 2008–09. One particular concern is the extent to which breaches of technical requirements represent the reason why a considerable number of young people are returned to court in the absence of any further offending. Sprott's (2004) study of the youth court in Canada captures something of the throughput of these cases. It reports that of 22,867 cases entered in court and involving failure to comply charges, over half did not include charges of criminal offending.[3] Furthermore, in almost half (46.1 per cent) of the 9,211 cases where a failure to comply conviction was recorded in 2002–03, the failure-to-comply charge was the only offence contained within the conviction. Overall, cases involving only one failure to comply conviction were more common in the western provinces of Canada and the pattern for males and females was broadly similar (ibid). Following the introduction of the YCJA 2003, Canada has made substantial progress in reducing the youth custodial population (Milligan 2010).

However, while custody cannot be used for the first breach of a community order, insufficient limitations within the current legislation have been attributed to a continued reliance on it as a response to technical violation offences (Solomon and Allen 2009). In 2008–09 for example, 16.3 per cent of young people found guilty of the offence of failing to comply, received custody and supervision in Canada (Milligan 2010: 33). The use of custody for offences of failing to comply is disconcerting given its reported ineffectiveness in reducing reoffending and its potential to negatively impact on young people's social and psychological development (Goldson 2010; Freeman and Seymour 2010) as well as the well-documented tendency for minority youth to be systematically overrepresented within its population (Bishop, Leiber and Johnson 2010; Denov 2004; Ministry of Justice 2011a; Sickmund *et al.* 2011).[4]

Variations within jurisdictions

Although the average national rate for breach of statutory orders in England and Wales was in the region of 6 per cent in 2009–10, the rate was found to be consistently higher at 8 per cent in the north west, the north east and Yorkshire, and consistently lower in others such as Wales (4 per cent) and the south west (5 per cent). Furthermore, within these areas, marked local variations were identified in the rates between different localities (Hart 2011). The differences outlined here suggest that other factors are at play beyond the overarching national legislative and policy influences. Muncie (2005: 55) argues that the process of translating policy into practice 'depends on how it is visioned and reworked (or made to work) by those empowered to put it into practice' and following from this suggests that a 'social work ethic of "supporting young people" may well subvert any partnership or national attempt simply to responsibilize the young offender'. In-depth local level analyses is required to explain differences in the breach rates between areas but Hart's (2011) study sheds light on one potential contributory factor. She identifies examples of practice within a number of YOTs that are indicative of a more flexible process to the use of enforcement procedures. For instance, some YOTs hold three-way meetings with young people, their families and staff members after warnings about non-compliance have been exhausted and before breach proceedings are initiated. In Newcastle in northern England breach meetings are convened as soon as young people are technically in breach of their order requirements.[5] Chaired by a YOT manager and attended by young people, their parents, carers and significant others, meetings are designed to explore the reasons for non-compliance and to identify ways to re-engage young people in the supervision process. If it is deemed that there is scope for re-engagement, young people are issued with a formal warning and permitted to continue. Where breach proceedings are considered to be the most appropriate measure, work continues with young people prior to the court appearance in an effort to secure their compliance. Other examples of negotiated practice include situations where YOT managers execute their powers to use discretion in making enforcement decisions, taking into account the young person's developmental stage, exceptional circumstances or the overall success of the order. In addition, a level of flexibility is extended through practices such as requesting an amendment to the conditions of a community order from the court, or seeking an adjournment period to monitor the young person's progress. Collectively these examples suggest that even within a stringent system of formal enforcement, space can be created in practice 'on the ground' to incorporate more flexible and responsive approaches when managing non-compliance in the community.

Broader cultural and socio-political differences can also mediate how youth justice policy is implemented in practice. Indeed, Field's (2007: 314) analysis of seven YOTs in Wales reported that despite changes to youth justice policy in the direction of increased punitiveness, social workers expressed 'a clear desire … to resist or limit the impact of political pressures for a "punitive turn" in youth justice'. Although England and Wales share the same legal system and governance structures for youth justice, recent research points to the distinctive nature of youth justice in Wales when compared with its English neighbour (Drakeford 2010; Hoffman and Macdonald 2011). Drakeford (2010:141) explains that when young people come into conflict with the law the Welsh approach is to try 'to put right flaws in the systems on which they depend, rather than on focusing on the "deficits" in young people themselves'. This approach, which was adopted by the devolved Welsh Assembly in 2004 as the foundation of all policy making for children and young people, aligns with the principles and ethos of the UNCRC. While gaps remain in service delivery and contradiction exists insofar as rights-inspired values co-exist with principles of public protection in the 'All Wales Youth Offending Strategy' (see Welsh Assembly Government 2004) (Drakeford 2010; Haines 2009), the case of Wales nevertheless counters the notion of uniformity and universality in the implementation of youth justice responses within England and Wales and beyond.

Conclusion

Responding to non-compliance is an important aspect in maintaining the credibility of community disposals in the eyes of offenders, the wider public and political and judicial stakeholders. It is also imperative in terms of promoting effective practice and seeking to reduce reoffending behaviour, and has particular resonance when working with young people who by virtue of their age and developmental level are more likely to engage in non-compliant behaviour (see Chapter 4). Balancing the need to take and to be seen to take non-compliance seriously while at the same time accounting for the exigencies of youthful immaturity is a particular challenge for the youth justice system. The evidence presented in this chapter suggests that considerable differences exist in the manner in which non-compliance by young people on community disposals is addressed between jurisdictions (and indeed within jurisdictions). The ethos and philosophy underpinning the operation of respective youth justice systems appears to be strongly influential in shaping the legal and policy structures and professional practice approaches adopted when responding to non-compliance. While there is a dearth of data on the outcomes for young people who do not comply with the requirements of community disposals, the available evidence indicates that recourse to formal enforcement procedures is embraced more vigorously in jurisdictions where public protection concerns and punitive attitudes towards young people in conflict with the law overshadow traditional youth justice objectives such as promoting rehabilitation and reintegration (Ministry of Justice 2011a; Sickmund *et al.* 2011). The effectiveness of such responses is questioned in light of Hearnden and Millie's (2004) research, which found that reconviction rates did not vary between areas where enforcement had been strictly imposed and those where a more lenient approach was adopted. Finally, variation in practice when responding to non-compliance within the same jurisdiction points to the conclusion that how national law and policy are implemented on the ground has the potential to influence outcomes for young people.

Overall this chapter highlights that young people with the same challenges, the same behaviour, and guarded by the same human rights standards, 'experience "justice" in fundamentally differential guises' (Goldson and Hughes 2010: 218). Recognition that securing young people's compliance on community disposals may require a shift away from enforcement-orientated practice towards greater attention to their motivations, abilities and willingness to comply is embedded in practice in some jurisdictions, but is only beginning to emerge in others (Robinson 2011). With this in mind, the following chapter provides a more in-depth exploration of the theory and research underpinning compliance.

3 Compliance theory, research and practice

The term 'compliance' may invoke philosophical notions of obedience and deference, but the literature on compliance in criminal justice, human rights and regulatory contexts suggests that its connotation in practice is far more wide-ranging and complex. In relation to state compliance with international human rights for example, Cardenas (2007: 6) asks if 'a compliant action represent[s] cooperation or an attempt to silence future pressure?' She suggests that states 'manage' their human rights obligations and engage in strategic action that enables them to be seen to comply and thus reduce future international pressure. Applying a similar lens to offender compliance with community disposals, it raises questions as to what compliance means and what are the processes that underpin compliance among offenders under supervision in the community. Understanding how offenders navigate their way through supervision on community disposals, as well as the factors that influence their motivation to comply, provides the basis from which to consider how compliance might be promoted and non-compliance responded to in the community. This chapter examines the main theories and perspectives that are relevant to explaining offender compliance with community disposals, the relevance of legal socialization *vis-à-vis* adolescent offenders, as well as the influence of offenders' interactions and experiences with the criminal justice system and its agents in shaping their perceptions of procedural justice and levels of engagement with the requirements of community supervision and the criminal law.

Defining compliance

As outlined in Chapter 1, Bottoms (2001) distinguishes between compliance with the legal requirements of community penalties (short-term requirement compliance) and compliance with the criminal law (longer-term legal compliance). In the policy literature, compliance with the conditions of community disposals has related primarily to attendance, with less emphasis on the extent to which offenders actually participate and engage at appointments (Youth Justice Board 2010; Ministry of Justice 2011b). The question arises if a distinction should be made between the offender who does the minimum amount to avoid breach action compared with the offender who attends appointments, participates actively in the process and is motivated to change. Robinson and McNeill (2010: 369) agree that there should be a distinction, and for this reason, propose that Bottoms' (2001) concept of short-term requirement compliance is divided into what they term 'formal' and 'substantive' compliance. In this configuration, formal compliance describes the type of compliance where the minimum requirements of the disposal are completed; in contrast, substantive compliance involves the offender's active engagement and participation during the supervision process. Hucklesby (2009) captures the essence of difference between formal and substantive compliance when she describes the example of an offender subject to an electronically monitored curfew order who complies in the formal sense by remaining indoors during curfew hours, but not in a substantive way, by directing criminal activity from his home once indoors. Differences in offenders' levels of compliance are likely to be underpinned by differences in their motivations to comply. In shedding light on what motivates offenders to comply, Bottoms (2001) outlines a conceptual framework made up of a number of mechanisms that he identifies as being relevant to offender compliance with the terms of community penalties specifically, and with the criminal law more generally.

A framework to explain offender compliance under community supervision

Bottoms' (2001) framework of compliance draws together theories and perspectives on social order and consists of four main components: instrumental/prudential compliance; constraint-based compliance; compliance based on habit or routine; and normative compliance (see Figure 3.1). Although the components

A Instrumental/prudential compliance
- (a) Incentives
- (b) Disincentives

B Normative compliance
- (a) Acceptance of/belief in norm
- (b) Attachment leading to compliance
- (c) Legitimacy

C Constraint-based compliance
- (1) Physical restrictions or requirements on individual leading to compliance
  - (a) Natural
  - (b) Imposed
- (2) Restrictions on access to target
- (3) Structural constraints

D Compliance based on habit or routine

Figure 3.1 An outline of the principal mechanisms underpinning compliant behaviour
Source: *Community penalties: change and challenges* (Bottoms, 2001: 90)

are presented as separate entities, Bottoms (2001) emphasizes that decisions about compliance frequently involve interaction and crossover between the various mechanisms. These issues are discussed later in the chapter when the dynamic nature of compliance is further explored.

Instrumental approaches to compliance are structured on the premise that individuals are motivated to comply with the law in response to incentives or sanctions built into the legal system and its structures. Accordingly, individuals' behaviour is believed to be shaped by perceived or actual threats of detection and sanction. Incentivized strategies, such as reduced frequency of supervision contact or early discharge of the court order, encourage offenders to comply with the conditions of community disposals, while formal warnings, breach action and the threat of imprisonment are the potential sanctions imposed for non-compliance. Constraint-based compliance manifests in a number of different ways. Offenders are naturally constrained due to the need for sleep, for example, and physically restricted from possible sources of offending by the use of situational crime-prevention strategies and devices. Opportunities for non-compliance are also reduced when offenders are detained by the police, in prison or monitored through technologies such as electronic tagging in the community. Increased compliance is not always inevitable however, because as Hucklesby (2009) describes, offenders, while tagged, may alter their offending activity to align with their curfew schedule. The final element of constraint-based compliance is described by Bottoms (2001: 93) as 'structural constraint' and comes about when 'someone is cowed into submission by the coercion inherent in a power-based relationship'. It has less relevance to the management of community disposals, but holds criminological interest insofar as it explains the type of 'compliance' that child sex abusers may seek to impose on their young victims (ibid.).

While instrumental and constraint-based mechanisms rely on external motivating factors to promote compliance, other mechanisms in Bottoms' framework are based on internal factors that influence regulation such as norms, values, attachments, habits and routines. Bottoms (2001) distinguishes between compliance based on routine and compliance based on habit. The example of sending children to school in compliance with the law on compulsory education is used to highlight that routines are an integral aspect of compliance because they have become an unquestioned aspect of daily life. Individuals also develop '*mental dispositions*, which may take the form of settled inclinations to comply with certain laws' (ibid.: 94). Internal motivations to comply are numerous and Tyler (1990) distinguishes between those that are connected to individual preference and feelings of commitment to others, such as a partner or child, and those that are associated with social values such as legitimacy and morality. Similarly, the final mechanism suggested by Bottoms (2001) refers to normative compliance. Divided into three sub-types, the first refers to conscious belief or acceptance of a norm that influences an individual not to engage in a particular way. On the basis that most, if not all, individuals hold some normative beliefs, Bottoms (2001) suggests that in principle at least, it should be possible to expand the range of beliefs held by offenders in the direction of increased compliance. In the context of community supervision, he suggests that this might be achieved through moral reasoning by the supervising officer or through the medium of victim–offender meetings whereby the process may offer the potential for offenders to reflect on the harm caused to victims. The second sub-type of normative compliance points to the importance of meaningful social relationships and emotional attachments to others as a mechanism of encouraging compliance. This aspect resonates in the broader literature where the development of positive attachments in the form of personal relationships or employment is identified with reduced reoffending and desistance (Laub and Sampson 2001). An individual, recognizing the stress caused to their family by ongoing contact with the police and the criminal justice system, for example, may try to stop offending. Bottoms (2001) refers to Beetham (1991) and Tyler (1990) in explaining the significance of legitimacy as the third and final sub-type. Tyler (1990) found that where individuals perceive that the procedures used and the treatment received by those who impose the law as just and fair, they are more likely to view authority, and the law, as legitimate. Procedural justice therefore appears to be an important precursor to legitimacy. Perceptions of legitimacy were in turn found to influence compliance, independent of other factors such as individuals' previous levels of compliance. Where the law and its agents are perceived to act in a procedurally fair manner, it is associated with increased legitimacy, and is positively related to compliance and cooperation (ibid.). General conditions associated with perceiving the law as legitimate and ultimately fair, include the opportunity to have one's perspective heard, to be treated with dignity and respect, and to perceive that laws are imposed consistently and without bias. Legitimacy is related to the fairness of the approach used by authorities when exercising their powers because when authority is brought to bear in these ways, individuals perceive that they are receiving procedural justice (Tyler and Huo 2002). Tyler (1990) suggests that legal authorities can activate feelings of legitimacy and obligation in the direction of compliance with the law by acting in a just and fair manner. Activation of these social values is identified with voluntary engagement in self-regulatory behaviour in the longer-term. As legitimacy develops, individuals are more likely to defer to legal authority, to increase their sense of obligation to conform and to be more compliant with the law (Sunshine and Tyler 2003; Tyler 1990; Tyler and Huo 2002). Robinson and McNeill (2010) explain that in the context of community disposals, the supervisor's task is to encourage the offender's transition from positions of non-compliance or formal compliance to substantive and longer-term legal compliance in order to achieve the objective of reducing reoffending. Existing models of change such as Prochaska, DiClemente and Norcross' (1992) model attest to the challenges associated with promoting and sustaining long-term change in offenders.[1] Supervisors' capacity to influence change with offenders on community supervision is compromised where the latter perceive that the order lacks legitimacy (Robinson and McNeill 2010). This may occur in circumstances where disposals are imposed without consent, penalties are perceived to be unduly harsh, where offenders believe that they have been unfairly treated or misrepresented during the sentencing process or where they have had previous negative or antagonistic experiences with the supervisory staff.

Much of the empirical basis for the findings in relation to legitimacy arises from Tyler (1990) and colleagues' work in a variety of US cities over the last 25 years. Current work through the EURO-JUSTIS research project is likely to shed light on the role of legitimacy and public trust in institutions of justice in a number of European countries in the near future (Hough, Ruuskanen and Jokinen 2011).[2] Other studies in the criminal justice realm lend empirical support to the importance of perceptions about the legitimacy of the law and the impact of procedural fairness on individuals' willingness to comply. In the context of policing McCluskey, Mastrofski and Parks (1999) report that the legitimacy associated with police intervention was the most significant predictor of compliance among citizens in Indianapolis and St. Petersburg. In Paternoster *et al.*'s (1997: 192) well-cited study, where perpetrators of domestic violence perceived that they were treated in a procedurally just and fair manner by the police at the time of arrest, it was associated with significantly lower levels of subsequent domestic violence and reduced re-arrests, leading to the conclusion that 'being treated fairly does indeed matter'. McIvor (2009) describes that the nature of the interactions that took place between sentencers and offenders appearing in the Scottish Drug Courts, motivated offenders to tackle their drug use and offending behaviour, thereby improving overall compliance. Using Tyler's (1990), work, McIvor (2009) identified ethicality, efforts to be fair, and representation, as factors that enhanced perceptions of procedural justice among offenders in the Drug Courts. Ethicality was observed in the way that offenders perceived that they were treated with dignity and commended by sheriffs in the court. Offenders appreciated the interest taken in their lives and the flexibility offered by sheriffs in making 'appropriate allowances' for relapses or setbacks (p.43). That people are concerned with the procedural fairness of the process of the law, more so than its outcome (Tyler 1990), was also evidenced in McIvor's (2009) study. Sheriffs' efforts were considered fair. Outcomes, albeit negative at times, were accepted by participants when they perceived that they had been given ample opportunities to progress and had not done so. For example, most of those who had their orders revoked following breach action recognized their responsibility in the process. Finally, offenders perceived that they were given a forum to have their progress acknowledged and to provide explanations for digressions (ibid.); this is an important aspect of procedural justice noted in other studies, including Crawford and Newburn's (2003) analysis of young people's participation in youth offender panels in England and Wales. Notwithstanding the central role of drug treatment, drug monitoring, sanctions and rewards in promoting change, McIvor (2009) concludes that procedural justice approaches may offer strong potential in promoting compliance for drug-reliant offenders.

Young people: legitimacy, procedural justice and legal socialization

The available evidence also suggests that children and adolescents' perceptions of the legitimacy of the law influences their decisions about compliance (Fagan and Tyler 2005; Tyler and Huo 2002). One of the major decisive factors in juvenile inmates' agreement or disagreement to follow staff requests in two correctional institutions for delinquent boys aged 10–16 years in the New York metropolitan area was identified as the perceived legitimacy of the directive (Jones 1964). A second factor related to a weighing up of the perceived benefits or deficits associated with compliance. Adopting Etzioni's (1961) terminology, Jones (1964) labelled decisions based on the legitimacy of the request as moral agreement or moral disagreement, and decisions made following a cost–benefits analysis as calculative agreement. Boys who complied out of moral agreement (normative compliance) recognized the legitimacy of staff requests, while compliance based on calculative agreement occurred following an assessment of the rewards and disadvantages available (calculative compliance). Non-compliers were most likely to base their assessment on the perceived illegitimacy of staff directives rather than on calculative reasons. By way of explanation, Jones (1964) suggests that the balance of power within correctional institutions is weighted in such a way as to favour agreement rather than disagreement where the incentives of compliance outweigh the disincentives.

'Legal' socialization refers to the process whereby attitudes towards the law and perceptions of the legitimacy of legal authority are shaped, developed and extended over the period from childhood through adulthood. Direct contact and interaction with the structures and agents of the law, such as the police, and indirect observation of family, peers and community experiences, make up the full realm of child and adolescent encounters with the law. It is the combination of these influences, it is argued, that shape adolescent perceptions of the law. Two US-based studies have focused particular attention on the legal socialization of children and adolescents. In the first of these studies, Fagan and Tyler (2005) interviewed 215 10–16 year olds from two racially and socio-economically diverse neighbourhoods in New York City. The first neighbourhood comprised 90 per cent African American and Latino residents, of whom almost 80 per cent lived in public housing; the second was more racially heterogeneous, had higher proportions of white working-class populations and more than 50 per cent of residents were recorded as foreign-born. Although individuals with direct experience of the criminal justice system were not specifically targeted, the high-crime profile and incarceration rate in one of the neighbourhoods suggested that participants were likely to have had higher than average levels of exposure to indirect (if not direct) contact with criminal justice authorities. Piquero *et al.* (2005) explored legal socialization with 1,355 adjudicated serious adolescent offenders in Philadelphia and Phoenix. Participants were predominantly male (86 per cent) and aged between 14 and 18 years (mean age 16.04 years). Twenty per cent of the sample was white, 34 per cent Hispanic and 41 per cent African-American. Unlike

Fagan and Tyler's (2005) study, Piquero *et al.* (2005) adopted a longitudinal approach over 18 months to measure change over time. Using measures employed by existing researchers in field (Srole 1956; Sampson and Bartusch 1998; Tyler 1990; Tyler and Huo 2002), both studies explored legitimacy and legal cynicism as dimensions of legal socialization. In this context, legitimacy was explained as a sense of obligation to defer to the rules of legal authorities even when these conflict with one's personal values and self-interests, while legal cynicism referred to the extent that individuals accept or reject the rules of law. Where legal cynicism is high, breach of the legal norms is considered reasonable.

Like adults, adolescent perceptions of the legitimacy of the law are drawn from their direct experience of interactions with the criminal justice system and their perceptions of how fairly they, and others, are treated by authority figures (Fagan and Tyler 2005; Piquero *et al.* 2005; Sharp and Atherton 2007). Fagan and Tyler (2005) report that participants gave higher legitimacy ratings when their interactions with criminal justice agents were perceived to be positive. Furthermore, legitimacy was identified as a significant predictor of self-reported delinquency behaviour with higher delinquency scores associated with weaker assessments of the legitimacy of the police by young people. Piquero *et al.* (2005: 296) also found that adolescents with high ratings of procedural justice regarding the police and the courts had higher legitimacy scores and lower legal cynicism scores, leading them to conclude 'that situational experiences with criminal justice personnel influence more general attitudes about the law and legal system'. Adolescent offenders with the highest legitimacy scores reported the lowest levels of legal cynicism and conversely, those with the highest legal cynicism scores reported the lowest legitimacy scores. Differences were noted between groups of adolescents. Younger adolescents were more likely than older youth to view the law as legitimate, suggesting that attitudes towards the law change in a negative direction as individuals move through adolescence and experience more direct encounters with the police and other criminal justice agents. Legal cynicism was higher for adolescents with more prior arrests and for Hispanic more than white youth. African-American youth and those who were locked up were more likely to report lower legitimacy rates than their white non-detained counterparts (ibid.). These findings are perhaps unexpected in light of the substantive evidence that certain groups of young people including minority youth and youth growing up in disenfranchised communities are frequently over-policed and subject to discriminatory and prejudicial treatment from the police (McAra and McVie 2005; Sharp and Atherton 2007).

Contrary to expectations, Piquero *et al.* (2005) reported stability in levels of legal cynicism and legitimacy over time. They describe that with few exceptions, there was little developmental change in the dimensions of legitimacy and legal cynicism over an 18 month follow-up period. In contrast, Fagan and Tyler (2005) found that legitimacy and legal cynicism changed over time from ages 10 through 14 when legitimacy declined and legal cynicism continued to increase. Differences in the methodological approaches used in both studies and age variances within the profile of the respective samples are possible explanations for the difference.

Piquero *et al.*'s (2005) sample was older, which may suggest that perceptions of the legitimacy of the law and procedural justice had already stabilized or that change occurs at other stages or over longer time periods during adolescence. Fostering legitimacy through fair treatment is an important aspect of development as it 'strengthens ties and attachments to the laws and social norms, as well as group membership among like-minded people' (Fagan and Tyler 2005: 222). However, as Fagan and Tyler (2005) point out, interaction with legal actors represents just one of a number of sources of adolescent values, and one of many processes of socialization. Furthermore, they suggest that perceptions of legitimacy must be considered in the context of adolescence when, during early adolescence especially, young people may reject the influence or intervention of authority figures in their lives 'with typically low stakes in conformity and a narrow social world, there is no easy offset for adolescents' predictable tendency to view social control as an infringement on their autonomy and therefore "illegitimate"' (ibid.: 223).

Offender attitudes and stances in relation to compliance

Structures and relationships of power are key dimensions inherent in the interactions between offenders, the criminal justice system and its agents. The way that offenders experience power while subject to community disposals is likely to influence their responses to it and their positioning within the dynamic of the supervisory relationship (Smith *et al.* 2009). Referring to the prison context, Crewe (2007: 265) suggests that if it is recognized that compliance is structured in relation to dimensions of power, 'it follows that individual prisoners will resist and comply in relation to the particular modes of power that address their values, aims and expectations'. Some evidence exists that usefully illustrates differences in the types of stances adopted by offenders in their interactions with various aspects of the criminal justice system including the probation and the prison systems (Crewe 2007; Ditton and Ford 1994). In Ditton and Ford's (1994) study of 43 probationers, half were described as highly committed and their involvement with probation was characterized by a willingness to actively work on their problems and to fully avail of the help offered. A smaller group was deemed to have a 'superficial degree of commitment' whereby they adhered to the requirements of the order, but demonstrated little knowledge or willingness to change their behaviour (p. 32). This group was identified as complying with the letter rather than the substance of the law. The remainder were categorized as having a 'low degree of commitment', they were uncommitted to change and only minimally compliant with the requirements of probation (ibid.). Overall, Ditton and Ford (1994) found that those who were committed to change and who perceived probation staff to be genuinely interested in their lives were more receptive to probation intervention, including monitoring, than other probationers.

Further analysis provided insight into probationers' attitudes towards probation. While the data do not directly speak to the issue of compliance, they nevertheless highlight that the manner in which individuals' experience criminal justice intervention in their lives may differentially impact on the way that they engage and comply with it. Ditton and Ford (1994) identify six sub-types or vignettes, of which four could be described as positive stances towards probation, and two as negative. Although outlined here as distinct categories, the sub-types are 'neither discrete or immutable' with overlap occurring between the different categorizations (ibid.: 39). The first positive sub-type – labelled 'a cry for help' – consisted of probationers who were not connected to any criminal networks and in the main were law-abiding. Offending occurred as a result of profound social, personal and financial problems. These probationers made the most of the help offered, viewed staff as key players in assisting them with their problems and reported positive changes in their lives as a result of probation intervention. The second sub-type was similar to the first with the exception that probationers saw themselves, rather than the staff, as the agents of change. For this group, the value of probation was that it gave them 'breathing space' and time to work on their own problems. The third sub-type, described as 'helpful deterrence', did not regard themselves as criminal or their problems as serious. Characterized as being marginally involved in offending behaviour, they demonstrated some commitment to avoiding future offending. For them, probation served as a positive deterrent and was seen as helpful in assisting them to 'keep on the rails' (ibid.: 39). Probation was perceived as a last chance and a 'turning point' to resolve serious difficulties and to avoid custody for the fourth sub-type. Made up of individuals with lengthy histories of offending associated with alcohol and drug abuse or personal and mental health problems, these probationers welcomed straight-talking approaches from their supervising officers. Overall, probation supervision was viewed as positive and linked to positive changes in their lives.

Not all probationers adopted positive stances to intervention. Ditton and Ford (1994) explain that for probationers categorized under the fifth sub-type, probation was 'irrelevant'. They neither perceived themselves to need assistance with problems nor considered that they had problems in the first instance. Neither did they intend to change and were 'lukewarm or even scornful' about the service offered. Offending was minimized, seen as something in the past or as an inevitable aspect of the present and probation supervision was useful only insofar as it was a mechanism to avoid custody. The final sub-type represented those who were resistant to change and who viewed probation intervention as 'intrusive' (ibid.: 40). Individuals in this category perceived probation as punitive and many were hostile to staff efforts to intervene in their lives. As expected, these probationers reported little change as a result of being on probation.

The dynamics that underpin and frame offender compliance tend to be context specific and this is most apparent in the contrasting circumstances of offenders under supervision in the community when compared to those in custody. Crewe (2007) reports on the different forms of compliance that exist in the prison setting using a four-category typology. Drawing on this analysis of the nature, organization and experience of power within a medium-security male training prison is not to suggest that generalizations can be made about the power structures and dynamics that exist across community and custodial environments. Rather, it is intended to demonstrate the diversity of the stances taken by offenders in negotiating power and compliance in different contexts. In the first category, described as 'committed compliance', Crewe (2007: 265) explains that prisoners structured their narratives in ways that demonstrated their commitment to change and their active compliance with the system. Incarceration was perceived as an opportunity for self-improvement and making amends and prisoners' normative commitment to comply was enhanced by instrumental mechanisms such as the prison-based Incentives and Earned Privileges (IEP) scheme.[3] Compliance among about half of the prisoners was categorized as 'fatalistic or instrumental' compliance (p. 267). While their level of compliance was similar to the committed compliers, their attitude differed in that their primary motivation to comply was to avail of the incentives offered by the prison for good behaviour, and to move expediently out of the system to be reunited with partners and children in many cases. Resistance to the regime was viewed as pointless in light of the incentives available and their perspectives were underpinned by their normative attachments to the outside world.

A small number of prisoners were classified under the third category of 'detached compliance' (p.270). These were generally former drug addicts many who had little to return to on release. Prison often represented a time of respite and security from the temptations and chaos of their lives outside. Although compliant, they were neither committed nor motivated by the goals of the establishment or its incentives nor indeed any normative attachment external to the prison. They progressed passively through the system and any minor deviation, where it occurred, was motivated by an opportunity to make life easier rather than a challenge to the regime. The final category 'strategic compliance and manipulation' consisted of one in four prisoners (p.271). This group was hostile to the prison and its staff but 'judging that the system could be neither ignored nor surmounted, they acted out an institutional script of active obedience in order to subvert its aims and advance personal rather than systemic objectives' (ibid.). They mendaciously engaged in activities which on the surface presented them as pro-social and committed to change (e.g. attending prison-based courses) while at the same time were actively involved in behaviours that were diametrically in contrast to the goals of the institution such as drug dealing and stealing from the prison kitchens and workshops. These prisoners viewed themselves as active and resistant and their primary goal was to deceive and exit the system without delay.

The dynamic nature of compliance: models, motivations and mechanisms

Building on Bottoms' (2001) work introduced earlier in this chapter, Robinson and McNeill (2010) outline a theoretical framework for community disposals underpinned by the perspective that individuals' responses evolve from their assessments of the treatment received from regulatory bodies with which they have dealings (see Figure 3.2). They also draw on Valerie Braithwaite's (2003)

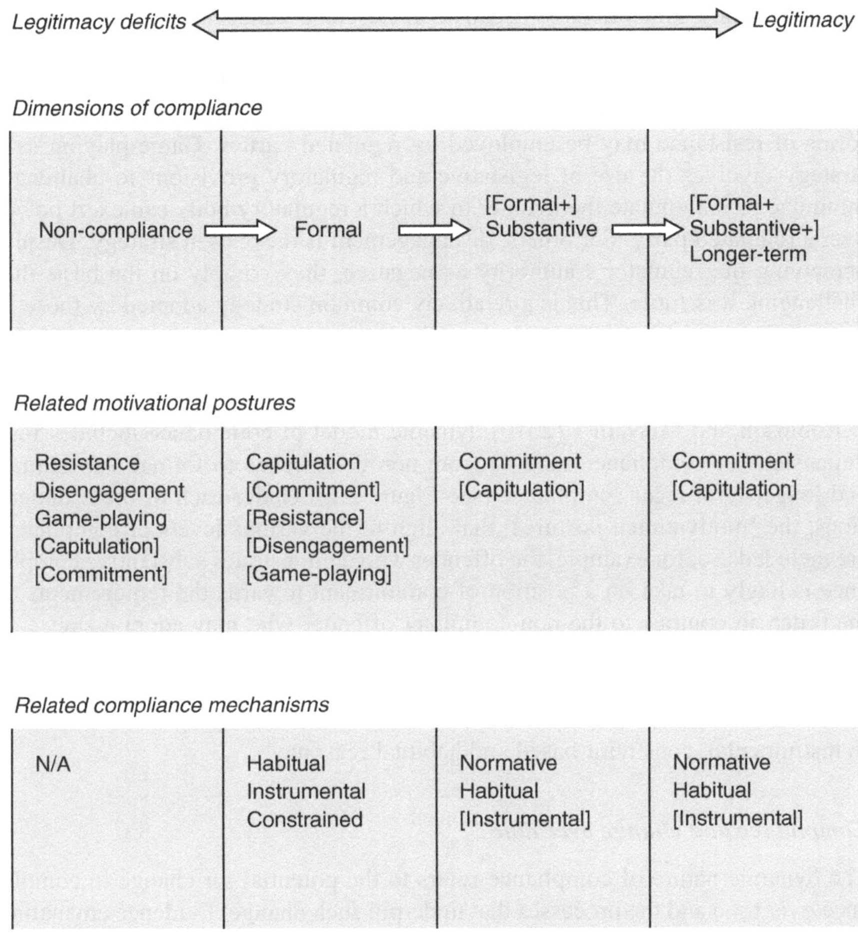

Figure 3.2 A dynamic model of compliance with community supervision
Source: *Offender supervision: new directions in theory, research and practice* (Robinson and McNeill 2010: 375)

research on tax regulation which suggests that authoritative power engenders different responses or 'motivational postures' in regulated parties. Described by Robinson and McNeill (2010: 372) as 'interconnected sets of beliefs and attitudes that are consciously held and openly shared with others', motivational postures are categorized into what Braithwaite (2003) terms 'postures of *deference*' and 'postures of *defiance*'. Postures of deference refer to commitment and capitulation and the difference between them lies in the level of willingness to accept and comply with the regulator's authority. On the other hand, resistance, game-playing and disengagement are categorized as postures of defiance (Braithwaite 2003, in Robinson and McNeill 2010). When the regulated party perceives the regulatory body's intentions as negative, a resistance stance is adopted. Bosworth and Carrabine (2001: 505–6) describe resistance as 'a form and use of power'. In criminal justice, as in other contexts, outright rejection of authoritative power risks the imposition of consequences for non-compliance; as a result more subtle forms of resistance may be employed by regulated parties. Game-playing as a strategy involves the use of legislative and regulatory provisions to challenge, minimize or manipulate the manner in which a regulatory body can exert power over a regulated party. For others, disengagement is the chosen strategy. Despite perceiving the regulator's authority as negative, they comply on the basis that challenging it is futile. This is a relatively common strategy adopted by those in institutional correctional settings where the incentives offered to comply with the regime, supersede the rationality of resistance in many, but not in all cases (Crewe 2007; Jones 1964).

Robinson and McNeill's (2010) dynamic model of compliance includes four dimensions of compliance ranging from non-compliance to formal, substantive and longer-term legal compliance (see Figure 3.2). Under each of these dimensions, the 'motivational postures' that align to the various levels of compliance are included. So, for example, the offender who demonstrates substantive compliance is likely to take on a position of commitment towards the requirements of the order, in contrast to the non-compliant offender who may adopt a stance of resistance, game-playing or disengagement. Drawing on Bottoms' (2001) framework of compliance mechanisms, the model suggests that the stances adopted by offenders are underpinned by a number of mechanisms ranging from normative to instrumental, constraint-based and habitual reasons.

Compliance and change over time

The dynamic nature of compliance refers to the potential for change in compliance over time and the processes that underpin such change. Evidence emanating from a range of criminal justice and regulatory situations indicates that the extent to which individuals comply, changes according to the interactions between regulators and regulated parties (Tyler 1990; Tyler and Huo 2002). Robinson and McNeill (2010) hypothesize that the notion of compliance as a non-static construct is applicable to community disposals. They propose that offenders will commence supervision at different points on the spectrum from non-compliance to longer-term legal compliance with the aspiration that offenders should progress in the direction of compliance (see Figure 3.2). The early stage of the supervision process has been identified as a period when non-compliance in the form of non-attendance and reoffending is more common especially among young offenders as they adjust to the expectations imposed on them (O'Mahony and Seymour 2001). Progression towards compliance is anticipated to be neither linear nor straightforward, given offenders' propensity for relapse and reoffending (Healy 2010). Moore *et al.* (2006) report that although 70 per cent of young offenders on intensive supervision and surveillance programmes (ISSP) in England and Wales were fully compliant by the sixth-month stage, a cluster of non-compliance re-emerged towards the end of the intensive period of the order when supervision and surveillance were reduced. There is a dearth of direct empirical exploration on offenders' perceptions of legitimacy and procedural justice in the context of community supervision. What evidence is available suggests that fair and respectful treatment in the relationship with their supervisor is highly rated by offenders on community supervision and central to successful progress in many cases (McCulloch 2010; McIvor 1992; Mair and May 1997; Rex 1999; Springer *et al.* 2009). Conversely, negative perceptions of the supervisory relationship have the potential to adversely impact on compliance (McCulloch 2010). Offenders value and attach greater legitimacy to interventions that are perceived to be meaningful and rewarding or that offer practical action-orientated responses to their problems (Farrall 2002a; Ditton and Ford 1994; McIvor 1992; Ugwudike 2010). Less is known about offenders' perceptions of other procedural justice indicators such as having opportunities to have their say and perceiving that rules are applied consistently and without bias. Few studies have focused specifically on compliance and therefore limited insight exists into the processes or practices that take place during supervision which may contribute or detract from greater levels of compliance among offenders.

Compliance and interaction effects

The complex make-up of compliance is further highlighted by what Bottoms (2001: 104) terms 'possible interaction effects'. The first effect relates to the interaction between the different mechanisms that underpin compliant behaviour. Here it is posited that the decision to comply may arise from a combination of instrumental, normative, constraint-based and habitual and routine mechanisms as described earlier in this chapter (see Figure 3.1). As an example, Hucklesby (2009) highlights that although electronically monitored offenders identified the main influence on their decision to comply as instrumental insofar as they wished to avoid potential punishment for non-compliance, some also reported concern about the consequences of punishment such as losing employment or being parted from their children. Their decisions to comply were therefore based on a combination of instrumental and normative reasons. The second interaction effect exists between compliance mechanisms and different types of individuals or groups. Bottoms (2001) references Sherman's (1992) research on policing domestic violence to illustrate that the same sanction shapes compliance among offenders in different ways. Sherman (1992) demonstrates that the subsequent violence rates following arrest for domestic violence were lower for married and employed perpetrators than for unemployed and unmarried offenders. Differences in the violence rates following arrest are explained with reference to individuals' 'stakes in conformity' whereby those with the strongest ties to others who disapproved of their behaviour were more likely to be deterred than offenders with fewer pro-social attachments (Sherman 1992, in Bottoms 2001:105). Lasley (2003) outlines similar outcomes among domestic violence offenders subject to intensive bail supervision. Those who were employed or were of Mexican origin were least likely to be re-arrested compared with other offenders. Fear of losing employment or the risk of being returned to one's home country acted as the main motivating factors associated with compliance. These findings further reiterate the point that individual decisions to comply are often based on a complexity of reasons arising from the unique circumstances of offenders' lives. The 'stakes in conformity' thesis also suggests that the potential for increased non-compliance among young people is likely to be greater given that they frequently have the weakest social attachments and stakes in mainstream society (Barry 2006; Griffin and Kelleher 2010).

Sustaining compliance in the longer-term

Although instrumental approaches – based on incentives and sanctions – often represent the primary mechanism for seeking offender compliance with community disposals, the relationship between deterrence and compliance is complex and mediated by a number of individual, social and situational factors (Nagin 1998; Sherman 1992). Furthermore, the success of deterrent sanctions in promoting compliance is based on offenders' perceptions of the certainty and severity of their implementation, as opposed to the availability of sanction *per se* (Nagin 1998). The implication is that instrumental measures and sanctions are likely to have substantial cost implications for criminal justice agencies where certainty of punishment depends on the level of resources available to monitor behaviour and to detect non-compliance in the first instance. Tyler (2006a) argues that a primary emphasis on instrumental approaches is not sustainable for the general functioning of democratic societies and contends that internal regulation generated through normative commitment is required:

> authorities cannot induce through deterrence alone a level of compliance sufficient for effective social functioning. Society's resources are inadequate to such a task and some base of normative commitment to follow the law is needed.
>
> (p. 65).

A reliance on instrumental mechanisms to bring about compliance also increases the risk that offenders will align their behaviour with the incentives/disincentives available to avoid punishment. Therefore where the purpose of community disposals is to influence positive behavioural change and reduce reoffending, a dominant focus on deterrence-based strategies may be detrimental to its overall integrity.

In contrast to instrumental strategies, compliance based on normative factors occurs where 'the citizen voluntarily complies with rules rather than respond to the external situation' (Tyler 2006a: 24). Here compliance emanates from the individual and is based on their internalized norms and values, attachments to others and/or perspectives on the legitimacy of the law and those tasked with imposing it. The evidence base that underpins individual motivation to comply points to the need for greater emphasis to be placed on supporting offenders to develop normative values and attachments, as strategies to promote compliance with the criminal law (Tyler 1990; Tyler and Huo 2002). Robinson and McNeill (2010: 377) develop the point with reference to community disposals by suggesting that supervision practice may require 'a much clearer focus on the deployment or activation of normative mechanisms in order to generate commitment to comply' by facilitating change in offenders' attitudes and beliefs, promoting and supporting their social attachments and working to improve offenders' perceptions of the legitimacy of the law and its agents. To promote normative compliance with the requirements of community disposals, offenders' recognition of their supervisor's legal authority of itself may be insufficient to activate meaningful change. Instead it is proposed that establishing '"psychological legitimacy"; that is, the moral right to influence another human subject with their consent (cf. Beetham 1991)' is a key facet of building compliance within the supervisory process (ibid.: 377). Although requiring further research and investigation, the indications are that engendering compliance through normative measures with young people may increase the likelihood of compliance with the criminal law. Jones (1964) for example, reports that the reconviction rate for juveniles detained in correctional institutions was 10 per cent after one year for those who mostly demonstrated normative compliance, compared with 56 per cent who exhibited calculative compliance. In a more contemporary example, Shapland and Bottoms (2011: 273) report that young adult offenders who 'had decided definitely to desist from offending were more likely to give "moral" rather than pragmatic reasons' for declining an opportunity to offend.[4] In contrast, those who did not express such views about desistance were more likely to provide practical reasons.

Conclusion

This chapter draws attention to the complexities involved in exploring compliance in the context of community supervision. It suggests that offenders comply with the supervision process to varying degrees and for different reasons, but neither their levels of engagement nor their motivations to comply are likely to remain static over time. Instead, it is posited that the impetus to comply is fluid insofar as it is influenced by changes in the dynamics within the professional relationship between offenders and their supervising officer, the changing circumstances of offenders' lives, as well as alterations in their subjective perspectives over time. These changes are likely to resonate strongly in the experiences of young people given the propensity for change in the social and psychological circumstances of their lives over the adolescent period (see Chapter 4). Where individuals perceive themselves to be treated in a fair and just manner by those in authority, their perceptions of the law as legitimate are enhanced and are seen to influence compliance in a positive direction (Tyler 1990). On the other hand, when procedural justice is deemed to be poor, individuals may cultivate weaker attachments to the law, including lower levels of cooperation with legal personnel. Such findings highlight the relevance of procedural justice in efforts to promote compliance with offenders on community supervision. Finally, the evidence presented in this chapter suggests that strategies which activate offenders' (internal) normative motivations to comply are more likely to succeed in maintaining compliance in the longer-term than those which rely on external strategies where 'someone or something else needs to keep on constraining, threatening or rewarding' (Robinson and McNeill 2010: 377).

4 The context of community supervision: adolescent development and social circumstances

Adolescence is characterized as a period of transition (Iselin, DeCoster and Salekin 2009) and a time of profound change, captured by Steinberg and Schwartz (2000: 23), who describe how 'other than infancy, there is probably no period of human development characterized by more rapid or pervasive transformations in individual competencies'. However, the process of development is complex and the biological, cognitive, social and emotional changes associated with the transition from childhood to adulthood manifest in different ways and at different times for all adolescents (Gillen 2006; Halpern-Felsher and Cauffman 2001). Such variances support the perspective that age alone is not a consistent or valid indicator of maturity (Graham and Bowling 1995). In recent years, there has been increasing acknowledgement that young offenders' contact and interactions with the criminal justice system must take consideration of the normative changes that occur during adolescent development especially in relation to cognitive and psychosocial maturity (Grisso *et al.* 2003; Scott, Reppucci and Woolard 1995). This perspective has gained momentum with researchers, primarily in the United States, where the stimulus surrounds the lowering of the age limit at which youths can be tried as adults in some states, automatic transfer statutes, and the subsequent rise in the numbers transferred to the adult criminal justice system (Altschuler and Brash 2004; Grisso *et al.* 2003; Scott *et al.* 1995; Scott and Steinberg 2008). Within these contexts, attention has focused on the influence of young people's developmental maturity levels on their capability to make socially responsible decisions about offending and competent legal decisions in police custody and in the courtroom. The evidence suggests that when compared with adults, adolescents differ in the processes and outcomes of their decisions, that these differences are related to immaturity and that they place young people in a weaker position relative to adults when making decisions. This chapter examines the manner in which cognitive and psychosocial immaturity influence young people's decision making in the criminal justice system before going on to explore its applicability to the context of community supervision. In this regard, attention is drawn to the ways that cognitive and psychosocial factors shape young people's decisions to comply with the conditions imposed on them while under supervision in the community. In seeking to locate individual decision making in its broader social context, the latter sections of the chapter focus on the role of the family, school and community.

Decision making and judgement: cognitive and psychosocial factors

Both cognitive and psychosocial factors are associated with the way that young people make decisions and consequently with how their decision making changes over time (Grisso *et al.* 2003; Cauffman and Steinberg 2000a). It is generally considered that by 16 years, most adolescents of average or above average intelligence have acquired a level of cognitive ability that enables them to reason, apply logic and problem solve in a similar manner to adults (Cauffman and Steinberg 2000b; Grisso 2000). It is well recognized that younger adolescents may be less competent in reasoning and problem solving abilities and more child- than adult-like in their functioning (Burnett, Noblin and Prosser 2004; Grisso 2000). Furthermore, adolescent deficits extend to having less insight into their own personality, motivations and behaviours than their older peers (Steinberg and Schwartz 2000). As a result, younger adolescents are more likely to make decisions that are less socially responsible in relation to offending and to their involvement and participation in the criminal justice system. Grisso *et al.* (2003) compared the capacity of 927 detained and community-based adolescents (11–17 year olds) and 466 young adults (18–24 year olds) to stand trial.[1] Using the MacArthur Competence Assessment Tool-Criminal Adjudication (MacCAT-CA), the study tested competency in the areas of understanding (comprehension of the defendant's rights at trial and court procedures), reasoning (the ability to process information for legal decision making and recognition of information relevant to a legal defence) and appreciation (the ability to recognize information as being relevant to one's circumstances). After controlling for social class and intelligence, the study found that those aged 11–13 years performed significantly lower on each of the three competency measures than older adolescents and young adults. Overall, the difference between the scores for adolescents and adults was moderate for 11–13 years and low for 14–15 year olds, while the oldest adolescents (16–17 year olds) did not differ significantly from young adults. Higher proportions of younger adolescents also demonstrated significant impairment on one or both of the MacCAT-CA scales relating to reasoning and understanding (30 per cent of 11–13 year olds, compared with 19 per cent of 14–15 year olds and just 12 per cent respectively of 16–17 year olds and young adults).

While noteworthy differences are demonstrated between younger and older adolescents, there are a number of caveats about the applicability of a cut-off point of 16 years for the full attainment of cognitive maturity. Grisso (2000) points out that the temporal dimension of cognitive development is not an exact science, and for some, development does not evolve fully until late adolescence or early adulthood. The evidence also suggests that, like other aspects of development, the pace of cognitive maturity may vary depending on intelligence (IQ), mental health as well as the psychological and social contexts where development occurs. Viljoen, Klaver and Roesch (2005) for example, found that in a study of adolescent legal decision making, defendants with a lower socio-economic profile were less likely to avail of their interrogation rights, while those with attention deficit disorders and hyperactivity were more likely to waive their right to counsel and were less likely to communicate with their legal representatives than other defendants. Irrespective of age, Grisso *et al.* (2003) found that juveniles with lower intelligence scores were more likely than those of average intelligence to be impaired in their capacity to understand the procedures of the court or their rights as defendants. They were also less likely to have the ability to process information relevant to legal decision making or to recognize where information was relevant to their case. Such findings are noteworthy given that a greater proportion of young people in the criminal justice system have low IQ scores than their non-offending peers (Hayes and O'Reilly 2007). Grisso *et al.* (2003) found that the IQ scores of detained (criminally involved) adolescents were substantially lower than those of their non-criminally counterparts from the same or similar types of communities. Of the detained adolescents aged 15 years and younger, between one-fifth and one-quarter had IQ scores ranging from 60 to 74 (extremely low to mild intellectual disability range) and a further 40 per cent scored between 75 and 89 (low average/borderline). Based on these statistics, Grisso *et al.* (2003: 350) surmised that in the region of two-thirds of detained youth had an IQ score that 'was associated with a significant risk of being incompetent to stand trial because of impaired understanding or reasoning or both'.

Kazdin (2000: 49) contends that the impact of mental health disorders on decision making by delinquent youth is not sufficiently understood 'to permit firm conclusions' but argues that the symptoms of disorders are very likely to have a bearing on decision making. By way of example, he suggests that impulsiveness associated with attention deficit hyperactivity disorder (ADHD) could obstruct young people's ability to deliberate, to engage in rational decision making or to seek out 'alternative courses of action' (ibid.: 50). The potential for mental health problems to impair decision making is pertinent for young offenders in light of the evidence suggesting that they are more likely than the general youth population to meet the diagnostic criteria for a range of psychological disorders and other mental health conditions (Hayes and O'Reilly 2007; Tolan and Titus 2009). Finally, Steinberg and Scott (2003: 1012) point out that many of the assertions about cognitive reasoning ability and decision making competency are based on studies where hypothetical situations are presented to adolescents 'under conditions of low emotional arousal'. In contrast, decisions made by adolescents in 'real life' offending or legal settings are frequently made under unfamiliar or stressful conditions of emotional arousal such as in police custody or in the courtroom (Peterson-Badali *et al.* 1999). The conditions under which decision making takes place are likely to impact on the quality of the decisions made and produce very different outcomes for real-life and hypothetical scenarios.

The 'Maturity of judgment' model

While cognitive ability is a key component in adolescents' competency to make legal and related decisions, it does not sufficiently account for the way that young people apply knowledge and information in practice or the social, psychological and emotional factors that influence their choices in the decision making process. Psychosocial factors such as the ability to control impulses, to establish autonomy, to develop perspective, to consider long-term consequences and to take into account the perspective of others have also been identified as core elements relevant to decision making.

A number of studies have hypothesized and examined the perspective that differences in psychosocial maturity result in differences between adolescent and adult decision making in legal contexts and in relation to involvement in criminality (Cauffman and Steinberg 2000a; Scott *et al.* 1995). Steinberg and Cauffman (1996) developed a 'Maturity of judgment' model based on three categories of psychosocial factors considered to be important influences on how individuals exercise judgement and make decisions. The three categories encompass *responsibility*, which includes self-reliance, clarity of identity, healthy autonomy and independence; *temperance*, which involves the ability to assess situations before acting and to control impulsivity; and *perspective*, which refers to the capacity to view situations from different standpoints, to understand the complexity of situations and to place them 'in broader social and temporal contexts' (Cauffman and Steinberg 2000a: 745). Although underpinned by psychosocial factors, Steinberg and Cauffman's (1996) model is based on the premise that acquiring maturity is a complex interactive process that incorporates cognitive and psychosocial influences. In further illustrating the complexity of decision making, a distinction is made between the process of decision making or 'judgment' described as involving a combination of cognitive and psychosocial factors relevant to decision making, and the outcome or 'the actual choices made' (Cauffman and Steinberg 2000a: 743). It is also posited that as adolescent development progresses, individuals will make less socially irresponsible decisions. However, in the absence of full maturity, psychosocial factors are likely to influence adolescent decisions in ways that differ from mature adults (Steinberg and Schwartz 2000).

Applying the 'Maturity of judgment' model, Cauffman and Steinberg (2000a) examined the role of psychosocial development on anti-social decision making among four cohorts of school and college students aged 12 to 48 years. When compared with other participants, they found that adolescents scored lower on measures of self-restraint (temperance), self-reliance (responsibility) and consideration of future consequences (perspective). Not only did they experience more difficulty in controlling their impulses and contemplating matters in the longer-term, but they were also less likely to view situations from the perspectives of others, or to have the same level of self-reliance and independence of thought as their adult peers. Overall, while there were significant differences in psychosocial maturity and decision making related to age, those who were more responsible, temperate and demonstrated greatest perspective were identified as having the greater 'maturity of judgment' regardless of age. A number of studies (Colwell *et al.* 2005; Cruise *et al.* 2008; Modecki 2008) subsequently used Steinberg and Cauffman's (1996) 'Maturity of judgment' model and produced broadly consistent results to those found in Cauffman and Steinberg's (2000a) empirical investigation. Colwell *et al.* (2005) explored the influence of cognitive and psychosocial maturity on adolescents' capacity to understand the Miranda warning.[2] Police in the US are obliged to recite the Miranda warning before undertaking any substantial questioning of suspects. Aged between 11 and 17 years (mean age 14.28 years), the male participants were drawn from a juvenile detention centre and a boot camp facility. Both age and intelligence were identified as factors related to adolescents' understanding of the Miranda warning with older and more intelligent individuals demonstrating greater knowledge about the procedures and their rights than their peers. Beyond age and intelligence, only responsibility was significantly related to adolescent capacity to understand the Miranda warning. Those who had greater clarity of identity, healthy autonomy and independence were better able to explain the warning in their own words, and to apply the knowledge in practice at a more advanced level than their contemporaries. Overall, the findings led Colwell *et al.* (2005) to conclude that in understanding decision making by adolescents, both intellectual and psychosocial factors are relevant.

Studies by Cruise *et al.* (2008) and Modecki (2008) also reflected Cauffman and Steinberg's (2000a) findings insofar as psychosocial maturity predicted delinquency and individuals who scored higher on the measures of psychosocial maturity demonstrated less anti-social decision making. Subsequent findings from these studies further highlighted the differences between adolescents and their older peers. For example, Modecki's (2008) research on the influence of psychosocial development on self-reported delinquency found that adolescents (mean age 16 for males and 15.71 for females) and college students (mean age 18.71 for males and 18.33 for females) were most delinquent in comparison with the adult groups. However, differences emerged when participants were informed that negative consequences were 'certain' to arise as a result of delinquent behaviour. In these scenarios, adolescents were more likely to pursue anti-social decisions than either the college students or the adults. These findings demonstrate clear differences in decision making outcomes between adolescents and their older peers, but what is less clear is whether adolescents behave this way because of 'a failure to consider negative consequences, an underestimation of such consequences, or an over-emphasis on positive consequences' (Modecki 2008: 89). In Cruise *et al.*'s study of 11–17 year old male and female adolescents detained in a boot camp (mean age 14.28 years) and a juvenile detention facility (mean age 15.28 years), temperance (as defined by Steinberg and Cauffman (1996) earlier in this chapter) was the factor found to be most strongly associated with frequency of delinquent acts. Specifically, those with the poorest impulse control reported that they committed delinquent acts more often, with their peers, and from a younger age than those with higher reported levels of internal regulation. These results are reflected in studies of self-control in the broader field of the social sciences. Gottfredson and Hirschi (1990) contend that the key component of criminality and delinquency is the absence of self-control. Individuals with high self-control consider the long-term consequences of their actions, whereas those with low self-control may act more on impulse and in response to temptation. It follows that individuals with lower self-control are more likely to engage in criminal and delinquent behaviour. Drawing on Gottfredson and

Hirschi's (1990) work, Grasmick *et al.* (1993) developed a psychometric scale to measure self-control and concluded that self-control is strongly related to offending. Wikström and Butterworth (2006) established that adolescents with low self-control got into trouble more often than others with high self-control.[3] Subjects with very low self-control were most likely to state that they were tempted to steal at least once per week and got angry with other young people on a daily basis. In terms of immediate gratification, the lower the level of self-control, the more likely it was that adolescents stated that receipt of £50 today was preferable to £200 after one year (ibid.).

Only a small number of studies have explored the role of psychosocial maturity and gender differences in adolescent decision making. The existing data unearth mixed results. Cauffman and Steinberg (2000a) found that females were less likely than males to engage in anti-social decision making across each of the following hypothetical scenarios: where participants were informed that adverse consequences would result from committing an anti-social act; that adverse consequences would not occur, and that the consequences were unknown. Females demonstrated more perspective and were more temperate than males, although there were no discernible differences in the psychosocial measure of responsibility. In contrast, Cruise *et al.* (2008) reported no gender differences in any of the three psychosocial factors: perspective, responsibility, or temperance. They suggest that as the mean age was higher in Cauffman and Steinberg's (2000a) study, it may be the case that gender differences emerge in late adolescence or early adulthood. This conclusion resonates in the evidence demonstrating that young females on average desist from offending at an earlier age than young males (Graham and Bowling 1995; Flood-Page *et al.* 2000). With some exceptions such as Grisso *et al.* (2003), even less attention has focused on psychosocial maturity and ethnicity, in some cases because of insufficient sample sizes and in others because of the demographics of the study locations (Modecki 2008, 2009).

Psychosocial development: perspectives on risk and peer influence

Adolescent decision making in medical, social and legal domains has had a somewhat controversial history, with some theorists arguing that policies underpinned by cognitive developmental differences between adolescents and adults restrict young people's rights to make choices about matters that affect their lives. Situations have ranged from decisions about health-related treatments, to consent for sexual activity, access to contraception and relational issues including marriage. Others have suggested that protective paternalistic policies, particularly for young people in the criminal justice system, limit the extent to which they are held responsible for their crimes. Against the backdrop of these criticisms, Scott *et al.* (1995) developed a model which they envisaged would provide a broader framework for considering adolescent decision making capabilities. Similar to Steinberg and Cauffman's (1996) model, Scott *et al.*'s (1995) model is underpinned by the premise that adolescent decision making is based on factors beyond the capacity to reason and to understand. To this end, while it incorporates the ability to reason and understand, it also includes three psychosocial dimensions: temporal perspective, attitude towards and perception of risk, and compliance related to peer and parental influence. The rationale for selecting these dimensions was based on the view that they would allow 'a comparison between the subjective values that drive the choices of adolescents and those of adults' (Scott *et al.* 1995: 227). According to Scott *et al.* (1995), temporal perspective and attitude to and perception of risk are closely linked. Cauffman and Steinberg (2000a) concur with this view in suggesting that developments in the psychosocial domains of responsibility, perspective and temperance may culminate in differences between adolescents and adults in risky decision making. Because adolescents' perspectives are more commonly grounded in the short-term, in making choices, their assessment and weighting of the risks and benefits of decisions may also be contextualized within this time frame. Adolescents' perceptions and attitudes towards risk are also seen to differ from those of adults, with adolescents using 'a risk-reward calculus that places relatively less weight on risk, in relation to reward, than that used by adults' (Steinberg and Scott 2003: 1012). The likelihood of adolescents identifying risks in particular situations is lowered in comparison with adults, as is the likelihood of them considering the prospect of negative consequences. Modecki (2009: 191) reports that even where risks are considered by adolescents, 'they may continue to underestimate hazards, and do not seem particularly swayed by perceived risk'. In addition, adults are more cautious and take considered and measured judgements in the decision making process. Halpern-Felsher and Cauffman (2001) for example, found that when asked to advise peers on making risky decisions, adults were more likely than adolescents to contemplate the risks and benefits and to suggest the prospect of a second opinion. Natural curiosity or the pursuit of peer approval (Ford *et al.* 1989) also motivates adolescents to act against risk awareness. Rodham *et al.*'s (2006) small-scale qualitative study of school-going adolescents aged 16 and over in the UK found that where adolescents wished to create a good impression with new people, they sometimes engaged in risky behaviour to be accepted, despite not specifically wanting to. Scott *et al.* (1995: 235) explain that 'loss and gain are defined according to the decision-maker's own values' and these factors influence decisions. Taking the scenario of a teenager who is invited to take drugs with her friends, they describe how the costs of refusing to participate – for instance, peer exclusion and perceived damage to self-image – may outweigh the risks of being caught or becoming addicted. In this context, Scott *et al.* (1995) suggest that the decision to take drugs is based on a 'rational choice' to avoid damage to self-image or isolation from the peer group. It further demonstrates, however, that adolescents' lack of life experience is likely to lead them to make decisions about risk behaviour that differ from adults and may not be in their long-term interests (Rodham *et al.* 2006). Given the premise that developmental change occurs over time, it is feasible that attitude and perception of risk will also change in tandem with developmental maturity. Less clear, based on current research, is 'whether attitude toward risk remains constant across decision making domains' (Scott *et al.* 1995: 230).

The remaining factor drawn on by Scott *et al.* (1995) to explain differences in adolescent and adult decision making relates to peer and parental influence. Steinberg and Schwartz (2000) describe how adolescents are most receptive to peer influence in early and mid-adolescence; thereafter, the influence of peers gradually declines with the move into late adolescence. Peer involvement and attachment represent important structures in the maturity process especially when the peer group holds normative, pro-social values (Steinberg, Chung and Little 2004). However, for many young people who offend, it is the negative influence of peers that is most commonly documented as a factor related to offending behaviour (Graham and Bowling 1995). It is widely supported that adolescents are subject to more peer influence than adults (Scott *et al.* 1995; Steinberg and Cauffman 1996) and this influence extends beyond offending-related decisions to all aspects of young people's lives. Peer influence can impact on adolescent decision making either explicitly when adolescents make choices based on direct peer pressure to behave in a certain way, or indirectly when the choice made is based on a desire for peer approval (Scott 2000; Steinberg and Scott 2003). Zimring (2000) argues that resisting peer pressure is a social skill not yet acquired by many adolescents. He contends that the capacity to avoid temptation while alone represents a different challenge to that where peers are actively enticing and encouraging participation in offending behaviour. Peer influence may overtake family influence at certain points of adolescent development (Pardini, Loeber and Stouthamer-Loeber 2005). There is a tendency among younger teenagers to question and object to rules and guidelines as part of the process of seeking autonomy and establishing independence, even from adults whose opinion they value (Steinberg and Schwartz 2000). Furthermore, Altschuler and Brash (2004) suggest that involvement with anti-social peers can interrupt normal parent–child relations and reduce contact with pro-social peers.

Psychosocial maturity and legal decision making

Grisso *et al.* (2003) examined the psychosocial dimensions of adolescent capacities in legal settings (in the contexts of responding to police questioning; disclosing information to a defence lawyer during consultation; and responding to a plea agreement). Differences in the choices made across ages by adolescents and young adults in legal settings and the relationship between choices and the psychosocial factors of risk appraisal, resistance to peer influence and future orientation were explored using the MacArthur Judgment Evaluation (MacJEN). Young adults (18–24 year olds) were significantly more likely to recognize the risk associated with legal decision making than any of the three adolescent groups (11–13 years, 14–15 years, 16–17 years). Overall, however, youth aged 15 years and under differed from 16 and 17 year olds who were seen to be broadly similar to young adults across most, but not all, dimensions. Younger adolescents, irrespective of age, gender and socio-economic status, were significantly less likely to recognize or to perceive the likelihood of risk in legal contexts or 'to consider the long-term, and not merely the immediate, consequences of their legal decisions' (ibid.: 357).

Adolescents' restricted ability to negotiate legal situations and take legally relevant information into consideration relative to their age is not uncommon. Viljoen *et al.* (2005) for example, found that adolescents aged 15 years and younger were more likely to confess during police questioning, to waive their interrogation rights and rights to appeal and were less likely to be influenced by perceived evidence against them when making decisions. It also emerged in Grisso *et al.*'s (2003) research that younger adolescents were more likely to make decisions that represented compliance with authorities such as confessing to the police rather than remaining silent, decisions which may not always have been in their best legal interests. Combined, the conclusions suggest that 'aspects of psychosocial maturation that include progress toward greater future orientation, better risk perception, and less susceptibility to peer influence' (Grisso *et al.* 2003: 335) may impact on young people's performance as defendants in addition to their capacity for understanding and reasoning (cognitive competencies). The implications from the research evidence highlight that adolescents are less future-orientated than adults (Cauffman and Steinberg 2000a; Scott *et al.* 1995), and as a result, short- rather than long-term consequences of decisions are likely to hold more weight (Bonnie and Grisso 2000; Steinberg and Scott 2003). Contemplating the long-term impact of consequences is a developmentally challenging process for adolescents and may considerably influence both the nature and underlying reasons for their decisions. One example reported by Peterson-Badali *et al.* (1999) refers to the cases of adolescents in police custody in Canada who admitted guilt or refused legal advice or access to their parents, in order to expedite their release time. Zimring (2000: 283) refers to adolescence as 'a period of "learning by doing" in which the only way competence in decision making can be achieved is by making decisions and making mistakes'. Because adolescents are less experienced in decision making than their adult counterparts (Steinberg and Schwartz 2000), consistency in the way that they apply logic and reasoning to situations is compromised, particularly in situations that are new, stressful and uncertain (Grisso 2000; Scott *et al.* 1995; Steinberg and Cauffman 1996). Scott and Steinberg (2008) suggest that even where adolescents have acquired similar reasoning capacities to adults, they are less capable than adults by virtue of their limited life experience, as well as being less efficient at processing information. Poor skill in this area has direct implications for adolescent offenders where 'in life, and particularly on the street, the ability to quickly marshal information may be essential to optimal decision making' (Scott and Steinberg 2008: 20). It also has important repercussions in legal contexts. Peterson-Badali *et al.* (1999) outline the scenario of a young person who reported that he understood what the right to silence meant, but made a statement while in police custody because he did not realize the right to silence applied to encounters with the police. In the same study, over 60 per cent of young people said they were informed of their rights regarding legal counsel, yet three-quarters reported that they did not contact a lawyer prior to police questioning. Of those, 76 per cent said that they did not believe access to a lawyer was possible. With regard to the right to silence, 59 per cent of those who were asked by police to waive their right to silence or to consult with a parent did so. The most common reasons reported were that young people thought they had to; they wanted to give their account of events, or because of police inducement or intimidation (Peterson-Badali *et al.* 1999). These findings highlight that awareness of rights alone is insufficient to counteract the situational pressures associated with involvement in the criminal justice system and furthermore demonstrate the impact of immaturity when making decisions in legal contexts.

Psychosocial maturity and young people's compliance with community disposals

Research on the links between psychosocial maturity and decision making is an emerging area where gaps in knowledge remain (Grisso *et al.* 2003; Fried and Reppucci 2001; Iselin *et al.* 2009; Modecki 2009). Grisso (2000: 160) cautions against making definitive statements about the relationship; he does, however, acknowledge that 'a good deal of theory, and some research, supports the general proposition that youths are in transition with regard to various psychosocial characteristics that could influence their preferences when they make choices'. More recently, Colwell *et al.* (2005) explain that the role of psychosocial factors is not clearly understood relative to other influences such as IQ or how factors interact across different settings. In other words, the skills and competencies associated with decision making in one setting are not necessarily applicable to all settings or generalizable across contexts (Scott *et al.* 1995).

Despite the limitations, the existing research offers promise in shedding light on some of the factors that influence young people's judgement about complying with the requirements of community disposals and the decision to desist from offending. It also further assists in understanding adolescent interactions with the structures and agents of the criminal justice system (Fagan and Tyler 2005). The circumstances under which community-based disposals are delivered and the interactions that take place are substantively different to the types of legal interaction that takes place in other aspects of the criminal justice system such as in police stations or in the courts. Community-based disposals for young offenders typically involve ongoing contact with a supervising officer, a team of specialist or programme staff or a combination of both. While subject to a community disposal, the supervision period can extend over a number of months or years during which the professional–client relationship and supervisory dynamics have the potential to develop and change over time (see Chapter 7 and 8). Against this, offenders are aware of the power vested in their supervisors to return them to court for non-compliance (Smith *et al.* 2009). Furthermore, the conditions of community disposals oblige young offenders to make compliance-related decisions (e.g. the decision to attend scheduled appointments, or not) on an ongoing and consistent basis over the entire supervision period. Lack of orientation towards the future, differences in attitude towards risk, and peer influence are likely to cause challenges for adolescents in their efforts to comply with community disposals. The temptation to opt out of supervision appointments or to engage in offending behaviour where the draw of peers provides more exciting alternatives may be a challenge for those who have not developed a sense of autonomy and resistance to peers. Contemplating the consequences of non-compliance may also be challenging for developmentally immature adolescents. Choices are also likely to be influenced by what young people perceive to be beneficial in the short-term as opposed to consideration of the long-term good.[4]

Young people's decisions about compliance in the context of community supervision are likely to change over time as their cognitive capacity and psychosocial skills improve with increased maturity. Pro-social behaviour and compliance do not automatically follow from maturity given that greater maturity may enhance offenders' capacity to manage or conceal their criminal activities or to present a façade of compliance with the requirements of community supervision (Crewe 2007; Little and Steinberg 2006).

Overall, the expectation is that adolescent preferences will shift in a pro-social direction as maturity evolves (Scott *et al.* 1995) based on the evidence that most adolescents, including those considered persistent offenders, will reduce their level of offending or grow out of crime in early adulthood (Rutherford 1992). The evidence relating to when full maturity is attained, although mixed, is increasingly shifting to the conclusion that developmental maturity continues into early adulthood (Bryan-Hancock and Casey 2011). Although Cauffman and Steinberg (2000a) found no substantial improvement in psychosocial maturity among adolescents beyond the age of 19 years, other evidence points to key differences in levels of maturity between young people in late adolescence and young adults (Bryan-Hancock and Casey 2010). Young people's cognitive and psychosocial development unfolds within the context of their social circumstances and relationships in the community; it is to these influences that the attention now focuses for the remainder of this chapter.

The social context of compliance: family, school and community

Fagan (2000) argues that in exploring young people's experiences, consideration must be given to the social and situational contexts that frame their daily routines in addition to the adolescent developmental factors as discussed above. Kazdin (2000) highlights the need to focus on adolescent decision making in the context of interpersonal relationships and the circumstances of young people's lives within the community environment. More broadly, it is argued that contextual factors interact with individual characteristics in shaping adolescents' capacity to make decisions (ibid.). The relevance of social context to offenders' decisions to stop offending is emphasized by Bottoms *et al.* (2004: 376), who assert that decisions must be viewed 'as being taken within specific social contexts, and not as disembedded and disconnected "confrontation(s) between the subject and the world"'.

Family support and monitoring

By virtue of their young age, vulnerability and limited opportunities for mobility, the family represents an important aspect of young people's social context and a force that is likely to directly and indirectly influence their decision making while subject to community supervision. Vogelvang and van Alphen (2010: 257) remind us that the probation client's role as an offender is only one dimension of the individual and sits within a broader set of roles that includes 'a child of his parents, and often as a sibling, partner, parent and extended family member'. This notion is particularly applicable to young people whose parents, as the primary caregivers, play a pivotal role in their lives. Successful development necessitates the involvement of supportive and consistent role models in addition to positive experiential opportunities to develop interpersonal skills, autonomy and perspective (Nixon and Halpenny 2010; Supple and Small 2006). Close and supportive bonds between children and their parents are associated with a reduced risk of delinquency (Graham and Bowling 1995). The association between social capital (parental support, teacher control and interpersonal trust) and self-reported delinquency was examined by Salmi and Kivivuori (2006) in a nationally representative sample of 5,412 Finnish adolescents aged 15–16 years. A 'robust link' between indicators of social capital and delinquency was identified whereby those who were least likely to report having parental support and teacher control were also more likely to be repeat offenders. Salmi and Kivivuori (2006) also uncovered some evidence pointing to the existence of an interactive effect between individual and family factors. Although the relationship remained significant when self-control and cognitive ability were controlled, the strength of the link weakened, leading to the conclusion that 'the social capital investments of parents and teachers may be partially influenced by the individual character of the adolescent recipient' (ibid.: 140).

Graham and Bowling (1995) identify that parental supervision is indirectly related to offending through its association with truancy and negative peer group involvement. Young people who engage in anti-social behaviour and truant from school are more likely to have parents who are unaware of their whereabouts or the identity of their associates (ibid.). Responsive parenting practices that monitor, respond and impose consequences for anti-social behaviour are important components in developing self-control (Gottfredson and Hirschi 1990). An appropriate level of parental monitoring is related to lowering the risk of delinquent behaviour (Griffin *et al.* 2000; Laird *et al.* 2003); conversely, the likelihood of becoming involved in offending behaviour is estimated to be approximately twice as high for young people with low to medium levels of parental supervision when compared with those receiving high levels of supervision (Graham and Bowling 1995). A low level of parental supervision is also linked to an increased propensity for adolescents to establish relationships with delinquent peers (Warr 2005). Some evidence exists to suggest that parental monitoring of itself may be insufficient to curb involvement in anti-social behaviour and that adolescents also need to perceive that consequences exist as a result of engaging in such activities.

Parsai, Marsiglia and Kulis' (2010) study of parental monitoring and substance use among 1,087 Hispanic and non-Hispanic adolescents aged 13–15 years old concluded that clear rules from their parents and a belief that consequences would follow reduced the likelihood of alcohol, cigarette and marijuana consumption. Similarly, findings based on secondary data from the American Drugs and Alcohol Survey (ADAS) involving 82,918 7th–12th grade students across 36 communities in the US also found that student involvement in drugs declines as perceived family sanctions rise (Kelly, Comello and Hunn 2002).

Family problems and parental input into the supervision process

Adolescents are reliant on parents and family members to provide for many of their physical, social and emotional needs and are therefore vulnerable when a nurturing and stable environment does not exist. A substantial body of literature strongly attests to the problematic family backgrounds and poor family functioning experienced by many young people in the criminal justice system (Barry 2006; Carroll and Meehan 2007; Wikström and Butterworth 2006). Among others, factors include: low levels of support and warmth, poor parental monitoring and supervision, harsh or inconsistent punishment or child-rearing practices, parental and family conflict and dysfunction, parental criminality and involvement in the criminal justice system (Loeber and Stouthamer-Loeber 1986; Loeber 1990; Moore *et al.* 2006). Childhood exposure to family and marital violence is a factor associated with increased adolescent offending behaviour, and involvement in the criminal justice system (Haynie *et al.* 2009; Herrera and McCloskey 2001). Kazdin (2000: 55) argues that although previous negative childhood experiences such as trauma do not necessarily influence future behaviour; he suggests that as adverse experiences accrue, 'they can greatly affect the probability of engaging in maladaptive strategies and can decrease the likelihood that rational decision making plays a central role in selecting courses of action'. Seymour and Butler (2008) identified that for a number of young people appearing before the courts, parental problems such as alcoholism, domestic violence, drug addiction, homelessness and parental imprisonment detracted from parental capacity to care and supervise their children. Professionals were generally of the view that parents' difficulties in maintaining control of their offspring were most often related to social and personal problems and a lack of parenting skills as opposed to an unwillingness to parent:

> There are families who have huge problems and they don't have a capacity to relate. There might be an alcohol problem, very poor education levels of parents, parents who are illiterate. Letters [are] sent out to families and they don't know how to respond because they can't read so there are all kinds of assumptions being made about the level of function of parents without checking it out.
>
> [P041, Probation Officer in Seymour and Butler 2008: 41]

To compound existing problems, family members risk being exposed to retribution arising from young people's criminality in the community or through their involvement with criminal gangs resulting in threats, violence, or arson against the home and individual members (Hourigan 2011). The impact of repeated offending behaviour and involvement in the criminal justice system has the potential in some cases to cause high levels of anxiety, stress and shame for parents and family members (Clear, Rose and Ryder 2001; Hillian and Reitsma-Street 2003; Shapiro and diZerega 2010). In these ways, young people's ongoing offending behaviour has the effect of damaging family relationships and further eroding what limited support structures exist for them. Research on the relationship between family structure and delinquency has unearthed inconsistent and at times contradictory results (Loeber and Stouthamer-Loeber 1986; Sampson and Laub 1993). While evidence points to a link between family structure and delinquency (Kierkus and Baer 2003), other research indicates that when factors such as parental support are controlled for, no discernible difference exists. Graham and Bowling (1995) for example, found that compared with others, young people in single-parent family and step-family configurations were significantly more likely to recall a poor relationship with at least one parent. They suggest that it is these differences in the quality of relationships and not the family structure itself that accounts for differences in self-reported delinquent behaviour.

Offenders' families are both an important factor leading to criminality and in supporting individuals to stop offending (Trotter 2010). While engaging families to work in partnership with youth justice supervisors might encourage young people's compliance and engagement with supervision, its strongest impact is likely to occur in situations where partnerships build capacity within the family to support compliance after the formal intervention has ceased (Shapiro and diZerega 2010). Vogelvang and van Alphen (2010) argue that family members cannot be compelled to engage in the supervision process and thus participation occurs on a voluntary basis. However, the problems experienced by young people and their families are noteworthy not only because they may be associated with young people's involvement in anti-social and criminal behaviour in some cases, but also because they are likely to hinder parental ability and willingness to engage in the supervision process or to support their children through the criminal justice system (Seymour and Butler 2008). Some parents with mental health difficulties such as depression experience considerable difficulty in their capacity to engage in partnerships designed to support their children (Sheppard 2002). Negative cognitions and feelings of hopelessness, helplessness and guilt inhibit participation and levels of involvement (ibid.). A number of studies indicate that a history of parental criminal involvement and substance misuse are not uncommon in the families of young offenders (Moore *et al.* 2006; Flood-Page *et al.* 2000; Graham and Bowling 1995). Schwalbe and Maschi (2010) identified that previous parental involvement in the criminal justice system and family drug misuse represented significant barriers to parental involvement in their child's participation in community supervision. As a result, officers reported that they had the lowest levels of contact with these parents in the course of supervising young people's cases. Similarly McGagh, Gunn and Lillis (2009) found that parental and youth substance misuse problems adversely impacted on the participation levels of young people and their parents on programmes designed to strengthen and improve family well-being.

The changing influence of family over time

Although adolescents at highest risk of reoffending are often those who encounter the most profound levels of family problems and dysfunction (Kazdin 2000; Little and Steinberg 2006), there is some evidence to suggest that the relationship between family-related factors and offending behaviour is not static and changes over time as young people move into late adolescence and early adulthood. Drawing on data from the Rochester Youth Development Study (RYDS) – a longitudinal study of the development of anti-social behaviour that tracked 1,000 young people from aged 14 years to adulthood – Ireland and Smith (2009) identified that while a significant relationship existed between living in 'partner-violent homes' and adolescent anti-social behaviour and aggression, the relationship did not extend into adulthood except in cases of witnessing severe violence.[5] Hoeve *et al.* (2007) found that family-related factors such as parental attachment, punishment and supervision were not related to delinquency and criminal behaviour among young adults. The only family factor strongly predictive of delinquency in early adulthood was a family environment with low levels of order, structure and rule governance. Following Sampson and Laub (2001), Hoeve *et al.* (2007) argue that the relationship between family-related factors and offending declines in early adulthood as change occurs in the nature of young people's social attachments. They explain that the relevance of social ties to family and to school, as factors that inhibit offending behaviour, become less important in late adolescence and early adulthood when their prominence is replaced by other social attachments such as a relationship with a partner or employment (Sampson and Laub 2001). These findings suggest that in promoting compliance in the course of community supervision, intervention might be best targeted at supporting family relationships in early to mid-adolescence and at the development of external ties including training and employment in late adolescence. Given that 'deterrence works best for those persons who have strong ties or attachment to familial or social groups' (Bottoms 2001: 104), it seems that developing strong social ties between young people, their family and social networks is central to encouraging both compliance with the terms of community disposals and compliance with the criminal law.

School and community

Disproportionately high numbers of young people in the criminal justice system exist outside mainstream education. Carroll and Meehan (2007) report that of a sample of 149 young people appearing before the Children Court in Ireland in 2004, just 21 (14 per cent) were still in school at the time of their first appearance.[6] Although not directly comparable, the significance of these figures becomes apparent in light of national statistics demonstrating that just 2 per cent of school leavers in Ireland leave school with no qualifications, 14 per cent complete the junior cycle of post-primary education, while the vast majority (86 per cent) complete their final senior cycle examinations following five to six years of post-primary education (Byrne, McCoy and Watson 2008). Excluded from a relatively young age, many young people have few alternative opportunities and on a daily basis spend long periods engaged in unstructured activity with peers and similar-minded associates. Their future prospects are bleak against the background of few formal qualifications, social prejudice and a criminal record. Smith and Stewart (1997: 101) describe exclusion from school as a formal mechanism for barring troublesome youth from 'participation in citizenship'. School exclusion removes an important source of opportunity for the development of the cognitive and psychosocial skills associated with maturity and it is also linked to increased risk of involvement in delinquent acts (Graham and Bowling 1995; McCrystal, Percy and Higgins 2007; Moore *et al.* 2006). In the longer-term, exclusion from the educational system has the effect of restricting young people's access to full labour market participation and hinders opportunities to expand social relationships beyond the narrow realm of their criminal peers (Berridge *et al.* 2001; Byrne and Smyth 2010). These effects are not insignificant given the association between pro-social bonds including employment, and desistance from offending (Laub and Sampson 2001; see also Chapter 9).

In the concluding reflections of their edited collection *Community penalties: change and challenges*, Bottoms, Gelsthorpe and Rex (2001: 238) suggest that one of the most important messages to emerge is that 'the effective pursuit of penal policy in relation to community-based sanctions needs to engage with the reality of the social lives of offenders, and the communities in which they live'. In the spectrum of community-based power relations, adolescents are often the most marginalized of groups (Brown 1995). That the majority of young people in the criminal justice system come from poor and disenfranchised neighbourhoods that are themselves marginalized from the state is evident. For many, their experiences of growing up in communities are characterized by few constructive social outlets and limited openings for advancement through pro-social avenues. At the same time, their environment is often replete with opportunities to associate with criminal peers, to access drugs and alcohol, or to be recruited or involved in criminal networks and activities such as drug dealing, storing weapons, couriering drugs and handling and selling stolen goods (Cloward 1959; Hourigan 2011). Little and Steinberg's (2006: 378) examination of the psychosocial correlates of adolescent drug dealing identifies that the incentives for pursuing 'criminal "careers" in illicit market activities' include exclusion from pro-social opportunities such as school and 'diminished expectations for conventional success'. Furthermore, crime and violence can impact on the development of social identity in adolescence (Fagan 2000). While the necessity of 'projecting the right image' and aligning oneself to certain groups may be an essential survival strategy, it invariably leads to increased risk of violence and victimization (ibid.: 384). It is against the backdrop of these types of circumstances and contexts that young people are required to make socially responsible decisions in complying with the terms of supervision in the community.

Conclusion

Age is used as an arbitrary definition of 'maturity', particularly with regard to decisions made about processing young people through the adult criminal justice system. Yet, on the basis of the evidence presented in this chapter, it is apparent that generalizing about the psychological competencies and skills of young people of the same chronological age is difficult and problematic (Steinberg and Schwartz 2000). Key differences emerge between young people's and adult's capabilities to reason and to process information, as well as in their perspectives on future consequences and risk-taking, consideration for others, independence, autonomy and peer influence. These differences are likely to impact on young people's ability to make consistent and socially reasoned decisions relative to their adult counterparts in legal and criminal justice contexts. While the challenge remains to 'define specifically how young people's cognitive and emotional capacities influence delinquent behaviour and abilities as legal decision makers' (Cruise *et al.* 2008: 179), the existing research demonstrates that immaturity and inexperience influence decisions in ways that lead to different outcomes for immature individuals compared to those who have the benefit of full adult maturity (Cauffman and Steinberg 2000a; Scott 2000). In summary, young people in the criminal justice system are required to make compliance-related decisions in the absence of the full social and psychological knowledge, skill and experience base available to adults. Furthermore, their decision making is often framed within social contexts characterized by dysfunctional or problematic family backgrounds, educational exclusion, anti-social peers and their location within marginalized communities where few pro-social outlets exist and criminal commodities such as drugs and alcohol are easily accessible (Steinberg *et al.* 2004). The nature of young people's lives is not automatically programmed towards compliance with the conditions of community supervision and their social and psychological circumstances form the basis for a number of potential threats to compliance during the supervision process. However, unlike 'mainstream' adolescence when poor choices may be dismissed or considered through the lens of youthful behaviour, in the criminal justice system, the decision not to comply with the requirements of community supervision or with the criminal law can have serious implications for young people including a deprivation of their liberty. It is from this standpoint that the following chapters focus on practitioners' perspectives on promoting compliance and responding to non-compliance when supervising young people in the community, before exploring young people's perspectives in later chapters of the book.

5 The social and criminal justice context of supervising young offenders

Exploring policy and practice on the management of offenders in the community must be located within its broader socio-political, cultural and criminal justice context. Goldson (2011: 16) argues that youth justice should be explored within 'its situational context' in order to understand the significance of historical and contemporary influences on the operation of the system and the extent to which policy and practice are shaped and mediated at local and community level. This chapter describes the contexts within which youth justice has emerged in Northern Ireland and the Republic of Ireland in recent decades. Although the respective systems are small by international standards, collectively they incorporate a number of legal, philosophical, policy and practice standpoints in responding to young people in conflict with the law. Commencing in the mid to late 1990s in Northern Ireland and somewhat later in the Republic of Ireland, both systems have, in diverse circumstances, undergone varying degrees of change. In exploring these contexts, the purpose is to shed light on the influences that have shaped the respective systems in both jurisdictions including the agencies responsible for supervising young offenders in the community. Piecing together these macro-level influences provides the foundation from which practitioners' responses to offenders' behaviour, including non-compliance, are explored in the course of supervising young people in the community in later chapters.

Northern Ireland

Following over 30 years of conflict in Northern Ireland, an international peace agreement between the UK and Ireland was signed in April 1998. Known locally and internationally as the Belfast/Good Friday Agreement, it provided the constitutional basis for devolution of power to the Northern Ireland Assembly. The Agreement, centred on principles of human rights, accountability and equality, contained a number of priorities including: economic growth and sustainability; social inclusion; representative policing; a review of the criminal justice system; normalization of state security; paramilitary disarmament; and the early release of politically motivated prisoners. The transition process has been supported with EU, US and other international funding which has been heavily invested in efforts to promote peace and reconciliation in the community (Magill and Hamber 2011). Despite this, the transition to a normalized society has often been a difficult and uncertain process.

The longevity and intensity of the conflict coupled with a modest population of just 1.8 million means that most inhabitants have been directly or indirectly affected either through death, injury, attack, intimidation or harassment (Hillyard, Rolston and Tomlinson 2005). Between 1969 and 1999, over 3,600 people's lives were taken and more than 45,000 were injured as a consequence of the 'Troubles'. Children and young people did not escape unscathed. Smyth (1998) documents that 257 individuals under the age of 17 years and 898 18–23 year olds were killed in the conflict (between 1969 and 1 March 1998) accounting for approximately one-third of the total who lost their lives. In some communities, punishment beatings and shootings were frequently meted out to young people perceived to be engaged in anti-social behaviour by local paramilitaries. Although the level of paramilitary attack has declined over the last decade, it has not disappeared completely (Eriksson 2009). Police data indicate that there were 83 casualties arising from paramilitary-style shootings and assaults in 2010–11 (PSNI 2011a). Furthermore, of 272 paramilitary-style attacks executed from January 2008 to December 2010, eight were perpetrated against young people under 16 years, and 121 against 16–24 year olds (PSNI 2011b).[1] Violence continues to be pervasive in some communities and here young people are often the subject of sustained community hostility. Sectarian attacks still occur and experiences of racial harassment and attack are not uncommon for some young people (Jarman 2003, 2004; Jarman and Monaghan 2003). The structures of division remain in many aspects of Northern Irish society. Over 90 per cent of public housing is segregated on religious grounds (*Belfast Telegraph*, 28 May 2010). In 2010, over a decade into the peace process, just 6.6 per cent of the total enrolment in nursery, primary and post-primary schools attended integrated schools in Northern Ireland (Department of Education Northern Ireland 2011). The arrangement of segregated Catholic and Protestant communities existing side by side in confined urban spaces has and continues to generate fear and anxiety about the threat of intimidation, attack and harassment. Furthermore, the evidence suggests that segregation of itself compounds alienation and marginalization, as Hargie, O'Donnell and McMullan (2011: 894) describe: 'the walls that were built to protect the two communities have in themselves contributed to the further social exclusion of those whose lives they were meant to enhance'.

The legacy of a recent and bloody past resonates with many and is consciously and unconsciously woven into the fabric of the present. Many of the children who witnessed or experienced violence first hand during the conflict, often without recognition of the trauma incurred, are now parents (McAlister, Scraton and Haydon 2009). The impact of past family experience and trauma is increasingly recognized as a factor that can profoundly influence and shape children and young people's well-being and mental health (Kerig *et al.* 2009; United Nations Committee on the Rights of the Child 2008). The need for improved mental health services and particularly child and adolescent mental health services is particularly significant in a post-conflict society where the standard factors associated with mental ill-health are compounded by the trauma associated with past experiences (Bamford Review of Mental Health and Learning Disability 2006). Like its counterpart in the Republic of Ireland, Northern Ireland has a higher suicide rate (13.9 per 100,000) than England and Wales, though lower than Scotland (NCISH 2011). The largest differences in suicide rates exist between Northern Ireland and other parts of the UK in relation to young people. From January 2000 to December 2008, 332 young people under 25 years lost their lives through suicide in Northern Ireland and of those, 78 were children and young people under 18 years (4.2 per 100,000). Those who died were more likely than other age groups to have lived in the poorest areas (10 per cent most deprived areas) and to have had the lowest rate of contact with mental health services (NCISH 2011).

The proportion of children living in persistent poverty (21 per cent) in Northern Ireland is over double that of children in Britain (9 per cent) (Monteith, Lloyd and McKee 2008). Poverty is heavily concentrated in certain neighbourhoods, and communities where the conflict was most profoundly experienced continue to be those with the highest concentrations of child poverty (Fay, Morrissey and Smyth 1998; McAlister *et al.* 2009). Youth unemployment is a bigger problem in Northern Ireland when compared with the UK average and also compares unfavourably to other OECD countries (Horgan, Gray and Conlon 2010). Youth have been disproportionately impacted by the current global recession and unemployment rates have increased significantly in recent years, leaving the prospects for those not already in employment, education or training particularly bleak. Horgan (2011: 453) argues that the 'corrosive effect that growing up in chronic poverty can have takes on added significance in a society emerging from conflict' where children develop against the backdrop of segregated communities characterized by high unemployment, physical and mental ill-health and long-term and sustained poverty. Hargie *et al.* (2011: 895) describe how the widespread nature of unemployment in interface areas has become normalized for many young people and expectations lowered to the point that 'they rarely raised their gaze above or beyond the horizons of the peace wall'. Despite the difficulties, children and young people's status in policy has been enhanced in the years following the Belfast/Good Friday Agreement. Although considerable progress is required to bring children's best interest to the heart of policy making in Northern Ireland, a number of steps have been taken to date. In 2002, the Children and Young People's Unit (CYPU) in the Office of the First and Deputy First Minister was established, followed by the appointment of the first Northern Ireland Commissioner for Children and Young People in 2003. Northern Ireland does not have a Minister for Children and Young People but the CYPU support the work of two junior ministers with responsibility for children and has responsibility for overseeing the implementation of Northern Ireland's children's strategy *'Our Children and Young People – Our Pledge: A Ten Year Strategy for Children and Young People 2006–16'*.[2]

Influences on the development of youth justice in Northern Ireland

Reform of the youth justice system in Northern Ireland is rooted in the processes that emanated from the 1998 Belfast/Good Friday Peace Agreement. Fundamental reform of the system followed a major review of the criminal justice system in Northern Ireland (Criminal Justice Review Group 2000), itself a central condition of the peace agreement. The integration and mainstreaming of restorative justice practices, and particularly the use of youth conferencing, formed the foundation of the recommendations and was legislated for under the Justice (Northern Ireland) Act 2002. The legislation provided for two conferencing options, a Diversionary Youth Conference operating as a pre-court diversionary mechanism and a Youth Conference Order which is imposed by the courts. With some exceptions, courts in Northern Ireland are now obliged to refer all cases for youth conferencing and the effect has been to locate restorative justice practice at the heart of the youth justice system.[3] Restorative conferencing has been positively endorsed within and outside of Northern Ireland (Independent Commission on Youth Crime and Antisocial Behaviour 2010; Campbell *et al* 2005; O'Mahony and Campbell 2006), though some concerns have been raised about its impact and effectiveness for persistent or prolific offenders who may be subject to repeat conferences (Criminal Justice Inspection NI 2008; Maruna *et al.* 2007). Youth justice in Northern Ireland is located in a justice-orientated framework and this is best reflected in its principal aim, which is to protect the public by preventing offending by children. Within the Justice (Northern Ireland) Act 2002 emphasis is placed on encouraging children to recognize the effects of crime and take responsibility for their actions. Agencies are directed to have consideration for the child's welfare but overt recognition and expression of children's rights are less apparent (Haydon 2009). The age of criminal responsibility is an important indicator of the extent to which age and maturity are taken into consideration in responding to offending behaviour by children. Northern Ireland does not fare well on this front by international standards. Although in line with England and Wales, when compared with its European counterparts, the age of criminal responsibility at 10 years is substantially lower.[4]

Many of the recent developments in youth justice in Northern Ireland have evolved in the context of post-conflict transition characterized by periods of political upheaval and ambiguity. The Northern Ireland Assembly was suspended four times since its establishment and governance reverted to the form of direct rule from the UK government. In 2007, when the Assembly recommenced, the UK Secretary of State for Northern Ireland retained responsibility for criminal justice and policing (Convery *et al.* 2008); it was only in April 2010 that these powers were devolved from Westminster. Unlike political protagonists of the past who came from the mainland to serve terms of office in Northern Ireland, the current political decision makers live, work and associate in the very communities to which they serve. It remains to be seen how local governance will shape the development of youth justice in Northern Ireland in the years ahead in light of 'a growing tendency within certain communities, media coverage and political commentaries to demonise children and young people, leading to calls for harsher policing and more punitive sanctions' (Include Youth 2008: 5). Against this, a preoccupation with punitive responses may resonate less within the political discourse in Northern Ireland where in some cases, politicians are representing communities who themselves have developed and nurtured community-based restorative justice projects to respond to crime and conflict in the community (see for example, McEvoy and Mika 2001). Grown out of concern to provide a non-violent alternative to punishment beatings and shootings from the late 1990s onwards, these community-based restorative justice projects engage with and provide supports and services to young people involved in criminal and anti-social behaviour, those at risk of involvement, and their parents and family members. The operation of such projects in the very communities most affected by crime indicate that a far more sophisticated narrative has developed within these communities about how youth crime should be understood and addressed (see Eriksson 2009 for a comprehensive account of the development and evolution of community restorative justice in Northern Ireland). In addition to community restorative justice, Northern Ireland has a strong and vibrant community and voluntary sector that has a long history of working with young offenders on a voluntary basis as well as in partnership with statutory criminal justice organizations (Department of Justice 2011; O'Mahony and Chapman 2007). Their role in youth justice discourse is not well documented but relationships established over time within and between communities lend recognition and legitimacy to their work with young people in conflict with the law. Equally strong has been the plethora of non-governmental advocacy and children's rights organizations that have played, and continue to play, a key role in lobbying to improve children's rights in the criminal justice system in Northern Ireland. In a jurisdiction that is necessarily localized by virtue of its small size, the impact of advocacy may be more concentrated and more difficult to ignore in policy making and practice circles as alluded to by a number of key informants in the current study:

> The Children's Law Centre, Include Youth, I mean that lobbying is certainly impacting on thinking on having under 18s in Hydebank [Young Offenders Centre for males up to 21 years]. There is an awareness that this is challengeable, if you like, there's a lobby out there that are basically saying 'this isn't right', you know, and not being written off as 'they would say that'. I think for me the rights' lobbyists are taken more seriously, I think partly because of legislation. In a sense we have legislation now that protects the rights of children. The other bit is because it's such a small place, you know things like the potential that you'll be judicially reviewed around decisions you take about issues, I mean in a larger place I think you'd just kind of go 'alright'. Here, people are genuinely thinking 'can I stand over what I have done and meet the standard of a court that is primarily probably looking at whether you are complying with the Convention or not'?
>
> [PBNI Key Informant]

Northern Ireland has not been completely immune to wider criminal justice discourses on individual responsibility (Muncie and Goldson 2006), public protection and risk management (Kemshall and Wood 2008). Anti-social behaviour orders were introduced by the UK government in 2004 though in what stands as an example of the negotiated space between policy direction and implementation in practice, few orders have been imposed in Northern Ireland since their inception. According to police statistics, a total of 60 orders were imposed on children under 18 years over a seven-year period between 2005 and 2011 (PSNI 2011c). One of the most significant manifestations regarding risk and public protection can be traced to the Criminal Justice (Northern Ireland) Order 2008 when provision was made for two public protection sentences for dangerous, violent and sexual offenders, both of which are applicable to young offenders.[5] A new determinate prison sentence has also been introduced for sentences of 12 months or more that do not come under public protection sentencing. Following the custodial period, each of the sentences requires that the offender is supervised under licence in the community for determinate and indeterminate periods of time, varying according to the nature of the sentence. Licences can be revoked where offenders are deemed to be dangerous, breach their licence conditions, or commit further offences. The same legislation also introduced curfews and provision for electronic monitoring to be used as a condition of bail or as a requirement of community orders, supervision under licence or youth-specific sentences such as Youth Conference Orders.[6] In the main, however, Northern Ireland has managed to resist or disregard many of the most intrusive actuarial, control and custodial practices that appear to be endemic within youth justice practices in England, despite its geographical proximity and constitutional embedding within the UK.

Responding to youth crime in Northern Ireland

In 2010–11, 9,096 referrals were made to the PSNI involving offending by young people under 18 years (PSNI 2011c).[7] Young males accounted for 78 per cent of the incidents referred. The police have discretionary powers to respond informally to low-level offences committed by young people, but in the majority of cases diversionary action must be sanctioned by the Public Prosecution Service (PPS). The PPS decides whether a youth case is dismissed, prosecuted or diverted from prosecution. In 2010–11, a decision to prosecute was the outcome for 25 per cent of referrals while a decision not to prosecute was taken in a further 27 per cent of cases (ibid.). Where a decision is taken to divert young people from prosecution, a number of statutory pre-court diversionary options exist in Northern Ireland. The most common are informed warnings or restorative cautions given by a trained police facilitator in the presence of young people, their parents or guardians and the victim in the case of a restorative caution. Young people are also diverted from prosecution through a recommendation to participate in a diversionary youth conference convened by the YJA (further detail on diversionary youth conferences is provided later in the chapter). Combined, informed warnings, restorative cautions, and diversionary youth conferences accounted for 33 per cent of the outcomes of referrals for offending behaviour in 2010–11 (ibid.)

The Youth Court in Northern Ireland has jurisdiction to deal with the majority of offences by young people from 10 to 18 years; however; very serious offences may be transferred to the adult Crown Court, a situation which occurred in 54 cases in 2010 (Northern Ireland Courts and Tribunal Service 2011). The Youth Conference Order is the most common statutory community-based order imposed on young people in Northern Ireland. It is a sentence of the court and counts as a criminal conviction. The procedures for delivery of a diversionary youth conference or a conference convened as part of a youth conference order are the same, with young people either admitting their guilt or being found guilty of an offence and giving informed consent to participate. For diversionary youth conferences, the Youth Conference Rules (Northern Ireland) 2003 stipulate that a report of the conference must be made to the Director of the Public Prosecution Service within 30 working days of a referral. Court-mandated conferences are completed within the period of adjournment which, depending on the individual Youth Court, is generally four weeks. All youth conferences are convened by a youth conference co-ordinator and a negotiated decision about how a young person should make amends is taken by the parties involved. A legal requirement is that the co-ordinator, a police officer, the young person and an appropriate adult must be in attendance for the conference to proceed. Victims have an entitlement to attend and participate, but are not legally obliged to do so and other attendees may include victim representatives, probation officers, legal advisors, advocates or supporters. An action plan is agreed at the conference and may include requirements for young people to apologize, to pay compensation, to undertake reparation or community service, to have restrictions placed on them through the use of curfews or electronic monitoring, or to take part in supervised or specialized programmes or treatments. All conference plans have to be approved by either the PPS in the case of diversionary youth conferences or the Youth Court judge for court-ordered conferences. For a small minority of young people who are considered unsuitable or unwilling to participate in youth conferencing, a number of other statutory community-based disposals are available including: attendance centre orders, community responsibility orders, reparation orders, probation orders, combination orders and community service orders.

There has been a dramatic fall in the use of custody for young people in Northern Ireland since the late 1990s, arising from provisions in the Criminal Justice (Northern Ireland) Order 1996 that placed restrictions on the use of custody to serious offenders as well as the introduction of determinate juvenile justice centre orders (JJCO) under the Criminal Justice (Children) (Northern Ireland) Order 1998. The juvenile justice centre order is the most common custodial order imposed. Extending for a period of six months unless the court specifies that a longer period, not exceeding two years, is required, half of the period of the order is spent in custody and the remainder under the supervision of the PBNI in the community. Most young males and all females under the age of 18 years are detained at the Woodlands Juvenile Justice Centre operated by the YJA. In 2010–11, a total of 40 JJCOs were imposed, of which 60 per cent were for three to six months and 40 per cent for seven to twelve months (Tate and Lyness 2011). Although the total average daily population of the Juvenile Justice Centre is 26, it is noteworthy that 65 per cent of the total average daily population consists of young people on remand – a pattern that has risen steadily in recent years. Some young males aged 15 years are detained within the Northern Ireland Prison Service (NIPS) estate at HM Young Offenders Centre (YOC) Hydebank Wood in Belfast, which caters for young male offenders up to 21 years. Between December 2010 and January 2011, there were a total of 92 committals (accounting for 74 individuals) involving under 18 year olds. Of those, 14 were under sentence, seven were fine defaulters serving seven days in lieu of a fine and the remaining 74 committals were detained on remand (Criminal Justice Inspection NI 2011). A series of review and inspection reports published throughout 2011 have highlighted previous criticisms of the continued use of Hydebank Wood for young people under 18 years due to the nature of the 'adult' custodial regime and dearth of appropriate educational and rehabilitative opportunities to meet their needs. All have recommended that the practice of committing under 18 year olds to this facility should cease (Criminal Justice Inspection NI 2011; Department of Justice 2011; Prison Review Team 2011).[8]

The Republic of Ireland

The Republic of Ireland has a population of over 4.5 million (Central Statistics Office 2011a). Beginning in the mid-1990s, a period of enormous and unprecedented economic growth – when the economy of the Republic was known as the 'Celtic Tiger' – greatly enhanced the prosperity of the country and its people. Reversing previous patterns of mass emigration, a vibrant and ethnically diverse society emerged as thousands of immigrants came to Ireland in search of work and a better life (Hughes *et al.* 2007). Despite substantial growth in wealth and prosperity, it was also a time of widening disparity in the economic position between rich and poor and relative poverty increased over this period (Nolan and Maître 2007). Furthermore, the rhetoric of prosperity served to mask fundamental problems in relation to equality of life opportunities and protection for children and the Republic of Ireland continued to have one of the highest levels of child poverty in Europe (Combat Poverty Agency 2004). The economic boom dramatically crumbled in 2008 against the backdrop of a global financial crisis. Much of Ireland's economic growth had centred on the construction and property sectors, markets that had been artificially inflated by grossly irresponsible lending practices by the banking sector. With lenders unable to repay, the Irish banking system was in severe crisis and the impact reverberated throughout all aspects of the economy. Unemployment rates rose significantly and consistently and by the third quarter of 2011 there were 314,700 unemployed persons in the country, an unemployment rate of 14.4 per cent and a notable increase in the numbers of long-term employed (Central Statistics Office 2011b).

A series of child abuse scandals in recent years has shaken what was once the bedrock of Irish society. Although the Catholic Church no longer retains its position as one of the most powerful institutions in the state, its status was severely damaged by a series of reports of inquiries detailing the litanies of emotional, physical and sexual abuse perpetrated by members of religious orders. Many cases emanate from previous decades, when large numbers of children were detained in religious-run institutions across the state (Raftery and O'Sullivan 1999); others relate to more recent times and involve cases where children were sexually abused by clerics in the community (Commission to Inquire into Child Abuse 2009). Despite public and political outrage following the publication of inquiry reports, the mistakes of the past have not necessarily been translated into lessons of the present. Child protection services, the vast majority of which are restricted to weekday office hours, typically 9am to 5pm, continue to be severely under-resourced and as recently as May 2010, the Ombudsman for Children reported that the statutory body charged with protecting children at risk in Irish society had failed in its duty to do so. Furthermore, sustained rhetoric and media reporting about the abuse of children by the clergy deflects from the strong evidence indicating that children continue to be most at risk of abuse and neglect perpetrated by family members in the family home (McGee *et al.* 2002; Office of the Minister for Children and Youth Affairs 2010).

Public anxiety about law-and-order issues and organized crime in particular came to the fore in Ireland in 1996 in the aftermath of the murder of crime reporter Veronica Guerin. In response to heightened moral panic about gangs and violence, a raft of legislation was introduced to enhance criminal justice powers in this area (O'Donnell 2007a). The proliferation of organized crime and associated violence centres on bitter struggles for control over the supply of drugs in the major cities, and partly explains increases in violent crime, particularly homicide in recent years (McCullagh 2011; Seymour and Mayock 2009). Campbell (2010: 428) explains that gun crime and specifically 'gun homicides' occur in those areas with the highest levels of profound and persistent deprivation and unemployment. Less well reflected is the role played by the drug consumption practices of ordinary citizens in fuelling criminal activity and networks (O'Donnell, 2007a,b). McCullagh (2011: 23) describes the source of organized crime and associated violence as 'the continued demand for illegal drugs and the willingness of ordinary citizens to pay high prices for them'. A more sinister development in recent years is that children and young people in certain areas are frequently exploited by criminal gangs to function as 'their eyes and ears' (Hourigan 2011: 129) and to store and act as couriers of drugs and weapons (*Irish Examiner* 14 October 2011). For those living in the shadows of violence and intimidation on a daily basis, recruitment as drug mules comes about through fear, the need to pay off drug debts, as well as the status afforded, and perceived protection offered by criminal gangs (Griffin and Kelleher 2010).

Influences on the development of youth justice in the Republic of Ireland

Youth justice law and policy making have been late developments in the Irish context. Throughout much of the 20th century and particularly in the early and mid-decades, thousands of children were removed from their families and communities and institutionalized within the industrial and reformatory school systems. Industrial schools housed destitute, neglected and orphaned children and those considered by the authorities to be at risk, while children deemed to have committed delinquent acts and petty offences were held in reformatory schools (Raftery and O'Sullivan 1999). A general inertia in relation to youth justice matters combined with a legacy of institutionalization left a vacuum of formal community-based criminal justice responses to young people in conflict with the law in the Republic of Ireland. In its place, the youth, voluntary and community sectors played important roles in working with young people in communities often on an informal basis with limited resources and formal recognition. The strength of these sectors has persisted over time and today statutory criminal justice services fund a number of non-governmental organizations to deliver services to young offenders on their behalf (Treacy 2009).

The first major legislative reform of the youth justice system in almost a century (since the Children Act 1908) only occurred with the Children Act 2001. The Children Act is perceived as a progressive piece of legislation that emphasizes diversion of young people from the formal justice system, the use of detention as a measure of last resort and the abolition of imprisonment for those under the age of 18 years. It also sets out a number of principles that offer guidance on the factors that should be taken into consideration when responding to young people in the justice system. These include their age and level of maturity, their right to privacy, and the desirability of building and strengthening links with family, school and community. The Act followed from a period of over three decades of reports and debate at national level about the need for fundamental change in the youth justice system (Committee on Reformatory and Industrial Schools Systems 1970; Burke, Carney and Cook 1981; Dáil Éireann 1992). The UNCRC was ratified by Ireland in 1992. In response to its first progress report to the UN Monitoring Committee in 1998, the government was severely criticized for its poor progress on implementing the UNCRC (McVerry 1998). According to one key informant for this research, the criticism provided momentum and impetus for greater focus and attention on child policy and children's rights in the Republic of Ireland.[9] As part of the response, the National Children's Office was established and the first National Children's Strategy (2000–10), *Our Children Their Lives,* was published. Espousing a 'whole child' perspective for policy development and service delivery, the Strategy emphasized a child-centred and family-orientated approach based on principles of inclusivity, equity and integration. Against these developments, it was not until a Review of the Youth Justice System in 2005 that serious consideration was given to the implementation of the Children Act 2001 (Department of Justice, Equality and Law Reform 2006). Responsibility for youth justice had traditionally been spread across the three government departments of education, justice and health and the absence of a lead agency or department was attributed to the unacceptably slow pace of its implementation. International experience suggests that the translation of legislation into practice is a complex process and contingent on factors ranging from the penal populist attitudes of the day, to the influence of the media and the professional background and value base of the relevant stakeholders. The approach taken by the group tasked with reviewing the youth justice system in 2005 was grounded in welfare principles and informed by the ethos of the National Children's Strategy, as well as experience garnered nationally and from other jurisdictions. In this regard, Scotland's integrated welfare approach to offending children was deemed to be influential. Following a dearth of action in the area of youth justice for over a century, a raft of key developments followed the Review. The Office of the Minister for Children and Youth Affairs (OMCYA) replaced the National Children's Office and took on responsibility for co-ordinating policy on children (including youth justice) across various government departments. The Irish Youth Justice Service was established in 2006 as an executive office of the Department of Justice, Equality and Law Reform. Its remit was to provide a co-ordinated approach to the delivery of youth justice in Ireland. Reiterating the principles of the Children Act 2001, the first National Strategy on Youth Justice, launched in 2008, emphasized the goal of reducing offending through diversion and rehabilitation (Irish Youth Justice Service 2008). In what may perhaps represent an additional step towards locating youth justice within a broader framework of children's policy and services, the government announced the transfer in June 2011 of the Irish Youth Justice Service into a newly established Department of Children and Youth Affairs (DCYA) headed by a Minister for Children and Youth Affairs with a full cabinet role (Dáil Éireann Debate Vol. 737 No. 6 12 July 2011).

Overall, the Republic of Ireland has resisted the prevailing punitive rhetoric that has overshadowed youth justice policy making in parts of the UK and the US, with some exceptions. The age of criminal responsibility was originally set at 12 years in the Children Act 2001; however, an amendment to the Act under the Criminal Justice Act 2006 lowered the age to 10 years for children charged with murder, manslaughter, rape or aggravated sexual assault.[10] The shift to the lower age of criminal responsibility was justified by the Minister for Justice of the time with reference to the experiences of other jurisdictions:

> there have been cases in other jurisdictions where there have been murders by 11 year olds. There have been serious offences committed here by 11 year olds … I do not think it is satisfactory for victims that the only sanction is for the perpetrators to be referred to social services. In addressing serious youth offending there is an obligation on Government to provide strong law together with good programmes if they are found guilty.
>
> (Dáil Eireann Debate Vol. 624 No. 3 Responses to Q.141 and Q.194, 3 October 2006)

Behaviour Orders (similar to anti-social behaviour orders (ASBOs) in the UK), also introduced under the Criminal Justice Act 2006, represented the potential for another retrograde development in Irish youth justice policy. Based on no more than the anecdotal evidence of politicians' accounts of the experiences of their constituents, one of their most noteworthy features has been their minimal use with young people. According to Garda Press Office statistics, just three orders have been imposed on under 18 year olds since their inception in 2008 to 31 August 2010 (Garda Press Office 2010). A plausible explanation put forward by youth workers and the police is that the network of youth services, crime prevention and diversionary initiatives in the Republic of Ireland diminishes the perceived benefit of Behaviour Orders as an effective response to anti-social behaviour by children and young people (Fitzpatrick 2011).

Responding to youth crime in the Republic of Ireland

In 2010, 17,986 young people, accounting for 27,257 offences, were brought to the attention of An Garda Síochána (police) in the Republic Ireland. Most were young males (78 per cent) and over half of all referrals related to 16 and 17 year olds (An Garda Síochána 2011). Official data on the nationality, ethnicity or cultural diversity of young people in the Irish youth justice system, and indeed in the Northern Ireland system, is not publically available, making it impossible to shed light on the extent to which young people from different backgrounds are represented in youth crime and criminal justice statistics. Two previous studies, one on the Children Court in Ireland (Carroll and Meehan 2007) and one on the Children Detention School system (Carr 2008), suggest that young Irish Travellers are over-represented in the system. In the latter study, Carr (2008) reports that young Travellers constituted approximately 12 per cent of the total male Children Detention School population over a 16 year period from 1991–2007 despite the Traveller population accounting for a tiny minority (0.6 per cent) of the national population.

The vast majority of decisions about how young people's cases should be dealt with are made centrally by the police at the Garda Office for Children and Youth Affairs in Dublin. In 2010, almost three-quarters of cases were dealt with using a formal or informal police caution, no further action was taken in a further 5 per cent of cases, and less than one-fifth were sent forward for prosecution. The Children Court in Ireland has jurisdiction to deal with all minor and most serious offences committed by persons under the age of 18 years under the Children Act 2001. Exceptions include manslaughter and those offences required to be tried by the Central Criminal Court, for example murder. In 2010, 107 cases were sent forward from the Children Court to a higher court for trial (Court Service 2011). With some exceptions, restrictions exist on the reporting, publishing or broadcasting of any information about young people under 18 years involved in any criminal proceedings that is likely to lead to their identification.[11] In contrast to Northern Ireland, restorative justice retains a peripheral role in youth justice in the Republic of Ireland. The courts have the option to divert cases away from the criminal justice system to the Health Service Executive through the use of family welfare conferencing or to use conferencing as a pre-trial diversionary option known as the family conference. The latter option is used only in a small number of cases. It is convened by the Probation Service, involves the young person, the family, the victim and/or advocates and subject to the young person's compliance with an agreed action plan, the court may dismiss the charge and a conviction is not recorded. The court has a number of community-based sentencing options at its disposal for young people (see Seymour 2012), but in practice, the most commonly imposed is the Probation Order (Court Service 2011). Healy and O'Donnell (2005: 57) describe how 'in the absence of a modern legislative framework judges have tended to innovate'. As explained in Chapter 1, adjourned supervision is a common judicial practice in the Irish context whereby the court adjourns sentencing until a later date, and directs that the young person is placed on probation supervision to assess their motivation to change. At the end of the adjournment period, the court will take into consideration how the young person has responded to supervision in deciding the outcome of the case. Probation Service statistics for young people supervised in 2010 demonstrate that 491 were supervised on probation orders with a further 361 on orders for supervision during deferment of penalty (Probation Service 2011a).

There has been a substantial reduction in the use of custodial orders for young people in the Republic of Ireland following the implementation of the Children Act 2001, which embodied the principle of retaining custodial options as a measure of last resort and placed strong emphasis on using the least restrictive option appropriate to the circumstance of the offence. The average occupancy of the Children Detention School system in 2009 was 39 with a total of 30 children (21 males and 9 females) committed under sentence during the year (Irish Youth Justice Service 2010). However, it is noteworthy that committals on remand accounted for 85 per cent of total admissions to the Children Detention School system in 2009 (ibid.). This is particularly significant given the complete absence of any formalized bail support programmes for young people on remand, a gap that leaves those most vulnerable at risk of further criminalization (Seymour and Butler 2008). Furthermore, delays in processing young people's cases are an unacceptable and persistent feature of the youth justice system. The extent of delays is uncertain in the absence of systematic data, but a study of 400 cases concluded in 2004 on the Courts Service Criminal Case Tracking System (CCTS) found that 43 per cent of young people made their first court appearance more than six months after the offence occurred and incurred an average of eight appearances in respect of each charge (Carroll and Meehan 2007). This practice is substantively at odds with the spirit of the Children Act 2001 and the UN Convention on the Rights of the Child. Although young females under 18 years serve custodial orders in the welfare-orientated Children Detention School system, it remains the case that young males aged 17 years are committed under sentence and remand to St. Patrick's Institution, an archaic institution operated by the Irish Prison Service whose closure was recommended almost 30 years ago (Committee of Inquiry into the Penal System 1985). Since then, national and international parties have continued to highlight the austere conditions of the facility, the inappropriateness of the regime to meet the needs of adolescent offenders, and reiterated calls for its closure (European Committee for the Prevention of Torture and Inhuman or Degrading Treatment or Punishment (CPT) 2007; Ombudsman for Children' Office 2011; St. Patrick's Institution

Prison Visiting Committee 2009). It is only since 1 May 2012 that the practice of sending 16 year old males to St. Patrick's Institution has ceased following an announcement by the Minister for Children and Youth Affairs in April 2012. In the same announcement the minister indicated that the capital funding had been secured to provide new facilities within two years, to end the detention of all young persons under 18 years at St. Patrick's Institution. In 2009, there were 227 committals of young males aged 16 and 17 years to St. Patrick's Institution, of whom 58 per cent were committed under sentence (Irish Prison Service 2010).

Agencies with responsibility for supervising young people in Northern Ireland and the Republic of Ireland

Growing evidence suggests that the quality of offender–practitioner interaction during the course of supervision is likely to impact on offenders' views on the usefulness of the disposal and perceptions of fair treatment and legitimacy (Rex 1999). Practitioners' professional background and values are seen to be influential in this regard. That said, most criminal justice practitioners operate within organizations which themselves have strategic purposes and goals that influence the expectations placed on staff in their work with offenders (Clear and Latessa 1993). The section to follow discusses the background history and contemporary approaches adapted in practice by the three organizations responsible for supervising young offenders on statutory community disposals on the island of Ireland – the YJA and PBNI in Northern Ireland, and the Probation Service in the Republic of Ireland. In so doing, it demonstrates how socio-political, cultural, organizational and professional factors merge to influence the shape of practice within and between organizations and jurisdictions. More specifically it provides the framework from which to explain how compliance is interpreted and promoted and how non-compliance by young people is responded to by practitioners in the respective organizations (see Chapters 6 and 7).

Before exploring each of the organizations in turn, it is worth reiterating that the professional backgrounds of all practitioners working in a formal supervisory capacity with young offenders in Northern Ireland and the Republic of Ireland are drawn from disciplines of care rather than control or law enforcement. YJA workers hold qualifications in social work, youth and community work or education. A requirement of appointment for probation officers employed by the PBNI is a social work degree qualification or equivalent while it is desirable for probation officers in the Republic of Ireland to meet this criterion. The PBNI also employ probation service officers to work directly with offenders. These officers are not required to have a formal professional qualification for the role, but they must achieve the Community Justice NVQ Level 3 within two years of appointment. Although used with adult offenders and for specific groups such as sex offenders, offending behaviour programmes are not routinely used with young people under supervision in Northern Ireland or the Republic of Ireland. Perhaps driven by professional orientation and a strong history of partnerships with community, supervision arrangements are most commonly centred on the one-to-one supervisory relationship between client and practitioner, supported by community-based programmes such as family support and mentoring, vocational and educational services, substance abuse treatment and in Northern Ireland, community-based restorative justice projects.

Role, purpose and culture of the YJA

The YJA was established in April 2003 and exists as an executive agency of the Department of Justice (DOJ). It followed from recommendations made in the aforementioned review of criminal justice that occurred in the aftermath of the Belfast/Good Friday peace agreement (Criminal Justice Review Group 2000). Described as signalling 'a comprehensive reappraisal of the structures and approaches to be used in Northern Ireland in dealing with young people at risk of offending or reoffending' (Dawson *et al.* 2004: 4), the principal aim of the YJA is to reduce youth crime and to build confidence in the youth justice system. As the lead agency that works with court-adjudicated cases in Northern Ireland, it holds direct responsibility for convening youth conferences, and supervising young people on bail support programmes, youth conference action plans and community orders as well as custodial services at the Woodlands Juvenile Justice Centre. The YJA also contributes to the supervision of young people who are subject to probation orders and juvenile justice centre orders, undertaking programmes and interventions to address offending. The YJA supervises a range of offenders from those diverted from prosecution by the PPS to those more heavily involved in the criminal justice system. The YJA operates throughout Northern Ireland through a network of eight regional community-based centres and a number of satellite premises.

A restorative, systemic and strengths-based approach

Youth conferencing as operated by the YJA is grounded in restorative justice principles and is most closely aligned to the family group conferencing model used in New Zealand, although more emphasis is placed on the victim than the family in the Northern Ireland model (Campbell *et al.* 2005). Youth conferencing accounts for the vast majority of statutory orders referred to the agency (92 per cent of 1,746 orders received in 2010–11) (Tate and Lyness 2011).[12] It is well documented that the way restorative justice operates in practice varies considerably and depends on the structures, personnel and philosophical underpinnings of the system within which it operates (O'Mahony and Doak 2006). The YJA describes the main aims of its conferencing service as meeting the needs of victims through a reparative justice approach, preventing youth reoffending through a rehabilitative justice approach, making amends for the harm done and repairing relationships and encouraging participation by stakeholders in the process (YJA 2008). The strong emphasis on meeting victims' needs is reflected in the high victim attendance rates (69 per cent) and victim satisfaction rates (O'Mahony and Doak 2006). The influence of restorative justice extends beyond the context of the conference and is a key dimension in practice when supervising youth conference and other statutory orders (see Chapter 6 and 7). In addition, a number of contemporary and historical influences have shaped the Agency's ethos in relation to the supervision of young people in the community. A policy shift towards the development of community-based provision, stimulated by concern about the numbers of young people detained within the custodial (training school) system in the mid-1970s, culminated in the establishment of Whitefield House under the patronage of the Northern Ireland Office (NIO) in 1977 (Dawson *et al.* 2004). Known colloquially as Whitefield, it offered service provision on a voluntary basis to young people at risk or engaged in offending behaviour using a holistic and systemic approach that located the problem of youth offending within the wider contexts of family and community. Central to this approach were the development of professional relationships with young people and their families and the advancement of partnerships with a range of voluntary, community and statutory agencies. These principles were retained and integrated into practice when Whitefield was replaced by the YJA (Dawson *et al.* 2004). More recently, key messages from the desistance research, such as an emphasis on developing a strengths-based approach when working with offenders, has shifted practice away from concentrating only on the risk factors associated with leading young people into trouble (Dawson, Dunn and Morgan 2007; Independent Research Solutions 2008). The YJA's history as an organization that has traditionally worked mostly with voluntary youth cases has required a shift in approach when working with adjudicated offenders. One key informant describes the change involved in the transition:

> As an agency previously we were Whitefield House which was an early intervention, prevention organization, with almost kind of the befriending role dealing with non-adjudicated young people. The big change for us as an agency is the shift and becoming a statutory agency that is mandated to work with young people who have offended and that has been a whole kind of culture change for staff with standards, with new ways of working, with responsibilities to courts, to victims and to young people much more.
>
> [YJA Key Informant]

Role, purpose and culture of the PBNI

With the exception of the YJA, the PBNI is the only other agency with statutory responsibility for supervising young offenders under 18 years old in Northern Ireland. The legislative onus on the courts to dispose of youth cases primarily through the conferencing process has resulted in a substantial decrease in the number of youth cases supervised by the PBNI in recent years. These changes have also had direct implications on the profile of young offenders under probation supervision. PBNI youth cases comprise of young offenders who are older, have exhausted other statutory community-based disposals or refused to consent to them, or where the nature or level of offending is deemed to necessitate a higher-tariff response. According to PBNI statistics for 2010, the majority of the young people (79 per cent) under supervision are 16 and 17 years and over 60 per cent have two or more previous convictions. Furthermore, 54 per cent are classified as high risk offenders on the basis of the Assessment, Case Management and Evaluation (ACE) risk assessment instrument, 32 per cent as moderate risk and the remaining 14 per cent as low risk.[13]

Community, rehabilitation and public protection

The basis for probation governance in Northern Ireland can be traced back to the Black Report (Children and Young Persons Review Group 1979) and a recommendation that probation should be administered by a state-appointed board, representative of a wide spectrum of community interests. A board of community representatives, rather than civil service management, was perceived to be the appropriate structure to retain greater legitimacy for probation work in the community against the backdrop of ongoing conflict during the late 1970s and early 1980s (Fulton 2008; O'Mahony and Chapman 2007). Established under the Probation Board (Northern Ireland) Order 1982, the PBNI continues to be overseen by a board of up to 18 members drawn from a wide range of representative community interests. Despite a previous recommendation to change its status to a government agency akin to the Prison Service (Criminal Justice Review Group 2000), the organization has managed to retain its structure of community-orientated governance and exists as a non-departmental public body (NDPB) in the DOJ in Northern Ireland.

As a criminal justice organization operating throughout the years of conflict in a context where the legitimacy of the criminal justice system and the state was often contested, negotiating relationships with communities was central to the organization's ability to engage with offenders. The most widespread manifestation of these efforts was in the development of partnerships and funding arrangements to community and voluntary organizations as well as the physical presence of PBNI offices in many neighbourhoods. Auld *et al.* (1997) suggest that the PBNI retained a relatively good relationship across the communities where it operated throughout the conflict, a view that was reflected by some PBNI staff:

> When you look at the years of the conflict, the Probation Board managed to continue to work in communities through the worst of the troubles, and we managed to do that through the strong partnerships that we had with community and in particular the community and voluntary sector.
>
> [PBNI Key Informant]

O'Mahony and Chapman (2007) point to two further issues that were relevant in enabling probation officers to work directly within the communities where paramilitary organizations were most active and violence most pervasive. A policy developed by the National Association of Probation Officers (NAPO) in 1975 to steer clear of completing courts reports on politically motivated offenders or supervising them on statutory orders allowed the PBNI 'to avoid political manipulation and to establish its non-sectarian credentials' (ibid.:165). Furthermore, the PBNI struck a delicate balance in cooperating with the police, the courts and the prisons, while at the same time retaining sufficient distance to maintain its position of neutrality in the community.

During the conflict, concerns about personal safety among offenders, associated with moving outside their community, required probation staff to arrange supervision in their clients' homes, in local PBNI offices or at other community locations in the vicinity where offenders lived. Fulton (2008) suggests that one implication of the PBNI's presence within the community was that it created a more nuanced and sophisticated understanding among staff surrounding the implementation of effective practice principles in their work:

> A paradoxical consequence of the conflict was that staff went out more into communities. The experience of working in communities meant that while adopting the cognitive theories PBNI was conscious of not neglecting the social dimensions.
>
> (pp. 730–1)

The tradition of established working relationships between the PBNI and the community and voluntary sectors (Stout 2007) has continued in Northern Ireland albeit with increased emphasis on partnerships that more directly relate to adjudicated offenders than in the past. This is reflective of a shift in emphasis from traditional probation values to an approach that reflects 'the dual responsibilities of public protection and rehabilitation of offenders' (Doran and Cooper 2008: 25) as outlined in the Criminal Justice (Northern Ireland) Order 1996. Legislative and policy documents may provide the framework for how criminal justice organizations operate in practice but less is known about how differing and sometimes conflicting principles play out in practice. In the following account, one key informant sheds light on how rehabilitative and public protection goals have been translated to inform current PBNI practice:

> We have held on to the social work base because [of] our belief in the person's ability to change, and that's fundamental, that's core to the work we do, we believe that offenders have the capacity to change. And whilst we have moved away from the 'advise, assist and befriend' role to rehabilitation of the offender and protection of the public, the 'advise, assist and befriend' role is still in there. We haven't lost that completely, we're prepared to assess what the needs of the offender are and to assist them in setting goals and changing their behaviour, and supporting them in doing that. We're still encouraging and enabling offenders to change their behaviour, but for those who aren't interested in doing that we will provide a service whereby we are monitoring them and holding them to account, and then breaching them or having them recalled if they don't comply with the requirement of their order or their licence.
>
> [PBNI Key Informant]

Although PBNI's community-based foundations have fundamentally framed the shape of probation in Northern Ireland, it has not been sheltered from the punitive influences that permeate criminal justice policy in England and Wales. Fulton's (2008: 751) description of criminal justice policy making in Northern Ireland as 'follow England – at a distance' provides the most succinct account of policy transfer in practice. Emphasis on public protection has been consolidated in probation work in Northern Ireland with the introduction of public protection sentences for serious and dangerous offenders under the Criminal Justice (Northern Ireland) Order 2008. Under the provisions of this legislation probation officers have a central role in preparing pre-sentence reports and supervising offenders under licence on release.

Role, purpose and culture of the Probation Service in the Republic of Ireland

The Probation Service is the primary agency with responsibility for delivering the vast majority of supervised statutory court disposals for young people in the Republic of Ireland. In 2006, YPP was created within the service and YPP teams, staffed by probation officers, were established in the main urban centres across the country.[14] Social workers employed as YPP officers have direct input into all aspects of young people's progression through the system. Their role includes assessing suitability for community-based sanctions, undertaking court liaison work, managing young people's cases while under supervision in the community, addressing the factors related to offending behaviour, providing support to their families, and working to provide for the needs of offending young people in conjunction with statutory, community and voluntary organizations (Seymour 2012). The majority of YPP cases are aged 16 years and over, with young people aged 15 years or under accounting for just 12 per cent of the caseload (Probation Service 2012).[15] The risk profile data, based on Youth Level of Service/Case Management Inventory (YLS/CMI) risk assessments completed between January 2009 and October 2011, identified that 56 per cent of cases were classified as moderate risk, 24 per cent were high risk and the remaining 20 per cent as low risk (Probation Service 2011b).

The probation services of Ireland and Northern Ireland share 'a common heritage in the Probation of Offenders Act 1907 and the commitment in it to "assist, advise and befriend"' (Donnellan and McCaughey 2010: 7). However, legislative, political and organizational factors have distinctly influenced the development of the respective services over time. Unlike Northern Ireland, the statutory basis of the probation order in Ireland remains as the 1907 Probation Act. Healy and O'Donnell (2005) suggest that the absence of updated legislation is indicative of a general inertia associated with criminal justice policy making in Ireland, while others have attributed a lack of reform with hampering development in the area of community sanctions (Expert Group on the Probation and Welfare Service 1999). Despite the legislative lacuna, the service has sought to symbolically and practically establish its position as one step removed from its tradition of advising, assisting and befriending offenders. The term 'Welfare' was dropped from the title of the service in 2008; furthermore, its purpose – 'to increase community safety and prevent victimisation by motivating, challenging and supporting offenders in leading a crime free life' (Probation Service 2008: 3) – reflects broader considerations for victims and communities. While there has been some movement in recent years to integrate effective practice principles, including the use of risk assessment instruments, the Probation Service has retained its strong social work tradition in the manner of their implementation. Fitzgibbon, Hamilton and Richardson (2010: 166) describe the introduction of 'What Works' principles into probation work in 2004 as bringing 'change only in the manner of implementation of its traditional rehabilitative goals'. Furthermore, National Standards for Probation Practice, commenced in 2008 for the management of adult cases only, provide the basis for more consistent practice while permitting officers to retain a considerable degree of professional discretion. Fitzgibbon *et al.* (2010: 167–8) report that the value attributed to risk assessment instruments by officers supervising adult cases in Dublin is in their use 'as a means of shoring up or confirming professional views rather than supplanting them'. Officers are permitted to use their clinical judgement where conclusions from risk assessments digress from professional perspectives on offenders' risk of reoffending. The value as described by O'Leary and Halton (2009: 109) is 'that professional discretion takes precedence over the actuarial data and it provides a safeguard when the aggregation of numbers just does not make sense. It also allows for the consideration of individual and local issues.' Overall, it might be said that while the Probation Service has adapted a public protection response to select groups such as sexual offenders (Donnellan and McCaughey 2010), it retains an approach that leans more towards rehabilitation than retribution or punishment for a majority of offenders. Young offenders are seen as a particularly distinct group in this regard. The ethos of the legislative approach as espoused in the Children Act 2001 has enabled the Probation Service to comfortably embed a welfare approach in its responses towards young people in conflict with the law:

> From our own perspective, we are social workers if you like working for the Department of Justice so that's our training. Now in some of our services for the management of adults we are becoming more risk managers. But we haven't really adopted that approach in relation to working with young people. I think within the Children Act now, we have the confidence to continue our social worker approach if you like, because it's seen as appropriate and the Act is saying that there's reasons for children coming to the attention of the courts and that those reasons need to be addressed and it allows us to bring our social worker skills and our social work approach to the fore.
>
> [YPP Key Informant]

Conclusion

This chapter provided an overview of how youth justice has evolved in Northern Ireland and the Republic of Ireland in recent decades. It commenced by exploring the way in which contemporary youth justice policy and practice in Northern Ireland has emerged in the context of a society in transition following a lengthy period of political conflict. While the criminal justice framework put in place in the aftermath of the Belfast/Good Friday Agreement provides the foundation for the system, it is equally apparent that the centrality of community in the policy discourse and the strength of community partnerships in Northern Ireland has provided the capacity and infrastructure to manage the vast majority of young offenders in the community. Youth justice in the Republic of Ireland has grown over the last decade following almost a century of political inertia and neglect. A historical reliance on the use of institutionalization for young people in conflict with the law for much of earlier part of the 20th century has now given way to a system that is firmly grounded in the ethos of retaining young offenders in the community save in exceptional circumstances. A long and established history of community and voluntary-sector involvement continues to play an instrumental role in service delivery to young offenders in the Republic of Ireland.

The differing origins of both systems combined with other socio-political influences are reflected in distinct systems of youth justice in the respective jurisdictions. In Northern Ireland, the youth justice system is grounded in a philosophy of restorative justice, and youth conferencing is the main statutory diversionary response to youth crime. However, Northern Ireland has not been immune from policy influences from other parts of the UK that emphasize strategies of risk assessment, management and control in the supervision of young offenders in the community. The youth justice system in the Republic of Ireland is located within a rehabilitative philosophy based on the premise that change is best facilitated within the context of diversionary pre-court options and thereafter through statutory court-ordered supervision in the community. Youth justice in the Republic of Ireland and in Northern Ireland is characterized by having low numbers of young people serving custodial orders within the respective child/juvenile detention systems for under 18 year olds (Children Detention School system in the Republic of Ireland and the Juvenile Justice Centre in Northern Ireland). Legislative principles and provisions introduced as part of the reform of youth justice in both jurisdictions have played an important part in retaining the use of custodial orders as a measure of last resort. Against this, both jurisdictions detain disproportionate numbers of young people on remand.

Eadie and Canton (2002) highlight the relevance of professional background, culture and organizational expectations in making sense of how youth justice policy is negotiated and applied in practice. They suggest that adequate attention is not always given 'to the organizational realities which stand between policy and practice' (ibid.: 15). In contrast to other jurisdictions, such as England and Wales, the professional training of those supervising young offenders in Northern Ireland and the Republic of Ireland is predominantly based in social work and to a lesser degree in youth and community work and education. However, as documented in this chapter, practitioners generally operate within organizations which of themselves are influenced by historical precedent and local and community factors. In identifying the manner in which each of the organizations has evolved over time, this chapter has provided the basis to explore how historical and contemporary influences weave into the fabric of day-to-day professional practice and decision making to be discussed in the following chapters.

6 Constructing compliance on offender supervision

Offender compliance is constructed within the policy and legislative parameters of individual jurisdictions and framed by the context of professional and organizational values and practices (Robinson and McNeill 2010; Eadie and Canton 2002). Expectations of compliance may also be shaped by the unique characteristics and exigencies pertaining to different offender groups. Supervisors' perceptions of what constitutes compliant and non-compliant behaviour on community disposals are significant as they are likely to influence how offenders' behaviour is interpreted and how compliance is promoted and responded to in practice (see Chapter 7). This chapter explores the perspectives of probation officers, probation service officers and youth justice workers (here on in termed 'practitioners') involved in the supervision of young offenders on statutory community-based disposals in Northern Ireland and the Republic of Ireland. The discussion commences by exploring practitioners' perspectives on the stances taken by young people in relation to their attitudes and behaviours during the supervision process. It is argued that these perspectives are based on a complex interplay between practitioner and organizational expectations and young people's behaviour, motivation, developmental stage and perceived commitment to change. Change in young people's circumstances, maturity and perspective on supervision means that compliance is a dynamic and shifting construct that alters over time. While young people may originally comply to avoid being returned to court, other reasons are likely to emerge as normative attachments develop within and outside the supervisory process. Conversely, negative changes in circumstances such as a relationship breakdown, unemployment, crises or bereavement can shift the compliance dynamic in the short- or longer-term. Overall, it is suggested that practitioners' narratives of compliance about young people are constructed on the basis of their interactions with them during supervision sessions and through their perceptions of how young people manage and negotiate compliance at home, at school and in the community. To this end, offender compliance not only changes over time, but its regulatory impact and control stretch far beyond the boundaries of supervision sessions into the realm of everyday life in the community.

Levels of engagement

Notwithstanding the dynamic nature of compliance (Robinson and McNeill 2010), practitioners' descriptions of the differing levels of young people's engagement with supervision were broadly similar to those found in previous research (Ditton and Ford 1994). The most atypical level involved cases where young people valued the opportunities offered to them in the supervision process. Such cases were characterized by consistent attendance and active commitment to change and were most likely to include individuals with less prolific criminal histories and with little or no prior involvement with the criminal justice system. More common were young people who demonstrated some level of commitment to change and who responded positively to ongoing encouragement, support and reminders provided by their supervisor. They were liable to digressions and to occasional offending relapses but in general they recognized the need for change and wanted something different in their lives. Despite expressing a desire to change, others were described as being unable to sustain a level of compliance that could credibly maintain their status on a statutory community-based disposal due to the profound nature of their social or personal problems. Some young people were similar in profile to what Crewe (2007) describes as strategically compliant prisoners. According to practitioners, these young people made strategic decisions about their level of participation and completed the minimum required of them to avoid being returned to court. Sometimes passive, sometimes hostile, they were perceived to be uninterested in making changes in their lives and 'played the game' as a mechanism to get through the order. For a final group, whose identity and aspirations were so firmly enmeshed in criminality that they explicitly flaunted their resistance to the rules and were neither interested in overt, nor covert, demonstrations of compliance. Although presented as distinctive categories of engagement, practitioners explained that there was a more fluid synergy between the categories, with young people shifting within and between different levels of compliance as time and circumstances unfolded. Furthermore, as outlined below, underpinning these categories of engagement was a myriad of practitioner expectations and offender behavioural factors that interacted to form and influence constructions of compliance over the supervision period.

Practitioner expectations and perspectives on compliance

In common with previous studies of community-based disposals (Ellis, Heddermann and Mortimer 1996; Farrall 2002a; Ugwudike 2010), non-compliance was most frequently described by practitioners as incidents where young people failed to attend scheduled appointments. However, the notion of substantive compliance (Robinson and McNeill 2010) was also strongly reflected in practitioners' perspectives and most were of the view that compliance also related to the way that young people participated and engaged during supervision appointments:

> Getting guys to show up at things, it's making steps, but the young people also need to know that they can't just stand still, just by showing up.
>
> [YPP practitioner group, Site 2]

> In terms of non-compliance, it isn't just about the young person showing up … so where a young person is showing up for individual work and clearly saying 'well I'm only here, because I have to be here and I've no interest in doing this work' or if they're turning up to do reparative activity and maybe someone from a charity shop is saying 'well they're coming in and standing there and they won't do anything that we're asking them to do'.
>
> [YJA practitioner group, Site 1]

Legislative, policy and organizational requirements, as well as best practice principles, require that practitioners have greater input into young people's lives during the supervision process than is normally the case for adult offenders. Developing and maintaining contact with families and liaising with addiction, community, education, employment, health and social services are therefore routine activities for many youth justice workers. Effective practitioners are seen to adopt a holistic perspective and are obliged to have in-depth knowledge about the extent to which young people are 'compliant' in other realms of their lives in the community:

> I'd be the first one to say that when I started contacting teachers originally, it was a case of 'are they [young person] showing up?' 'Yes', 'grand', type, type, type into my report, you know, young Joe Bloggs is showing up to school; whereas now I'm kind of going it's a bit more than just showing up.
>
> [YPP practitioner group, Site 2]

Although not always forming part of the formal requirements of statutory court disposals, young people's behaviour in the home, their attendance at school, alternative education, training or employment, the presence or absence of problems in these contexts, the extent to which they associate with anti-social peers or consume alcohol and/or drugs and the issues that arise were perceived by practitioners as indicators of compliance and collectively they contributed to the overall script of each young person's compliance. Being non-compliant in other aspects of their lives was likely to impact negatively on practitioners' perceptions of young people's commitment to change. Furthermore, practitioners' reports that notify the courts of continued alcohol or drug use or poor attendance at school are likely to evoke more negative perceptions of young people by the judiciary, particularly when combined with other aspects of non-compliance such as non-attendance at appointments.

Moving away from offending was strongly identified as an expectation of compliant behaviour during the supervision process. Efforts to stop were described by practitioners as requiring young people to make radical change in their lives that had to be negotiated within the minefields of their circumstances and social networks. It involved, but was not restricted to, distancing themselves from criminal peers, stepping outside the endemic cultures of criminality that existed within some families and some communities, saying no to drug dealers and older criminal adults, to drugs and to cheap alcohol, and to the range of weapons and implements available to them. Moving away from offending was characterized by practitioners as demanding, complex and subject to setbacks. Recognizing that relapse is 'a highly probable initial outcome for individuals who attempt to change their behaviour' (Healy 2010: 98), a distinction was made by practitioners between young people who were perceived to be committed to change but experienced a temporary lapse into offending behaviour and those who continued with a repeated pattern of such behaviour. The behaviour of the latter group was clearly constructed as non-compliance, in contrast to the former where reoffending was seen as an inevitable part of the shift towards desistance (Farrall and Calverley 2006) rather than as a fundamental act of non-compliance.

Young people's stances on compliance: practitioners' perspectives

Adolescent experiences of community disposals are similar to those of adults in that they are structured on power relationships and interactions that take place within the realm of the supervisory process (Smith *et al.* 2009). Unlike adults however, the relationship dynamics with authority figures are also framed around the differential power base between teenagers and adults. Raby (2005: 168) suggests that the positioning of power and identity is distinct for young people because 'they experience a temporary inequality that intersects with other significant identifications ... are shaped by discourses of a fluid, becoming self, and are also diversely shaped through the material inequalities of their diverse lives'. With reference to a study of 12–19 year old adolescents detained in correctional settings in Canada, Cesaroni and Alvi (2010) suggest that conflict may arise from the tension between a time characterized by seeking out independence and individuality while at the same time being subject to the power of a regime and 'relegated to being child-like, dependent, and strictly controlled' (p. 313). Cesaroni and Alvi (2010: 315) explain that youth resistance was demonstrated through direct confrontation with staff such as physical resistance and 'through symbolic and expressive acts of trivial subversion'. These types of resistance manifested in behaviours such as engaging in stand-offs and threats against staff, instigating fights with peers and refusing to obey directions. Involvement in these incidents was based on instrumental decisions, with the motivation, in some cases, driven by the desire for fun or to ease boredom. Unlike the strategies of resistance employed by adult prisoners in previous research who masked their deviance through engaging disingenuously with staff and prison programmes (Crewe 2007), the adolescent detainees in Cesaroni and Alvi's (2010) study engaged in confrontational resistance that culminated in very direct consequences for them, including segregation. In the current study, practitioners were also of the view that when compared to adult clients, young people were more vocal and less subtle in their repudiation of requests made to them:

> They [young people] definitely do tell you 'no, I'm not doing it' more so than adults. Adults will be like, even though you know they're not going to do it, they'll tell you that they will, whereas ninety per cent of the time children would be like 'I'm not doing it'.
>
> [PBNI practitioner group, Site 2]

Practitioners reported that young people had a greater tendency to raise their objections to participation at supervision by storming out of appointments or by verbally protesting in a loud and sometimes forceful manner. Not all practitioners thought that behavioural differences during supervision could be delineated along gender lines, but those who did, said that verbal objections were more commonly raised by female clients than by their male counterparts. Young people's frame of reference often did not extend beyond their immediate circumstances in terms of assimilating information about supervision expectations and aspirations for the future. For example, a commonly described objection was where young people compared their supervision requirements with those of their peers and objected to participation when they perceived that more was demanded of them:

> I mean it could be what they'd say, they would say 'well I've a friend on probation and he doesn't have to do this or she doesn't have to do this so why do I and I'm not doing it'.
>
> [PBNI practitioner group, Site 2]

Cesaroni and Alvi (2010) reported similar findings, suggesting that the strategies adopted by adolescent detainees appeared to reflect their immediate needs such as a desire for entertainment, rather than longer-term concerns about being released and reunited with family members.

Young people's stances in relation to supervision were sometimes directed by other external influences. The presence of established criminal figures in a young person's life was reported by practitioners to have a profoundly disruptive impact on the supervision process. Experiences were recounted of young people being discouraged from attending appointments or conversely, ordered to attend and undertake the minimum requirements to avoid drawing extra attention to themselves:

> A lot of the juveniles are usually the runners for the more serious criminals, so we'd have a lot of that stuff to deal with, hiding and stashing drugs and all those kind of things. So they're either being encouraged by the more serious criminals to engage in services or told not to. So that is a huge factor. They're told 'you go to probation, go to every single appointment, that way you're

> not getting attention', you know what I mean? So you're complying, you're the perfect client.
>
> [YPP practitioner group, Site 1]

While avoiding appointments was the most obvious demonstration of non-compliance by young people, more subtle manifestations were similar to those used by offenders in previous studies of supervision practice (Ditton and Ford 1994; Rex 1999; Worrall 1990). These included turning up late or on different days and times to scheduled appointments, sitting in silence or restricting communication to one-word answers and limiting opportunities for disclosure. Reflecting practice experiences elsewhere (Ellis *et al.* 1996), some flexibility was generally provided to those who sought to rearrange an appointment in advance; however, cases where rescheduling was sought on an ongoing basis were more likely to be perceived by practitioners as attempts to hamper the supervision process. Attendance under the influence of alcohol or other substances was described as a strategy employed by some young people to avoid engaging at supervision while in other cases it was associated with addiction problems and chaotic lifestyles; for others, negotiating the supervision process involved memorizing the professional jargon and repeating it back during supervision:

> Even the language they use on occasions, you know, 'I know I'm subject to negative peer influences' and I'm looking at them saying 'what did you say?'... 'I know I'm subject to negative peer influences' - you know, they've heard it, the words mean nothing to them, it's just rhetoric and they're repeating it. And, you know, again it's back to surviving the system, it goes back to surviving, but not managing.
>
> [PBNI practitioner group, Site 2]

Although potential indicators of a lack of full engagement, the above strategies used by young people were not automatically perceived by practitioners as evidence of non-compliance, as discussed in the following section.

Resistance to change or youthful resistance?

Previous research suggests that passive strategies are employed by offenders to circumvent direct challenges to their lack of enthusiasm about supervision (Ditton and Ford 1994) and to avoid direct confrontation with their supervisors (Worrall 1990). This is because such forms of resistance are less amenable to being formally categorized as non-compliance (Crewe 2007). In this study, practitioners reported that differentiating between behaviours that are associated with active or passive forms of resistance from those that are characteristic of the developmental stage and circumstances of young people's lives required them to draw on their professional skills and to engage with line managers in working out the underpinning narrative within each story of compliance or non-compliance. Acknowledging the difference between adolescent defiance and more calculated resistance was an important aspect of defining what constituted non-compliance. The interpretation of such behaviours was located in a much broader context that took into account factors such as age, maturity, learning difficulties and stage of supervision. Age has long been a defining feature of the cut-off point at which young people are deemed responsible for offending behaviour in the criminal justice system. Although the evidence suggests that older adolescents (16 years and older) tend to have more advanced cognitive and psychosocial skills than younger adolescents, it is well documented that chronological age is not always a reliable indicator of young people's maturity levels (Cauffman and Steinberg 2000b; Graham and Bowling 1995). Practitioners explained that differences in developmental immaturity manifested in supervision and their expectations of young people therefore had to be tapered accordingly on a case-by-case basis. One practitioner, in describing the differences between two 17 year old female clients highlighted how differences in maturity levels can manifest in practice:

> They are both extremely bright, like it's not anything to do with intellect it's just where they are developmentally. Like [with] one of them, I'd say 'okay let's put a plan in place' and she's way more able to go with the plan, she'd be more mature and stuff. The other one is like 'no', like yesterday I was up in her house trying to get her to go back to her addiction counsellor and she was screaming at me like a 13 year old, do you know? Whereas the other one would have her outbursts but it wouldn't be like that, she'd be just very mature.
>
> [YPP practitioner group, Site 2]

The inimitability of working with young offenders was highlighted in practitioners' accounts that demonstrated the importance of distinguishing between 'non-compliant' and adolescent-orientated behaviour:

> If an ADULT came in to me and he started standing up and walking around and poking at things and lifting books off the shelf and asking questions 'what's that?', I'd be getting a bit, you know, what's going on here? But young people do that because they're naturally inquisitive. In terms of their age, you know, their chronological age might not necessarily reflect their psychosocial stage or their cognitive development.
>
> [PBNI practitioner group, Site 2]

> I have a young person and yesterday we were up at his house doing a session and after that he was coming to meet the linkage worker about employment and training that he wanted. But like I don't know how many times he said that he wasn't going to go to the linkage worker. I arrived and he said 'I'm not going', during the meeting he said 'you know I'm not going' and I just completely ignored it and then we left the house and he said 'I'm not going you know'. Now he went, he was going, but if that was an adult, this is the difference, and he said 'I'm not going' that would have been it. I would have

> left it at that. But with adolescents your intervention is different, there's more decision making going on, you as an adult being responsible.
>
> [YPP practitioner group, Site 2]

The limitations created by developmental immaturity were compounded where young people had learning or behavioural difficulties, which was not uncommon given the target population (Chitsabesan *et al.* 2007). Expectations about the level of work that could be completed within one session were revised by practitioners for young people with learning or behavioural problems. Learning difficulties or behavioural problems were seen to hinder young people's capacity to engage in the supervision process manifesting as problems with assimilating information and concentrating on defined tasks. Where learning difficulties or behavioural problems such as ADHD or hyperactivity were identified, there appeared to be general recognition that the limits of young people's capacity to concentrate or sustain concentration were considerably lower than their peers':

> With conditions like ADHD attention deficit or an inability to focus, we're looking at about twenty minutes that we could possibly get some meaningful work done. After that they're either not listening, they're anxious to leave so it's being mindful of what they're capable of along with what we want to get through to make sure both agendas are met.
>
> [YPP practitioner group, Site 1]

Finally, most practitioners explained that they adopted a more tolerant attitude to their expectations of young people at the beginning of supervision when young people were less aware of the expectations on them (see Chapter 7).

Organizational expectations and constructions of compliance

Eadie and Canton (2002: 23) argue that where practice standards are applied uncritically without consideration of 'constraints upon young people' or awareness that the same sanction may differentially impact on different individuals, the prospect for unfair and oppressive treatment arises. Recognizing the need for balance, they suggest that reflective practitioners will explore ways of 'legitimately interpreting' practice standards. Ugwudike (2010: 335) reports on probation practice in Jersey and Wales and suggests that an individualized approach to non-compliance that recognizes the exigencies of particular cases is 'more responsive to the practical problems that can impinge on compliance' and more likely to encourage future compliance. In the current study, practitioners across the three organizations tended to adopt an individualized approach with young people. Within that, certain organizational parameters existed that influenced the way in which young people's behaviour was formally conceptualized by practitioners as non-compliance. For example, YJA practitioners described that the main emphasis on compliance in their practice was focused on honouring the commitments given to victims as part of youth conference action plans or community orders. Non-compliance with victim-related requirements of the action plan was therefore seen to represent a serious aberration and a compromise to the credibility, integrity and legitimacy of the conferencing process:

> I see non-compliance as very different from lack of motivation and I think non-compliance in the way in which I practice is where a young person is contravening the wishes of the victim and the actions that they've agreed to with the victim at the conference.
>
> [YJA practitioner group, Site 1]

Legislative provision also had an input in influencing YJA practitioners' descriptions of what constituted non-compliance. Under the Justice (Northern Ireland) Act 2002 a distinction is made between the threshold of non-compliance for diversionary youth conferences and youth conference orders. In legal terms, young people subject to diversionary youth conferences are only deemed to be non-compliant when they fail to comply with the requirements specified in their conference plans to a 'significant extent'; in contrast, a failure to comply with any requirement of a youth conference order constitutes non-compliance.

Differences around the management of attendance requirements also varied between organizations and impacted on the way in which non-compliance was constructed. For instance, at the time of conducting the research in early 2011 supervision practice by the PBNI operated within the Northern Ireland Standards and Service Requirements (Doran *et al.* 2010).[1] Described by Doran and Cooper (2008: 28) as 'the framework for accountability to government', the standards set out guidelines on probation officers' work, from offender assessment to all aspects of supervision and management of offenders. The standards in relation to attendance stipulated that weekly contact with offenders was a minimum requirement for the first 16 weeks of the order and included one home visit per month. Thereafter, the potential existed to reduce to fortnightly contact for the next 16 weeks and to no less than monthly contact for the remainder of the supervision period. Reduced contact was not automatic but rather was contingent on the offender's progress with the supervision plan and risk assessment score. Where an offender failed to attend and did not provide an acceptable reason, the incident was recorded and a formal written warning noting a failure to comply was issued to the offender. A second incident of unauthorized non-attendance within a six-month period resulted in a final written warning and breach proceedings were activated where subsequent non-attendance occurred within the same time period. While standards provided direction on what constituted acceptable reasons, qualitative scope remained for practitioners to consider the circumstances of individual cases. Underpinning the objective fact of non-attendance at appointments is the subjective minefield of what defines an acceptable or unacceptable excuse. Discretion was therefore afforded in determining what constituted the acceptability of reasons for non-attendance. Acceptable reasons varied but broadly included unexpected events in the offender's life including illness or bereavement or in crisis situations where circumstances made compliance difficult for the offender in the short-term:

> If somebody's granny is ill and they've been sent off to stay with their granny and look after her, or if there's a funeral, or if they're not well and they're in bed with a really bad dose of the flu, you might accept any of those explanations this time as an acceptable explanation, but you might be saying 'look on the next occasion you need to be phoning me, the responsibility is on you to let me know, in advance not afterwards, and not when I chase it up'. So it's all about them taking responsibility.
>
> [PBNI Key Informant]

Management played a key role in sanctioning discretionary decisions and their understanding of the challenges of working with young people was therefore perceived by practitioners as a central dimension in supporting their work:

> I have one young person whose mummy misuses alcohol and she's not available at all to him, and he was first of all placed in residential care but then the placement broke down so social services moved him back to the house and there was no support. On the home visits, myself and social services did joint visits, the mummy was never there, she's never available. Probation has very strict standards of contact, but say in an emergency, like the week that he moved from the children's home back home, I just went to my manager and said 'look, there's no point in me seeing him this week, he's being shipped about and whatever' and she said 'that's fine'. But other than that you'd be expected to see them every week.
>
> [PBNI practitioner group, Site 2]

For each of the three organizations, level of risk mediated attendance requirements and was also influential in determining what was considered to be non-compliance. All practitioners said that attendance requirements were elevated for higher risk offenders and their failure to attend was perceived as being more serious and necessitating more responsive action due to concerns about public protection and the young person's safety. This was particularly so where young people were living out of home in hostel or temporary accommodation and had few stable connections in their lives. The extent to which non-attendance was framed as non-compliance by all of the organizations was escalated where young people could not be contacted or went missing from their place of residence. Each of the criminal justice agencies had to balance competing responsibilities to, on the one hand, retain young people on community supervision and on the other, to address concerns for public protection.

Regardless of whether non-attendance was formally constructed as non-compliance, many practitioners described that absences were challenged, recorded on offenders' case files (see Chapter 7) and were included in the overall narrative of the offender's progress when writing future court reports.

Non-compliance was likely to have direct implications for many young people especially those who encountered multiple court appearances. It was of particular relevance to young people in the Republic of Ireland where cases are often adjourned before being finalized – for periods varying from weeks to months – to monitor offenders' responsiveness to probation supervision (see Chapter 5). Healy and O'Donnell's (2010: 5) analysis of judges' decision making based on regional newspaper reporting in Ireland suggests that adjourned supervision is used by judges 'to give the defendant an opportunity to demonstrate willingness to reform … as ways of discouraging those who appeared before them from reoffending … to create a relationship of trust between the offender and the judge'. The consequence for young people is that they are often required to re-appear before the judge and to have their progress – as articulated in their supervisor's report – examined and taken into consideration as part of the decision making process. The significance of this practice was not lost on the young people in this study, who attached considerable importance to the court report in their narratives of negotiating compliance on supervision (see Chapter 8).

Conclusion

This chapter demonstrated that the concept of compliance is a complex construct that extends far beyond the standard expectation to attend supervision sessions. Compliance involves young people's active participation in supervision and demonstrated commitment to change through their behaviour at home, at school and in the community. Constructing compliance is not a uniform process and for practitioners working with young people, it involves a requirement to distinguish between adolescent-related behaviour and genuine resistance to the supervision process and behavioural change. Making decisions about what constitutes non-compliance is a negotiated process involving the practitioner and the line manager and is influenced by factors such as the age and maturity of the young people, their circumstances, motivation, risk level and the relevant organization's expectations and standards. From what practitioners said, it is apparent that interpretations of incidents of non-compliance, unless extremely serious, are seldom viewed in isolation but rather are contextualized within a narrative based on the young person's overall level of compliance with supervision. It is this narrative that holds the strongest significance not only in its influence on the contents of subsequent court reports, but in the way that it informs practitioners' approach in adopting strategies that promote compliance and respond to non-compliance over the supervision period.

7 Promoting compliance and responding to non-compliance as part of the supervision process

Addressing issues of compliance requires that approaches are balanced and responsive to the needs of the target audience (Ayres and Braithwaite 1992; Bottoms 2001). Transferring across to the context of young offenders on community supervision, the suggestion is that responsive strategies must be cognisant of young people's social and developmental status as adolescents, their involvement in criminality and criminal sub-cultures, their level of civic involvement, social capacity and relationships in their lives. Farrall (2002b: 263) captures the challenge in explaining that community sentences need to be perceived 'as both effective in helping those so sentenced address their offending behaviour, and additionally able to ensure that the vast majority of them complete the requirements of their sentences'. Moving aside from young offenders for a moment, recent research suggests that 'compliance-orientated practice' may offer more promise in retaining offenders on community supervision and in reducing reoffending than approaches which seek compliance through deterrence-based strategies including the threat of custody (Ugwudike 2010; McCulloch 2010). The absence of evidence to link strict enforcement practices with promoting long-term compliance with the criminal law is noteworthy (Hearnden and Millie 2004), with one explanation being that offenders are reasonably impervious to the deterrent aspects of punishment in the first instance. Opportunities to talk, to discuss problems and solutions and to have someone to advocate on their behalf are more commonly cited motivators of compliance by offenders than deterrent concerns related to enforcement (Ugwudike 2010). The threat of being returned to court for failing to comply remains the ultimate armoury in the discourse of community supervision and a key motivator for some offenders; but as Bottoms (2001) explains, compliance is likely to be motivated by a complex range of interacting influences. In other words, the decision to comply may be partly motivated by instrumental reasons such as a desire to avoid being locked up; in turn this may be influenced by normative reasons such as having attachment to one's child or recognition of wanting a better life. Strategies to encourage compliance therefore must be sufficiently flexible to accommodate differing and changing motivations and barriers. This chapter is rooted in the premise that for many young offenders the threat of being returned to court or detained in custody as a result of non-compliance has limited leverage, especially for those young people who are most disengaged and with the lowest levels of social capacity and connectedness to society:

> I mean the other thing, for some of them, is that they have no interest in complying, because of how they feel about themselves basically. You know 'I've no loyalty to anybody'. I'm thinking particularly of young people in care at times who probably think 'What will I lose? I've lost everything anyway. What am I going to lose by not doing this?' I think with a lot of young people, they've given up on themselves.
>
> [YJA practitioner group, Site 2]

Where the final deterrent of custody does not act as a responsive strategy for non-compliance, an alternative approach is required that engages with young people in a way that promotes short- and long-term compliance yet responds fairly and consistently to non-compliance. The discussion below commences with the young person's transition from the court to the community; this is followed by practitioners' accounts of their practice in engaging and sustaining young people's motivation to comply as well as the policies and practices employed in managing non-compliance.

From the courtroom to the community

The early stages of supervision are frequently a challenging time as young people become accustomed to the statutory requirements placed on them by the court disposal. It coincides with higher reported levels of non-compliance (Moore *et al.* 2006) and reoffending in some cases (Seymour 2003).[1] In the current study, practitioners explained that the majority of young people commence supervision with limited insight into the expectations on them despite information being conveyed during the pre-court assessment process. Weijers (2004) suggests that the courtroom provides an important but often under-utilized platform for communicating messages about the consequences of offending behaviour. He argues that enhancing explanations and participation opportunities to young people in the courtroom and engaging in 'moral communication' with them creates a more realistic basis from which the implications of offending behaviour are understood (ibid.: 27). Courtroom conditions including poor acoustics, heavy court lists or limited communication between young people, judges and their legal representatives have been previously reported as inhibiting the quality of participation for young people in the court system in Northern Ireland and the Republic of Ireland (Kilkelly 2006; Department of Justice 2011). Considerable disparity in judicial practice and communication has also been reported, ranging from high levels of engagement to very limited, if any, interaction (Kilkelly 2005). The use of conferencing as a forum for collectively agreeing how the majority of young people should be dealt with in Northern Ireland was perceived by YJA staff to enhance young people's level of understanding by virtue of the preparation and participation involved in the process. That said, it was also reported that the level of understanding varied between cases. The status of adolescents as young participants who have not yet attained full adult maturity was a key factor in mediating levels of understanding in both the conference and court process. In this regard, practitioners described that many young people's restricted capacity to assimilate information and to comprehend longer-term consequences were factors that hindered their level of understanding. With few exceptions, a court report on the young person's suitability for a community disposal including details of their circumstances, offending behaviour, criminal history and motivation is required before a sentence can be imposed on a young person in Northern Ireland or the Republic of Ireland. Practitioners perceived that knowledge of an imminent court date assisted some young people to focus in the short-term on getting a good report for court; however, the longer-term significance was less apparent:

> I think a lot of them can see it up to the report stage, getting the report to court and you see the solicitor is saying, 'get a good report, make sure you get a good report'. So they can sometimes focus on attending appointments, getting that report, going to court and then they kind of think that's where it will end, that's it and anything after that is just muffled. If you ask them to repeat back, 'what are your conditions?' very often they won't be able. I don't think that they can understand long-term what actually is involved, not all of them, but most. Even though you have discussed with them at the assessment stage that 'look, these are the conditions that will be recommended for you when you go to court on a certain date' and then they go to court, they get placed on probation and then you touch base with them after and you're checking in, 'okay what happened in court'? They can't remember, 'oh I just signed [the court order] and it ends there'. Then you have to go back and try and discuss what the conditions were, because sometimes the understanding is not there or maybe they're not taking in everything, they're so busy in their heads that they're not taking in what's being discussed in court or what they're been told.
>
> [YPP practitioner group, Site 1]

Encouraging compliance through engaging with young offenders

Trotter (1999: 2) explains that working with offenders under court-ordered disposals involves supervising 'involuntary clients' who do not choose to avail of services and may be opposed to intervention. Involuntariness takes on added meaning when supervising marginalized and difficult-to-reach young people whose resistance to intervention is well documented (Chapman 2000; Eadie and Canton 2002; Hollin 1996). Not dissimilar to other studies of young people in the criminal justice system, practitioners described that many of their clients are typically involved in offending and anti-social behaviour for considerable periods of time prior to commencing supervision. Some are entrenched in offending behaviour and have had repeated contact with the criminal justice system.

Marginalization and a sense of hopelessness coupled with experiences of exclusion within and beyond their own communities characterize the lives of many and present as significant challenges for staff tasked with promoting change and compliance:

> The underlying notion from a lot of the young people we work with and young men in particular, is having no place and they have no sense of future and there is that drive and hopelessness which makes our job quite difficult in terms of bringing them up to the point where they're hopeful enough to want to achieve and be ambitious for the future.
>
> [YJA practitioner group, Site 1]

The unpredictability, indifference and impetuousness associated with adolescence was perceived to create unique challenges in attempts to promote compliance and respond to non-compliance. The space within which practitioners' efforts to reinforce future consequences occurs is frequently occupied by adolescents whose primary reference point is the present – 'what happens to me today?' This disjuncture means that working with clients whose time frame is developmentally programmed towards the short-term makes messages about long-term consequences far less significant. Furthermore, the influence of peers, differential perceptions of risk, and an increased tendency towards impulsivity necessitates an entirely different platform from which to commence the supervision journey when compared with adult clients. Immersed in the throes of adolescence and with few meaningful attachments to society, for young people in the criminal justice system, the social and psychological stakes in conformity are low (Bottoms 2001) and the challenges of engagement high (Hammersley, Marsland and Reid 2003). It is often in these circumstances that supervision commences and participation is required.

Offender participation relates not just to compliance, but as Chapman and Hough (1998) outline, it is intrinsically linked to effective practice. Without engaging offenders in the process, the prospects for behavioural change, including reoffending, are reduced. The rationale for engaging offenders is perhaps best contextualized within Prochaska *et al.*'s (1992) model of behavioural change. Consisting of five stages (pre-contemplation, contemplation, preparation, action and maintenance), it posits that those at the pre-contemplation stage are least motivated, have not personally acknowledged a need to change, or consider that the benefits of offending outweigh the consequences for them. Those at the contemplation stage have acknowledged the possibility of a need for behavioural change, while the preparation phase involves developing the skills to avoid risk situations. Action and maintenance are the phases when behavioural changes occur (Prochaska *et al.* 1992). Chablani and Spinney (2011) suggest that many of the most marginalized young people are at the pre-contemplation stage and require a strategy that involves building relationships with them and establishing trust before any programme of behavioural change commences. Reporting on a programme to engage very high risk disaffected teenage mothers, they describe a retention rate of 90 per cent after one year when working with a total of 81 cases. The outcome was attributed to a strategy that combined 'relentless outreach' and relationship building:

> what we're saying is that we want to target people who are really disengaged and disconnected so we have to go after them and do whatever it takes and use ourselves to build relationships that feel real to people and that are trustworthy enough so that young people connect so that we can actually get to the hard conversations.
>
> [Deputy Director of Roca, in Chablani and Spinney, 2011: 375]

The approach articulated by Chablani and Spinney (2011) resonated with the majority of practitioners, albeit within the confines of the expectations imposed by the criminal justice system. Among practitioners, there was a sense that responsibility could not be loaded onto young people in the same way as adults and that engaging with them required practitioners to 'keep at it' and to reach out again and again. The approach did not seek to abdicate responsibility from young people; instead emphasis was placed on practitioners' ability to identify the barriers to compliance and reasons for non-compliance and to work with young people to overcome those obstacles. Reasons for non-compliance were similar to those recounted in previous studies (McCulloch 2010; Ugwudike 2011) and included unstructured lifestyle; lack of motivation; transport problems; childcare issues; timing of appointments; criminal history; personal and social problems; accommodation problems; unemployment and conversely work/training commitments. According to the majority of practitioners, proactive strategies such as arranging transport to sessions, meeting young people in their communities or calling to their homes were employed throughout the supervision process. The latter involved a combination of home visits or, on occasion, efforts by practitioners to ensure young people's attendance at early morning events. This approach facilitated contact with young people while also providing opportunities to identify and address barriers to attendance. Frequent mobile (cell) phone and text contact was also identified as an important mechanism for engaging and communicating with young people. With the exception of a small number of practitioners who restricted the use of mobile phones for exceptional cases, texting was commonly used by most to remind young people about appointments. It was also considered as a practical strategy that facilitated compliance:

> We all have work phones so we share numbers and can text them [young people]. Or I would phone them a lot as well to wake them up for appointments because even getting them out of bed for a morning appointment can be a struggle, you know, because they're not used to that structure. So we do what we have to do to get them to appointments usually. But texting I think works well and a lot of them would communicate that way.
>
> [PBNI practitioner group, Site 1]

In addition to reminders, texting enabled practitioners to convey messages or to check in with young people between sessions. Despite a reluctance to use their phone credit to contact their supervisors, there was a general view that by communicating with young people in a way that they were familiar, it increased the likelihood of them responding. For example, some practitioners explained that they frequently received text messages from their young clients with a 'call me' message asking them to return a call. Fear and uncertainty are reasons attributed to problems of engaging young people and so texting was seen to be a less confrontational method of communication, especially at the early stages of supervision:

> They'll always respond to texts because they feel safer, if you ring them up, 'ah yes, what what what?' you can hear the panic in their voice straight away. If I've an established relationship I'll ring them, but if it's a new order it'd be a quick text, you know, 'hi there if you get a chance give me a quick text back and then I'll give you a call, is everything ok?' where you're showing empathy with them, you're showing concern, you're not coming down like a ton of bricks on them. That sort of calms the waters and that opens the door for you.
>
> [PBNI practitioner group, Site 2]

Communicating compliance in the supervisory relationship

Practitioners described the development of positive working relationships with young people as 'the key ingredient' and 'the cornerstone' of any strategy that sought to encourage their attendance and participation at supervision appointments. The characteristics identified with working relationships were in line with other studies of practitioner–client relationships (Boswell 1996; Rex 1999; Trotter and Evans 2010) and included establishing rapport, demonstrating empathy, and being genuine, honest and respectful. Although identified as the basis for engaging in any work that seeks to affect behavioural change (Marsh and Evans 2009), previous research suggests that the development of such relationships is a slow process requiring high degrees of resolve from staff (Seymour 2003) and leading Ditton and Ford (1994) to suggest that persistent offenders might need to be won over by persistent staff. As will be outlined when discussing young people's perspectives, the supervisory relationship has the potential to be an important catalyst for change (see Chapter 8). However, building its foundations with young people who often have a suspicious and distrustful disposition towards adults in authority necessitates a high degree of professional tenacity in persevering with the process:

> You must stick with these young people, its like 'stick-ability' and when they're pushing you away, realizing that it's not you, it's them building the wall. If young people don't have good attachment, they will put everything up to build walls around themselves, actually a huge percentage of the body of our children have attachment issues and trauma and sometimes kind

of a combination of both. So that's where you're looking at real difficult situations.

[YJA practitioner group, Site 1]

It was not uncommon for practitioners to describe working with young people for a number of months before change occurred in their participation and engagement at supervision sessions. Change was therefore an incremental process that shifted over time. As described in the following example, recognition of the nuances of young people's demeanour and differentiating between poor communications skills, social awkwardness and genuine resistance to change requires professional insight from supervising staff:

> Practitioner 1: We were working with a young person and if you got four words out of him it was a good session …
> Practitioner 2: I remember that
> Practitioner 1: And it must have taken two, two and a half months …
> Practitioner 2: Easily
> Practitioner 1: And then you got a few more. And then by the end of it, he was with us about eight months, and by the end he came in and chatted away and sat for about an hour and a half and for us we felt that was the persistence of working with him, seeing where he was at and we just kept going with it and I think that was a big break, because I wasn't long started when I had that case and it really showed me that you have to work like that with a young person.
>
> [PBNI practitioner group, Site 1]

Engaging with young people through the medium of the practitioner–client relationship was not seen as an end in itself, but was perceived as the vehicle to effect change and as a legitimizing force in a context that required staff to combine a caring and controlling role (Trotter 1999). Fostering legitimacy in the supervision process has central relevance in light of the evidence demonstrating a positive relationship between perceptions of legitimacy and willingness to comply (Fagan and Tyler 2005). It also resonates strongly with Bottoms' (2001) theoretical model of compliance which suggests that compliance is more likely to occur and be sustained where offenders are motivated by normative reasons such as perceiving the system to be legitimate or from a sense of moral obligation (see Chapter 3). Rex (1999) provides practical application to Bottoms' (2001) theory in her findings that suggest probation officers' demonstrations of commitment towards their clients and clients' positive perceptions of this commitment 'was crucial in preparing probationers to take quite directive guidance from supervisors' (p. 380). Identifying the underlying reasons for non-compliance with young offenders is seen as a key task for supervisors (Eadie and Canton 2002), is central to developing effective responses to non-compliance (Bottoms 2001) and is best facilitated through the medium of positive working relationships with young people.

Front-end compliance

Communicating expectations, roles and consequences of non-compliance to offenders represent standard practice at the onset of supervision (Mair and May 1997) and in many cases during the assessment process, when offenders typically 'consent' to the community disposal recommended. Less is known about the quality and context of this communication or the extent to which principles of informed consent are integrated into the practice. The rationale for such practices are found in the evidence which suggests that compliance rates are higher for those who have a clear understanding of what is expected of them (Ditton and Ford 1994). 'Front-end compliance' was a term coined from the words of one practitioner in this study who used it to describe the notion that non-compliance is greatly reduced where work prior to or at the beginning (front-end) of supervision is focused on ensuring that young people have an opportunity to participate and to fully understand their options and the expectations that will be placed on them. The corollary of front-end compliance is not only that informed individuals are likely to be more compliant individuals but perceptions of fairness in the process are enhanced where clear and informed messages have been communicated and reiterated. The notion of front-end compliance shares similarities with Trotter's (1999) concept of role clarification which is described as one of the key skills when working with involuntary clients. Role clarification involves an exploration of the client's expectations and understanding of the disposal, discussion on what is negotiable and what is not, limits on confidentiality, the nature of the professional relationship and the nature of the supervisor's authority (Trotter and Evans 2010). Particular emphasis is placed on the need for supervisors to communicate the dual care and social control aspects of their role to avoid any misconceptions that might act as a barrier to engagement and to assist clients in understanding that they have a helping as well as a legalistic role (Trotter 1999). Communicating expectations and explaining the supervisor's role was identified as a key role at the commencement of supervision:

> You explain to young people in the beginning 'my job is to help young people not get in trouble again' so let's look at how we do that, and 'if you have this to do and if this doesn't happen, then this is what will happen'. So it's about that honesty from the very beginning, both in terms of support, but also in terms of compliance and taking other action.
>
> [YJA practitioner group, Site 2]

Reminding young people about the requirements of their disposal was not restricted to the early stages of supervision. It was a continuous task for practitioners, and one that necessitated encouraging as well as challenging young people about their behaviour during supervision appointments. Many described the process of reiterating similar pieces of information on different days and in different ways. Typically conversations recalled by practitioners involved a process of explaining and often confronting young people about their behaviour while outlining negotiable and non-negotiable aspects of supervision (Trotter 1999). Engaging in dialogue with young people was the primary communicative mechanism favoured by practitioners in the supervisory context. The use of dialogue resonated strongly with the professional philosophy of many of the practitioners, who viewed their role as working together with young people to overcome barriers to compliance. It also created the type of active and participatory context identified within the principles of effective practice (McGuire and Priestly 1995) and provided a platform for listening, giving advice and guidance, problem solving, and coaching in a directive but non-judgemental manner (see McCulloch 2005). With some exceptions, practitioners described that many young people's perspectives about their responsibilities with regard to supervision were filtered to some degree by their level of developmental maturity. Addressing these perspectives through an ongoing process of role clarification (Trotter 1999) was a core process throughout the supervision period:

> I'd have young people that would arrive up to the office and go 'I can't stay, because my friends are going into town to buy a jumper'. It's not even your jumper, but it's, 'oh my pal is doing this' or 'I have to go to my friend's he's getting [his] cast off' or 'my friend's mother is sick'. So it's the most random excuses, but they are priority to probation, to court. That's completely relevant to them, because that's their focus right now. And they don't get that it's not a real excuse particularly with the court, I'm like 'you signed up to this, I don't think the judge is going to accept that as a reasonable excuse', but it is *the* most important thing to them right there and right now.
>
> [YPP practitioner group, Site 1]

A number of practitioners described how they engaged young people in role play as a way of reminding them about the expectations of supervision. These scenarios typically centred on issues that most frequently led young people into trouble and to this end, role play was a strategy that sought to model what compliance meant in practice. Efforts to minimize young people's future involvement in the criminal justice system – particularly as a result of altercations with the police formed the basis of much of this work. Below, the process of role playing a police–youth encounter with a client is described by one practitioner as a way of raising young people's awareness of their behaviour and reducing the potential for further criminal charges:

> I would be saying to him 'right I'm the police officer now … and I'm coming up to you and you KNOW why I'm coming up to you' – 'no, I don't know why you're coming to me' – 'I'm coming up to you because you're known to us, you have a record, you're in the town, I see you now, it's Friday night, it's eight o'clock, things are starting to pick up in the town and I see you, I say right I'm going to go over and see what he's at tonight' – 'now what do you think of me saying that?'. 'That's not fair' – I say 'no, no, think about it, how is it not fair?' What I do is I build them to a stage where I say 'expect

> that, and understand that that's a reasonable reaction, and understand that that's part of the price you have to pay for your offending to date and work through that; so if you're expecting that, this is what you say': 'yes officer I'm going here, I'm making my way to here' so 'you give an explanation and that's how you will survive that'. So you're trying to pre-empt silly disorderly behaviour where they WILL be arrested and charged with disorderly behaviour, if they're cheeky or they're aggressive or they're pushing. They'll often say 'I don't know why they've got me up for this [charge] 'cause all I did was kind of held myself against the car door, sure that's nothin', that was nothin'. And in their lifestyle in terms of how they interact with their peers, in terms of pushing and shoving and just generally a rough-and-ready life, that IS nothing. So they don't understand that, you're trying to just give them an understanding of where their social location is, what the expectations are from the police and what they should be expecting from the police, you know? And that helps to a degree.
>
> [PBNI practitioner group, Site 2]

Demonstrating compliance through pro-social modelling was a strategy outlined by some practitioners in accounts of their work with young people. Previous research suggests that the impact of pro-social modelling and other approaches associated with effective practice may be greater when offenders perceive their relationship with their supervisor as positive and legitimate (Rex 1999; Ugwudike 2010). This is because offenders are likely to be more receptive to the messages communicated when they value the perspective of their supervisor:

> A guy we were working with I took him to the leisure centre and the lady was quite rude and I actually found myself, you know, if the young person hadn't have been with me I might have been rude back, but I thought no, we'll deal with this properly. So I decided then I'd demonstrate how to deal with it properly. It's about being really upfront and candid with them 'cause I did say it to him, I said you know I felt like shouting back at her, so they see that you're human too, and that you're being honest and upfront and saying 'look I was going to approach it that way but I actually allowed myself to think, to deal with it differently'. So you're actually demonstrating what you're looking for them to do.
>
> [PBNI practitioner group, Site 1]

Another approach used by practitioners was to motivate compliance through the use of moral appeal. Moral appeal involved reminding young people about the impact of offending on family members most commonly their children for those who were already parents, their parents or their grandparents (typically a grandmother). For young people in Northern Ireland who were subject to youth conferencing plans and orders, moral appeals to comply extended to reminding them about the commitments they made to victims. The following example outlines one practitioner's description of encouraging a young person to undertake the promises given to a victim of his offending:

> 'At the time do you remember when we were in the conference you wanted to do this, because you knew it would make [victim] feel better for what you did to him? You said you would do this, remember what you said, remember how that felt' and keeping that momentum with them can really sort of spur them on at times as well, even if it is to write that apology letter that's hard to do, or to undertake whatever amount of reparation that they need to do.
>
> [YJA practitioner group, Site 2]

Negotiating the parameters of supervision and providing a sense of ownership in the process was considered an important element in encouraging compliance. Negotiation can have mutual benefits for clients who are given a role in the process and supervisors who have the opportunity to exercise their role in terms of the treatment plan and organizational expectations. Practitioners' accounts reflected an emphasis on involving young people in the process of seeking solutions where barriers to non-compliance arose. In the following example, one practitioner describes the process of negotiating the timing of appointments with a young client in an attempt to facilitate attendance and to imbue a sense of responsibility in the outcome:

> Some kids see a power struggle in this that we have the court order. We can go back to court and they're just kind of this poor subject to it, whereas if you can say 'well, look, we'll try and work on that, I'll negotiate with you'. If they're saying 'well I'm not attending my appointments, because they're at nine o'clock on a Monday morning forget it', I'll be 'okay, well listen, if you're telling me that that's the issue I'll put it in for three o'clock on a Tuesday'. So you're facilitating them and letting them assert themselves in this relationship and try and even out that power balance that they perceive it to be. So it's negotiating things with them all the time and giving them a say, because then it's easier to go back, if they missed it on Tuesday at three I'm like 'well you told me you could make this'. So now it's back [to them]. It's having them take responsibility all the time and that's what a lot of my conversations [are] with them.
>
> [YPP practitioner group, Site 1]

Responding informally to incidents of non-compliance also involved reminding young people of the consequences of their actions and what the next steps would be:

> We have to be discussing custody and spell out 'look, this is what will happen if you don't', do you know? And to be very open, if they're not doing it I'd say it. I'm very straightforward; I would say you're not doing it and so that

> it's out in the open like, I'd share that with parents, that it will result in breach to the courts because do you know you write your own report? I'd say that to them, that the report reflects what you're doing and your behaviour. So I would say 'look now you're not doing what you're supposed to' and I'd name it.
>
> [YPP practitioner group, Site 2]

> I would generally, for children, give them a couple of verbal warnings saying 'look, this is not acceptable, if you're going to come to the office like this we can't work with you'.
>
> [PBNI practitioner group, Site 2]

Despite efforts to apply the concept of consequences to scenarios that were applicable and relevant to the young person's life, it remained an ambiguous notion for some. According to practitioners, immediate and tangible consequences, such as losing one's driving licence, were far easier to assimilate than long-term consequences such as being returned to court or the prospect of custody. These were perceived by practitioners to be considerably more difficult for some young people to fully comprehend and process. Similar findings were reported in a study of young people on bail from the Children Court in Ireland where young people attached limited importance to the consequences of breaking their bail conditions and many reported that the realization of the seriousness of their situation arose only after they had been detained in custody for failing to comply (Seymour and Butler 2008). Finally, some practitioners explained that young people in residential care often encountered difficulties in comprehending the mandatory nature of supervision requirements and the consequences of non-compliance in the criminal justice system due to their experiences in the care system where they could exercise more autonomy:

> When they've been through the care system as well, because you know the way, like I've worked in residential care and sometimes they'll say 'I'm not going to that doctors appointment' or 'I'm not going to that' and there's no consequence, so when they're on probation then they don't realize that there is a consequence when you don't come to probation, it's a different system that you're in now, it's not the care system, you can't just go 'I'm not going'.
>
> [PBNI practitioner group, Site 2]

There was uniform recognition that clear messages about the unacceptability of certain non-compliant behaviour had to be consistently conveyed to young people. In practice, this meant that while incidents of non-compliance did not necessarily result in a formal sanction, it did require that they were discussed with the young person. McIvor (2002) suggests that a consistent approach to enforcement may enhance offenders' perceptions of procedural fairness and positively influence their commitment towards compliance. Conversely, inconsistent responses are likely to reduce their sense of legitimacy in the process and ultimately their level of compliance. Practitioners described the importance of them following through with young people on what they had communicated about expectations and consequences surrounding non-compliance. Being consistent in responses to non-compliance was also seen as an important factor in maintaining integrity and stability within the professional working relationship:

> I think the honesty too around if you miss an appointment or you don't attend and it's not colluding with the young person saying 'ah sure that was only one appointment missed, we'll let that go'. It's from the very start being honest and having very clear boundaries around it. If you let young people away with missing a couple of appointments and then the next time you start non-compliance proceedings, the relationship sort of goes down. There's no point in telling them one thing and acting another way, because you wouldn't want them to do that, so it's like [us] behaving that way as well.
>
> [YJA practitioner group, Site 2]

A number of practitioners also commented that responding in a consistent manner to incidents of non-compliance represents an important dimension of coaching young people as part of their transition towards adulthood and efforts towards getting and holding down employment: 'you have to be accountable, you have to be responsible, you have to be where you say you're going to be when you say you're going to be there if you want to hold down a job or training or anything like that' (YJA practitioner group, Site 1).

Barriers to compliance: addressing problems and crises

Eadie and Canton (2002: 22) suggest that any efforts to address offending behaviour must take into consideration the reality of young people's 'lived experiences' and arguably the same principle applies when addressing personal problems that directly or indirectly threaten attendance and participation at supervision appointments. Sometimes, discordance between supervisors' assessment of offenders' problems and offenders' own perceptions of their problems required practitioners to connect with young people through a series of dialogues and active cajoling in bringing together an agreed plan for change. Reaching treatment agreements between practitioners and clients that include 'the collaborative identification of problems, goals and possible solutions' (Raynor, Ugwudike and Vanstone 2010: 117) is an integral part of effective practice and central to successful completion (Eadie and Canton 2002; Trotter 1996). Referring a client to an anger management programme when he or she does not consider anger to be a problem is likely to have considerably less impact than in situations when it is at least considered that it may be a problem. The business of making referrals to appropriate agencies – a core factor in problem solving approaches (Dowden and Andrews 2004) – frequently required practitioners to advocate and negotiate with external agencies on the young people's behalf. Accessing and sustaining service provision for high risk young offenders is challenging and placement breakdown frequently occurs, particularly where services are not orientated specifically towards working with challenging young people (Seymour 2003). A considerable part of practitioners' work therefore involved ongoing liaison, advocacy and sometimes mediation. Getting the appropriate supports that were responsive to young people's needs served both to address problems and in turn, supported compliance. The example outlined below of the type of support provided to a young person living in supportive accommodation best illustrates the point:

> The main thing with compliance is the support because like I've a young person who's now living in supportive accommodation, he's been allocated what's called an Intensive Support Social Worker who sees him two or three times a week, it's her now that facilitates us with attendance at probation appointments, so it's not just ANY kind of support, it's not just someone in the family, it's someone who's willing to take the time and effort to get him there.
>
> [PBNI practitioner group, Site 2]

In contrast to working with offenders on the routine problems of their lives, crisis situations necessitated an immediate and reactive strategy to minimize the risks for young people's well-being, safety and reoffending. According to practitioners, crisis situations typically centre on some form of breakdown in the family relationship or to a lesser degree an external threat of serious harm or violence against them. The prospects for compliance where young people are unable or unwilling to remain at home following a breakdown in family relationships are poor (Seymour and Butler 2008). Young people who end up in temporary hostel accommodation or on the streets become quickly immersed and enmeshed in a street lifestyle of alcohol and drug use, violence, victimization and further criminality (Mayock and O'Sullivan 2007; Mayock and Vekić 2006; Seymour and Costello 2005). Minimizing the risks for young people in these circumstances was described by practitioners as requiring intensive work with young people and their families, liaising with their line managers, liaising with external agencies to access services and co-ordinating responses with the key stakeholders involved.

It was mostly practitioners based in the main cities of Belfast and Dublin who explained that situations where threats of violence were perpetrated against young people created considerable difficulties in maintaining them under supervision. The sources of the threats varied within and between the two cities but appeared to emanate from vigilante or dissident paramilitary groups in a small number of localities in Belfast and as a result of family feuds or more commonly drug-related violence in some areas of Dublin. In the latter scenario, this involved threats arising from unpaid drug debts where young people had used, misplaced or had drugs confiscated from them by the police. The challenges of working with young people under some form of threat were compounded by their limited awareness or unwillingness to grasp the seriousness of their situation. Cases were described where young people returned to areas knowing that threats could be executed against them or engaged in petty, but potentially inflammatory actions, against perceived perpetrators. Practitioners described that young people's level of appreciation of their circumstances varied considerably from case to case; overall however, they demonstrated less insight than their adult counterparts:

> These kids, they're definitely being used and manipulated and they again are completely unaware and they think that they're in. But also this protection afforded by their association with these more senior members, so it's almost a means to an end, 'I'm not going to be targeted or I'm not going to be hurt because I've got all these people behind me'. They don't realize. They'd be like 'well he put in my windows, so I'm going to burn down his house'. And I'm saying 'well then what's going to happen?' I'm saying 'you could kill somebody'. 'So what? And if he kills me, I'm going to ...'. I'm saying 'if he kills you, you're dead'. But they have this idea that they'll bounce back and their attitude is 'and so what if he puts in my windows?' I'm like 'well your mam will be pissed off'. I've had people like settin' fire to people's houses and families left on the streets, there's notoriety in saying 'well I got a hiding' or 'I got stabbed' and 'I was there'.
>
> [YPP practitioner group, Site 1]

Threats against young people sometimes extended to the family home and practitioners recalled incidences where windows were smashed, cars were vandalized and threats were issued to other family members. The destabilizing impact of such threats served to further weaken the family unit and solutions were frequently out of the control of young people, their families and supervisors. There was often ambiguity surrounding the nature and the length of the threat, therefore contributing to further uncertainty for young people and their families. With regard to drug debts, the threat remained until the debt was repaid and it was not uncommon for practitioners who encountered these situations to explain that already poor families were forced to borrow money or to use social welfare payments to repay their child's debts. The complexity of problems emanating from threats of violence necessitates a far broader inter-agency and community-based strategy than that which can be facilitated within the confines of the supervisory relationship (Griffin and Kelleher 2010). In that context, it appeared from what practitioners said that their primary focus was on minimizing risk to the young person's and other clients' safety by facilitating appointments in alternative locations or arranging transportation to, and from, scheduled sessions. However, sometimes the circumstances that arose from ongoing threats compromised the young person's ability to such an extent that it was unsustainable to continue with supervision.

Building capacity for the future

The motivation to remain engaged in supervision is enhanced where young people have some normative attachment or investment in the process and perceive a benefit from their continued involvement. Graham and Bowling

(1995: 72) argue that in seeking to move young people away from anti-social influences and towards desistance they must 'be offered escape routes in the form of legitimate opportunities for growth and self-development'. McNeill (2006: 134) reflects a similar perspective and suggests that in facilitating desistance, 'practitioners may need to assist young people in navigating transitions; both by acting as a conduit to "social capital" and by seeking to build it'. Perhaps expectedly, given the professional background of practitioners in social work, youth and community work and education, a fundamental belief in the capacity of young people to change emerged strongly from accounts of their work. Through the communicative processes of supervision, some practitioners described how they sought to convey a sense of possibility and hopefulness to young people as well as attempting to develop their aspirations for the future. Others explicitly stated that their practice was aligned to a strengths-based model that worked towards giving young people opportunities to see themselves as capable of changing the direction of their lives for the future (Burnett and Maruna 2006; McNeill 2009).

Building capacity with young people was an incremental process (such as working on a curriculum vitae or completing an employment application with them) that sought to build up their aspirations for the future. Practitioners explained how they drew on their professional skills to identify situations that may result in future opportunities for young people. For instance, one described that she retained a copy of her young client's exam timetable and texted to remind him to attend. The real significance of such action is most clearly demonstrated in a later account in this book from a young woman who describes how her supervisor's support during exams at a time in her life that was characterized by chaos and persistent offending has now enabled her to continue her studies as she becomes a mother and moves towards desistance (see Chapter 8).

Adopting an advocacy role and negotiating access to accredited vocational, educational or personal development programmes targeted to the interests of young people was identified by practitioners as the main approach used in bringing about practical application to ideas about the possibility of achievement and aspirations for the future:

> There's this barrier in their own head, I can't do that, because they've been told from parents to teachers beforehand you're nobody and you're never going to amount to anything. And even just doing the process and there's no pressure of exams … they're told you're going to get a certificate if you complete, and they actually get it and then they learn that's how you get these things … so it gives them that sense I can actually be something else other than what people are telling me I'm going to be.
>
> [PBNI practitioner group, Site 1]

Practitioners described that participation in and completion of programmes sometimes had a knock-on effect for young people and motivated them to continue to develop their knowledge and skills. Moreover, it provided an added dimension to the value and legitimacy attached to their experiences of supervision (see Chapter 8).

The role of parents and family in encouraging compliance

Much of the literature on parents and families in the criminal justice system is strongly orientated towards their deficiencies and shortcomings (see Chapter 4). The concept of the irresponsible parent has been fervently propagated in some policy contexts to the extent that it has obfuscated the nuances that underpin parenting difficulties (Arthur 2005). This disjuncture between rhetoric and reality has resulted in considerably less attention being focused in criminal justice contexts on providing support systems to build strengths within family networks. The desistance literature provides the strongest foundation in attesting to the importance of fostering meaningful social bonds as a strategy for supporting compliance. The theoretical and empirical literature on compliance with community penalties (Bottoms 2001) further substantiates the need to build strengths within young people's social networks on the basis that those with the strongest normative attachments to society are more likely to comply.

A commitment to involving families, through home visits and family meetings, was reflected by all practitioners across the three organizations. Practitioners described parental support for the supervision process as being pivotal to the success of sustaining momentum and young people's compliance. The cases with the most successful outcomes were those where a responsible adult was seen to be 'pushing behind' the child throughout the supervision process. According to practitioners, parents' commitment to the process was mirrored in their child's behaviour in many cases. The most practical support provided was where parents facilitated compliance by reminding their son or daughter about appointments. This was most effective where parents also had the ability to impose boundaries and to exert some persuasive or authoritative influence on their child. Requirements such as ensuring that the young person was woken in time to attend appointments, that their safety was maintained within the home, and that they were adequately cared for, were further indicators of parental support. These contrasted with common situations described by practitioners where through chaos, crisis or dysfunction, the level of care provided by parents was minimal and young people often took care of themselves. Parental support also involved a willingness to communicate openly with the supervisor about the young person's behaviour between appointments and to assist in identifying the underlying factors where non-compliance occurred. It was in this area that expectations sometimes became enmeshed between parents' loyalty to their child and the professional relationship with the supervisor. Practitioners explained that some parents concealed negative information in an effort to protect their child which later emerged either through police reports in the case of offending or other community sources:

> Sometimes what's happening is that mothers in a protective way collude with the young people and conceal information. Say for example they were out

> late and they were drinking at the weekend the mum might say, 'don't be saying anything, sure it'll be alright, we'll ignore it'.
>
> [PBNI practitioner group, Site 2]

From the practitioners' perspective, when parents condoned behaviour, it gave mixed messages about the acceptability of their actions and also compromised the practitioner's legitimacy in the eyes of the young person. These types of incidents were more challenging when parents not only overlooked non-compliant behaviour but attempted to take responsibility for it themselves. Minimizing young people's role in the process was perceived by practitioners to diminish their efforts to hold young people accountable for their actions:

> I had an incident yesterday where an 18 year old didn't turn up for his appointment and his mother was phoning me to apologize because she hadn't got him out of bed, so the parent can sometimes take on the onus. It's my fault if he doesn't get in, if he doesn't go where he has to go, you know and it's hard to challenge that then with the young person if it's been set up that way that well you haven't been compliant, but my mum didn't get me up and the mum is at home taking responsibility or the dad is at home taking responsibility for the young person not doing what they have to do. But that collusiveness or collusion has been why they're in trouble in the first place, somebody has made excuses for their behaviour and let them away with it and I think that's why this situation arises, we all, most of us encounter it.
>
> [YJA practitioner group, Site 1]

Frequently parenting alone, with limited or no supports, in circumstances of poverty and isolation, with histories of chronic personal and social problems, sometimes fearful of aggressive or violent behaviour from their teenage son or daughter, and imminently fearful of the next caller to the home, many of the parents were described by practitioners as being disempowered and 'the forgotten person' in the criminal justice process. In spite of the difficulties, their potential value in supporting the young person through supervision was recognized and engaging with parents was perceived to be an important aspect of practitioners' work. Not all parents were willing or able to involve themselves in the process, due either to the extent of their own difficulties or a reluctance to engage. Others, particularly those with criminal histories or for personal, social or cultural reasons, were more openly hostile and resistant to any form of intervention. For parents who were open to receiving support, the challenge was to engage with them in a way that supported and strengthened their parental role in the longer-term. Building working relationships with parents and working towards strengthening the family dynamic was the primary purpose of family work. As the following example indicates, the value of intervention with parents often unfolds over time and where successful is seen to promote compliance through strengthening parents' role within the family:

> Practitioner 1: When the parent comes to youth conference generally, it's the first time maybe they have really engaged with this agency and I have

had a parent recently, she was extremely aggressive to the point where I was reluctant to go out and see her initially and we have worked with her now for about seven months and it emerged in the most recent conference that her ability as a parent, she always felt that it was being questioned. There's been a kind of transformation with her, we reinforce the positives and work really hard with her in saying 'you are a bloody good mum', you know 'stop doubting yourself'. And she actually challenged her child in the conference about his behaviour, something she has been afraid to do for a very long time and she walked out of there bouncing, she felt so fulfilled. Now I know it's not an evangelical experience for her, but at the end of the day we're getting there . . . small steps. You do walk alongside the parents and I think that's where non-compliance comes in, get them on board, help them strengthen themselves as a parent so they can say 'you are going to this appointment', simple things, 'you are getting out of bed, here's on the fridge the things you have to do this week, you will do them' and not to be afraid of that.

Participant 2: And sometimes if there's not a partner, it's more difficult if you're a mum on your own so that's where it's almost like we become a partner in some ways, ok I'm going to say to him tonight about getting his backside in to wherever it is tomorrow, you say it to him too so they're not on their own. It's a very lonely world when you're a mum who lives down some of the streets that we work in and they've got no other support and their whole history is I'm not really that good a mother, do you know?

Participant 3: We are not going to change where young people live, we are not going to change the parenting roles, but what I hope we can do is instil with the parents the support to help them to continue on the road, long after we have left.

[YJA practitioner group, Site 1]

The role of extended family

In Northern Ireland and the Republic of Ireland, changes in family structure and housing development in recent decades have contributed to a decline in the level of extended family networks and support available to families within their neighbourhoods (Corcoran, Gray and Peillon 2007; Fawcett 2000). While the level of involvement of extended family may have diminished, some practitioners reported that it continued to play an important role in supporting compliance in some cases. The main medium through which extended family involvement was facilitated was through family group conferences or family meetings. Situations where extended family members provided practical or social support that alleviated the strain between young people and their parent(s) were perceived to be very effective in supporting compliance. For instance, one practitioner described how tension levels in the home were considerably reduced as a result of a client's uncle agreeing to take him to indoor football a few evenings in the week and another uncle who committed to doing some work with the young person at weekends. This type of support was also seen to have wider implications in providing pro-social activities and positive role modelling for the young person.

The use of family involvement in establishing reparation placements was identified as another beneficial strategy to encourage compliance. These placements, often in a local youth, recreational or sports club, were seen to be more effective as a result of 'getting someone in the community to take them [young person] under their wing' [YJA practitioner group, Site 2]. In these cases, family and community ownership and commitment to the process was deemed to be an influential factor in encouraging compliance and successful completion. Extended family was seen as a useful resource in young people's lives in times of crisis where practical assistance such as the provision of temporary accommodation reduced the risk of homelessness. The nature and diversity of family circumstances meant that the capacity for families to provide support varied substantially between families and communities.[2] Despite the difficulties for some families, there nevertheless appears to be considerable merit in identifying extended members of the family network to promote compliance in appropriate circumstances. Indeed, McNeill (2006: 134) reminds us that promoting desistance and building and sustaining momentum with young people involves developing the young person's strengths 'at both individual and a social network level'.

Other strategies

According to practitioners, minimal use was made of constraint-based strategies for supervising young people. Where strategies such as electronic tagging – available for young people in Northern Ireland only – were employed, their use was generally organized around a specific period of time when young people were deemed to be at risk of engaging in offending behaviour. Certain incentives, such as reducing levels of contact with offenders who are deemed to be progressing well, are formally and informally integrated as standard practice when supervising offenders in the community in many jurisdictions, including Northern Ireland and the Republic of Ireland. Beyond this practice, incentive-based strategies were not frequently used by practitioners to promote compliance in this study. Some key informants suggested that where incentives were employed, it was important to conceptualize them as mechanisms to reinforce positive behaviour rather than as a reward *per se*. Conscious of the need to retain public credibility, explicit reference to incentives or rewards was perceived to fit uncomfortably within a discourse that sought to reduce offending and to hold young people accountable for their actions. Similarly, where leisure or creative activities were used with young people, they were generally conceived by practitioners as mechanisms through which the work of supervision was facilitated rather than as incentives or rewards for compliance.

Promoting and responding to non-compliance: formal approaches and enforcement

As outlined in Chapter 2, the use of breach proceedings in response to non-compliance on statutory community disposals is more common in some jurisdictions than in others and is a contributory factor in increasing the youth detention population as a result (Bateman 2011). It was not possible to establish the extent to which breach action was routinely initiated across the three organizations due to the absence of available statistics; however, practitioners' accounts provided some insight into its location within practice. For young people under the supervision of the PBNI, breach action is initiated as a consequence of failing to attend supervision appointments without an acceptable reason on more than two occasions within a six-month period. Formal responses to non-compliance for those supervised by the YJA are provided for under the youth conference service guidelines and other agency guidelines on the supervision of community disposals. Similar to provisions for addressing non-compliance with conferencing plans in other jurisdictions (O'Dwyer 2005), the guidelines outline that at the stage of a third incident of non-compliance with the youth conference action plan, the youth conference co-ordinator should arrange a family group conference. Attendees of the original youth conference and those involved in the delivery of the youth conference plan are included in the conference. The purpose of the conference is to remind young people about their commitments in their original action plan and the consequences of not complying, to consider the obstacles for compliance, to identify supports to overcome them and to agree a plan for successful completion. If non-compliance persists the case is referred to the co-ordinator for a decision regarding the initiation of breach non-compliance proceedings.

According to YJA practitioners, breach action is not commonly employed as a response to non-compliance on youth conference or other community-based disposals supervised by the agency. Previous research on the agency's practice reported that revoking youth conference orders was a measure of last resort that followed extensive efforts to encourage compliance (Campbell *et al.* 2005; O'Mahony and Campbell 2006). Among these efforts was the option for practitioners to temporarily suspend certain aspects of the disposal in 'circumstances beyond the young person's control – such as family conflict or homelessness' (Campbell *et al.* 2005: 116). One practitioner in this study described the rationale underpinning the use of this option on supervision:

> If a young person, for a variety of reasons is not able or ready or is de-motivated we would record it, that we are nearly almost suspending part of the order at that particular point in time. And we would do a lot of work on building the relationship again, hopefully to recommence work with the young person, to then continue with their order, rather than I suppose threatening them with court or implying if they don't do this next week then that means court.
>
> [YJA practitioner group, Site 1]

Overall, breach proceedings initiated by the YJA are reserved for those cases where all other responses to non-compliance have failed or where young people's actions breach the commitments given to victims:

> So, for example, if a young person has breached a restricted area because of the needs of the victim, that they want to feel safe so the young person has to

> stay away, I would go straight to non-compliance proceedings and therefore straight to court.
>
> [YJA practitioner group, Site 1]

> I think there is a point where some young people will say very clearly, you know 'I'm not doing' and it doesn't matter what you say the response is 'I'm not doing'. In that instance you've gone through the stages of getting parents to try and influence, you try to influence yourself and you do all that bit, but there comes a point where you say that's not going to happen.
>
> [YJA practitioner group, Site 2]

Unlike the case for adults under probation supervision in the Republic of Ireland, YPP does not operate within a framework of standard practice guidelines. As outlined in Chapter 5, practice is strongly embedded in the ethos and principles of the Children Act 2001, which promotes the use of community-based disposals in response to young people's offending behaviour and reserves detention as a measure of last resort. According to practitioners, breach action is rarely employed as a strategy and may only be initiated following discussion with the senior probation officer on their team. As explained in the following account, YPP practitioners operate within a context where there is a strong expectation from the courts that young offender cases should be managed in the community, save in exceptional circumstances:

> The courts want us to stick with the young people that are referred to us for as long as possible. The end point is when they end up in detention and I don't think the courts want that to happen if that can be avoided, but they also expect us to use our judgement as to when we can no longer stand over some of the behaviours that young people are involved in. And while we haven't set it down as a policy, I think in practice it's around where they are a danger to themselves or are posing a danger to others that we would pull the plug and bring the matter back to court. The reality is we don't work in a vacuum, we are representatives of the state and employees of the Minister, so we do have a context of what we can accept in terms of risk. We have a public protection responsibility as an organization, and while you balance the amount of leeway you can give a young person, you know there are times when you have to make a judgement call that it's come to a point where it's not healthy and you have to do something about it.
>
> [YPP Key Informant]

Breach proceedings are most commonly initiated by way of a summons in both jurisdictions whereby an application is made by the supervisor to the court ordering the young person to appear within a specified time period, usually four weeks. When issued, the summons is served in person by the police. The process was described as slow and elongated in both jurisdictions and it was not uncommon for lengthy time periods to elapse before breach cases were finalized.

To successfully serve the summons, prompt police action and the availability of the individual to take possession of the documentation are required. As a result, delays occurred where higher policing priorities superseded the task of serving summons and where young people or their families did not cooperate with the process:

> When the summons server goes out, the young person will probably know, or they'll recognize the summons server. The parent might collude in saying he's not in; he might be upstairs, he might be looking through the curtains, or they might not open the door at all. So they'll attempt to serve it and then the summons is returned and you're into that whole rigmarole.
>
> [PBNI Key Informant]

In exceptional cases where high risk young offenders failed to attend and their whereabouts was unknown or their actions were seen to present a danger to themselves or to the public, practitioners in Northern Ireland explained that breach proceedings could be initiated by warrant where appropriate. Recourse to warrants was described as a rare occurrence, but was nevertheless considered to be a more responsive approach where serious concerns existed about risk and safety.

Breach proceedings and compliance

Echoing the findings of previous research on compliance and enforcement (Ditton and Ford 1994; Hearnden and Millie 2004), the use of breach proceedings was identified by practitioners as a mechanism to encourage compliance, rather than as an end in itself in most cases. The time period between issuing a summons for breach proceedings and the corresponding court hearing was viewed as an opportunity 'to renegotiate the contract of engagement' and 'to win young people back onside'; to this end, appointments continued to be offered to young people during this period. Being returned to court was described as 'a wake up call' for some young people and as one practitioner explained, it reminded young people of the consequences of being subject to a statutory court disposal:

> I think that it can serve as a reminder to the young person that this is a court order at the end of the day. This is important and you know I'm not going to be let away with not completing it just because I don't want to.
>
> [YJA Key Informant]

However, as outlined at the beginning of this chapter, returning to court and the threat of custody for non-compliance was not perceived by practitioners to have any substantive deterrent impact on most of their clients who were not cooperating. The challenge therefore was to present breach proceedings not as a threat but as an opportunity for young people to re-engage in the supervision process in advance of the court hearing. Practitioners explained that their communication with young people who were subject to breach proceedings had to be framed in a positive way that would encourage them to comply with the order:

> It's how it's pitched to them, I always put it to them as a period of opportunity. I mean if they came into me and I said 'ah well sure that's it now you've breached, what do want me to do about it?', if I said that to them they'd say 'ah sure if that's it so, I'm away', you know? But equally if you sell it to them as an opportunity they'll respond to it that way. What I do then in the interim is I say 'look, this is what you've done, this is what's happened, now you still have an opportunity to turn this around because I'm going to offer you weekly appointments and you now have the chance to come in and do that work with me and what you have here is an opportunity for me to walk into court in four weeks' time and say to the Magistrate he has not attended however he has attended consecutively since the time of the breach and he hasn't missed an appointment and he's engaged in the following activities'.
>
> [PBNI practitioner group, Site 2]

This strategy was similar to that outlined by Hedderman (2003: 191), who suggested that persuading offenders 'to appreciate "what's in it for them"' is an important dimension of promoting compliance. Where young people re-engaged in the supervision process prior to the breach hearing, practitioners explained that they frequently sought for the breach action to be withdrawn or for the imposition of a short adjournment period to monitor their progress.

Although it was perceived that some judges and magistrates adopted more hard-line approaches, overall practitioners were strongly of the opinion that judges and magistrates in the Children Court (Republic of Ireland) and the Youth Court (Northern Ireland) were keen to retain non-compliant young people under supervision in the community, even in cases where practitioners believed that they had exhausted all options to stimulate compliance and cooperation in young people:

> The magistrates very much take on that you're taking a case back for breach, but they are almost looking down at you going 'what are you going to do here?' You know? They don't want to revoke the orders because they don't want the young person not having the community supervision, so they are looking to you to know 'what's your solution to this?' We're just sitting there thinking 'custody' because it's just gone on so long but still here's another chance. But the judges always do want to try and give the kid a chance, and give us a chance because they know we're genuine in what we're trying to do.
>
> [PBNI practitioner group, Site 1]

According to practitioners breach proceedings were an effective strategy for some young people whose behaviour changed as a result of the process. For others who remained unable or unwilling to change, breach proceedings acted as no more than a marker on their pathway through the criminal justice system. Where young people in these cases were ordered by the courts to continue under supervision in the community, practitioners thought that it sent out conflicting messages about the significance of consequences. It was also seen to compromise the credibility of the respective organizations in the eyes of families and communities:

> They [young people] just think 'what's the point, if I don't comply again the judge will just give me another load of probation'. So they don't recognize any consequence and the thing is we always use it as a threat, so when we've exhausted that there's absolutely nothing.
>
> [YPP practitioner group, Site 1]

> It can be a difficulty for parents and for communities if they see a young person coming back out, no consequences as such; at least that's what the young person is saying: 'well sure I've gone to court, I've got away with it and nothing happened. I can just do as I like'. And I think that potentially can have a loss of reputation in terms of ourselves within the communities and yet we can only take it as far as we can take it, you know?
>
> [YJA Key Informant]

Two factors were identified as potential influences on the overall approach adopted by members of the judiciary in seeking to retain non-compliant young people in the community where possible. The first was attributed to legal reasons insofar as judges and magistrates in both jurisdictions operated within the parameters of legislation that sought to limit the use of custodial orders for young people to offences of a serious nature or as a measure of last resort (see Chapter 5). Secondly, a number of key informants and practitioners explained that opportunities to engage in formal and informal discussion with members of the judiciary at local level had facilitated greater shared understanding between both parties surrounding the challenges of responding to non-compliant young people in the criminal justice system.

Conclusion

Young people commenced supervision with limited insight into the expectations placed upon them, and often with low stakes in compliance by virtue of their marginalized status, involvement in offending behaviour, social circumstances and developmental stage. The key task of encouraging offenders to comply therefore involved consistent efforts by practitioners to engage and communicate with young people in a manner and style that ignited motivation and commitment to comply. Building positive working relationships was identified as being centrally important to the process of engaging young people and the basis for successfully promoting compliance. Relationships were not only linked to the effectiveness of approaches such as pro-social modelling, but they were also seen to legitimize the requests for compliance made by practitioners. Data presented in this chapter suggested that an emphasis on promoting compliance at the 'front-end' or early stages of the supervision process paid dividends in sustaining young people's compliance over time. Explaining roles and requirements, communicating expectations and highlighting consequences were standard tasks of the supervisor's role. However, it was in their descriptions of the strategies used to communicate with young people that practitioners most clearly illustrated the dynamic and active processes involved. Through engaging in dialogue, negotiating the parameters of supervision, using role play and pro-social modelling practitioners sought to involve young people in discussions about compliance as well as demonstrating what compliance meant in practice. Furthermore, the emphasis placed on being seen to be fair by practitioners was reflected in the way that ongoing reminders about expectations and consequences were communicated to young people. This is an approach that resonates strongly with procedural justice research, which highlights that offender perceptions of fair treatment in the criminal justice process may contribute to a greater sense of legitimacy in the system and reduce the likelihood of future non-compliance (Tyler 2006a; McIvor 2009).

Supervision entailed a holistic approach that required practitioners to work with young people on problem solving and removing obstacles to compliance. It also necessitated the use of professional skills to negotiate the crises of young people's lives from violence to family breakdown and homelessness. Addressing practical and personal problems associated with compliance is an important factor for a number of reasons. As well as assisting offenders to resolve problems, Ugwudike (2011) suggests that supervisors' acknowledgement of the challenges faced by offenders may enhance their perceptions of fair treatment and, in turn, positively influence compliance. Promoting compliance also involved building capacity by linking young people into training or vocational services that would offer opportunities to have their achievements acknowledged and to provide accreditation. Recognition of the potential of some parents to support their child's compliance with supervision was a strongly valued dimension outlined by practitioners. Where extended family had the capacity to provide support, it was seen as an invaluable resource to alleviate stress and tension in the family home and in turn to encourage compliance. Practitioners viewed their role as working alongside parents to encourage young people's sustained involvement in supervision. Organizational differences existed in the threshold and nature of the behaviour that triggered breach proceedings, but what was common across the organizations was a view that breach proceedings were sometimes useful to encourage compliance. To this end, breach action was perceived as an opportunity for young offenders to re-engage in the supervision process. Taking breach proceedings was often an elongated process slowed by the length of time for summonses to be served by the police and exacerbated when offenders were unavailable or intentionally absent to take delivery of the documentation. With some exceptions in both jurisdictions, practitioners were of the view that judges and magistrates were eager to retain young people in the community and to respond to non-compliance using community-based, rather than custodial disposals.

Overall, the perspectives presented in this chapter suggest that when working with young offenders where threats of being returned to court or detained in custody often carry limited deterrent value, the possibilities for change and compliance are firmly located within a relational approach that seeks to engage with young offenders, embrace the principles of 'front-end compliance', address problems and barriers to compliance and build capacity and strength within young people and their families.

8 Young people's perspectives on the supervision process

The nature of one-to-one supervision sessions between the practitioner and the client is an underexplored area of criminological research (Springer *et al.* 2009; Trotter and Evans 2010). Evaluations of initiatives to manage offenders in the community have focused primarily on the effectiveness of programmatic interventions with less emphasis on knowledge creation about one-to-one supervision and the supervisory relationship. Some noteworthy and informative exceptions exist in the work of Farrall (2002a), Farrall and Calverley (2006), Healy (2010) and Rex (1999); however, for the most part these studies concentrate on adults currently or previously under probation supervision. Although it is documented that young offenders are often the most challenging clients to engage and the most likely to violate technical requirements associated with community-based sentences and sanctions (McCluskey *et al.* 1999; Moore *et al.* 2006), less is known about their experiences of negotiating compliance on supervised community disposals. This chapter seeks to address the gap by exploring the social, emotional and legal dimensions of supervision including the dynamics in the relationship between probation officers and young people that may influence the latter's decision to comply with the conditions of supervision and avoid further reoffending. Bottoms (2001) alerts us to the subjective nature of criminal justice interventions with a reminder that a considerable distance is likely to exist between the anticipated outcome of regulators' intentions when seeking to induce compliance and the manner in which such measures are experienced in practice by regulated parties. In attempting to capture the subjective nature of the supervision experience, young people's perspectives on power are also explored, focusing on their interpretations and efforts to manage compliance within the legal parameters imposed on them. The manner in which compliance changes over time is examined by drawing on young people's retrospective accounts of the supervision process.

Perspectives on the early stages of supervision

Commencing probation supervision was described by young people as a stressful time characterized by uncertainty about what would be expected of them, distrust of their probation officer's motivation and in many cases, resistance, or at least ambivalence, towards changing their criminal behaviour. Having their probation officer visit them at home or being required to attend supervision appointments was perceived as an unnecessary intrusion in their lives and something they sought to avoid. They described meeting with adults unknown to them in unfamiliar contexts, without the presence of their family or friends, as a difficult challenge at the beginning of the supervision process. In their view, the social distance between their lives and those of their probation officers was marked, and many described negative or at best indifferent attitudes towards probation. Sarah, aged 18 years, reflected the views of a number of participants in recalling her initial outlook at the time she was placed on probation supervision when she was 15 years old:

> They're [probation officers] telling you that you are not allowed rob, you're robbin' off someone else, you're not allowed do that, don't be doing that. And you're like 'what's it got to do with you?' … the way I was like I just didn't care … you're just childish. You don't want to be coming into a sophisticated place like this [probation office] and sitting down listening to someone, a big posh person, that's the way you put it, I'm putting it the way I put it a few years ago. You're sitting down with someone you think their life is just they have everything, they have all the money, they're working here just sitting down and they're getting paid for it. That's the way you looked at it back then.
>
> [YP86]

Explaining that they 'hated' attending probation when they first started, it was not uncommon for young people to describe their behaviour as cheeky, scornful and disruptive. Not unlike strategies reported in other probation contexts (Svensson 2010), some explained their approach as being withdrawn and saying little or nothing in response to their probation officer's questions. Young people attributed their attitude at the early stages of supervision to their being anxious and fearful of the process in some cases, while others said it was due to not trusting their probation officer, not wishing to disclose information or because they could not see the purpose of probation. Episodes of non-attendance at appointments in the past had frequently coincided with times when their living arrangements had broken down or in situations where they were heavily enmeshed in criminal behaviour, were associating with (often older) criminal peers, using excessive quantities of alcohol and drugs, and returning to the family home on an intermittent basis only. Avoiding interaction with their probation officer by not attending appointments was a strategy attempted by some young people when they started, but as they recounted, they soon realized that persistent non-attendance would result, and in some cases had resulted, in them being returned to court for non-compliance proceedings.[1]

Young people who reported a history of alcohol and drug misuse problems explained that their addictions had previously overshadowed their attitude towards probation. Negotiating their way through supervision in the midst of heavy substance misuse involved efforts to avoid using or consuming substances prior to appointments with their probation officer in the hope of diverting attention from their behaviour. However, they suggested that their ability to maintain this façade declined as their addictions deepened and gave way to behaviours such as turning up for appointments under the influence of alcohol or drugs, persistent attempts to reschedule appointments and more commonly, not attending at all. During these times, young people described having little concern for the consequences of non-compliance. Gaining access to alcohol or drugs through whatever means necessary took precedence over all else and probation, if given consideration, was a low priority in their lives, as Claire described:

> I'd get up and the first thing you'd think about was the heroin like. You wouldn't be able to move without doin' it. You'd like, you'd be in pain an' all like. I'd smoke it, I'd get dressed an' go back out an' just get more. That would be just me whole day. Just gettin' it, smokin' it, I used to sell it as well like in town. I never really went before [to probation]. If I was in the area I'd go like, I wouldn't go out of me way for anybody. I just didn't listen an' she [probation officer] used to bring me back to court an' all an' get me put back [have her case adjourned to monitor progress].
>
> [YP80]

Changing perceptions of supervision

Change in young people's perceptions of probation supervision occurred over time, supporting Robinson and McNeill's (2010) hypothesis that attitudes towards compliance and compliant behaviour are not fixed or static for offenders on community disposals. While probation officers described having concerns about some young people's motivation to comply with the terms of community supervision in the past, they reported that levels of compliance improved considerably for most of the research participants as they progressed through the supervision process.[2] Kevin – who was described by his probation officer as 'initially very resistant and a repeat offender who wasn't prepared to change' – spoke of the change in his level of engagement at appointments from the time of commencing supervision:

> Before now I'd come in an' walk around this room around in circles like an' she'd [probation officer] ask me to sit down an' I'd say 'no I won't sit down', an' just walk out the door. I just let it in one ear an' out the other you know? But now it doesn't bother me comin' down an' talkin' or whatever. I don't mind like you know? I've been down here nearly every week you know, like for the last six months I'm attendin' all me appointments an' all an' goin' with your man every Monday, the mentor every Monday like you know?
>
> [YP79]

Drawing on Robinson and McNeill's (2010) dynamic model of compliance with community supervision (Figure 3.2), it could be said that many of the young people's accounts demonstrated 'commitment' to comply with the requirements of probation supervision. For them, improved attendance, an openness to participate at supervision appointments and readiness to take advice and direction from their probation officer typified the kinds of changes they outlined. Their descriptions, as captured in Kevin's case above, suggested that they had moved beyond undertaking the minimum effort in order to fulfil the requirements of supervision (formal compliance) to a situation where they more willingly and actively participated (substantive compliance) (Bottoms 2001). Their changed perspectives on compliance brought with it a more positive outlook towards the supervision process.

The nature and extent of change varied between cases, affirming the notion that offenders commence and progress at different levels during the supervision process (Seymour 2003). Probation officers indicated that there was no noteworthy difference in the frequency of attendance between those who continued to offend and those who did not, reflecting similar findings from previous research (Healy 2010) and giving support to the view that formal compliance is unlikely to be the most effective way of measuring genuine compliance with the criminal law. For a small number – all of whom reported recent reoffending – it appeared that problems with substance misuse and continued involvement in offending behaviour blocked pathways to substantive compliance as a desire to conceal their activities sometimes resulted in reluctance to participate openly at appointments. Their level of engagement was more likely to involve a haphazard effort to negotiate and manage involvement in the criminal justice system against the backdrop of ongoing offending. For example, Jason explained his motivation for attending appointments; he saw it as an opportunity to establish if his offending had been brought to the attention of his probation officer:

> What's goin' to happen an' what's gonna get said. Did anythin' get said back to me probation officer? [did] new charges or anythin' get put in. Like, see did the copper [police] send new charges down or anythin' and there's more trouble there waitin', 'cause she'll [probation officer] tell me like.
>
> [YP78]

Being apprehended for further offending and mindful of the inevitability of subsequent court appearances, official scripts of compliance in the form of a good attendance records were seen as important assets by those who continued to offend. Involvement in ongoing offending was also more likely to contribute to the perception that supervision was a mechanism for controlling and monitoring rather than assisting them. Explaining his view of probation supervision, Joseph commented:

> It's kind of like being locked away, but you are not locked away. It's hard like, because you can't really go and do your own thing, you are not free like, you are still under the law like you know what I mean? You can't go away and do what you want like. It's a bit annoyin' [weekly appointments], it wouldn't be too bad if it was once a month kind of thing or once every five

> weeks even to come in and see them. Sometimes it's kind of awkward like bein' asked weird questions, just questions that you don't really feel comfortable answering. He [probation officer] tries to ask me did I get into any more trouble and stuff.
>
> [YP71]

Compliance in these cases might be categorized as a reluctant acceptance, or submission to their probation officer's authority (Robinson and McNeill 2010). This was particularly the case where differences existed between probation officers' and young people's perspectives on barriers to desistance. In these cases, probation officer directives tended to be perceived as burdensome and coercive. The point is highlighted by Henry who described his rationale for attending Alcoholics Anonymous (AA) meetings despite perceiving himself not to have an alcohol problem:

> I just probably just go [to AA] 'cause she [probation officer] wants me to go there. She knows that I drink. She thinks I've a problem, but I don't think I've a problem with drink. I don't want to be off drink because there's nothin' wrong with me like. I'm not addicted or anything, just she makes a big deal out of it like so I said 'right to make them happy I'll go'.
>
> [YP72]

Motivation for change and the supervisory relationship

Young people's changing attitudes to probation supervision were rooted in the changes that occurred in the relationship with their supervising probation officer. With a few exceptions, such as Wild (2011: 65), who outlines lower rates of probation violations and recidivism where juvenile offenders reported 'a positive helping alliance' with their supervisor, there remains a dearth of empirical investigation on the role of supervisory relationships when working with young people (Prior and Mason 2010). Matthews and Hubbard (2007: 113) suggest that supportive relationships with adults can moderate the impact for youth in high risk environments by altering their self-perceptions, including their vocational aspirations, by influencing their perceptions of other relationships in their lives, and through promoting resiliency. Of specific relevance is the literature on adult offender supervision which highlights the importance of positive working relationships in increasing retention rates, reducing reoffending and promoting desistance (Berman 2005; Burnett and McNeill 2005). Not unlike the experiences of many offenders in the criminal justice system (Eadie 2000), social exclusion, alienation and stigmatization characterized the young people's lives leading them to be suspicious and wary of authority figures. As a result, building relationships with their probation officer commenced from a low baseline. What was most striking about the young people's accounts was the recognition they gave to their probation officer's continued efforts to work with them despite their earlier resistance and negative attitudes towards supervision. Their perspectives aligned with those of practitioners (see Chapter 7) in describing change in the relationship as a gradual process that frequently involved considerable perseverance on the part of their supervisor:

> My probation officer was always there for me, that's what it was. I never really had anyone there for me, and it's like I can look up to [her]. She practically put me on the narrow [straight and narrow] road like. I don't know how she put up with me like. I just laughed at her really at the start. And then she just stuck with me like. She just stuck with me.
>
> [YP86]

Remaining a consistent presence in their lives, supervisors sent the message to young people that they were genuinely interested in what happened to them, supporting the existing literature about the importance of practitioners remaining steadfast in their efforts to engage with the most challenging young people (Chablani and Spinney 2011; de Winter and Noom 2003; Milbourne 2009).

Advocacy and encouragement

Balancing the provision of advice and assistance with enabling adolescents to exercise independence is a challenge when working with young people (de Winter and Noom 2003). However, the aspect of probation supervision that was central to the entire supervision process, according to participants, was their probation officer's ability to advocate and access services on their behalf. Looking to the wider context of probation practice in the Republic of Ireland, Healy's (2010) analysis of the case files of 73 adult male probationers, reports that where supervision plans were in place, two-thirds of them referred to addressing addiction issues and one-third aimed to provide assistance with education and employment. Furthermore, for over half of the participants in Healy's study, assistance was provided through referrals to external agencies (n=39) or by direct practical help from the probation officer (n=40). Taken together, the evidence suggests that probation practice for young people and adults in the Irish context is heavily focused on addressing offenders' problems through practical and direct action. Farrall (2002a) suggests that probation officer efforts to address barriers to desistance with offenders result in greater benefits when an action-based approach is adopted. In demonstrating the point, he explains that obstacles were overcome more frequently when officers reported that they had provided probationers with 'some' or 'a lot' of assistance with employment and family related issues.

Readiness to change is a core element in successful behavioural change (Farrall 2002a; Stephenson, Giller and Brown, 2007); however, individual commitment and agency is insufficient of itself without the availability of structural or service opportunities to support change. This is especially true in the case of young people seeking to address problematic alcohol and drug use. Although attributing the decision to attend as their own, those who had completed alcohol and drug treatment explained that their probation officer had played an important role in accessing the relevant services for them. Peter's account encapsulated the essence of what other participants recalled about the type of assistance received:

> She [probation officer] set up a lot of the things for the [alcohol] treatment and she helped me by getting me in there. Like the [alcohol treatment service] now they were dragging their feet with getting me in there d'you know they were and she'd [probation officer] ring them and kind of give out to them really like and kind of speed them up a bit. And she always gave me things to do like, she could say 'if you want to while you are waiting, you can come up to our office and there's somebody there that will set up CVs and stuff'. So she was always kind of trying to keep me busy anyway like, so I found that good. I used to hate her calling down, because d'you know I thought she was wasting my time like. But she ended up setting up a lot of things and I'm grateful for that like.
>
> [YP73]

The dominant influence of the risk factor paradigm in some youth justice contexts has often overshadowed perspectives that seek to build and develop existing capacities within young people's lives (Case and Haines 2009; Murray 2010). In addition to accessing new avenues of opportunity, the usefulness of probation officers' assistance was acknowledged in areas where young people had previously sought to achieve and had not succeeded. James, a young man who lived in a small rural town with limited access to public transport, explained that he had made a number of attempts to pass the written aspect of his driving test, an exam required under Irish law to acquire a full driving licence. For him, the most useful practical aspect of supervision was the assistance arranged through his probation officer that culminated in him successfully passing the test. In addition to the accomplishment itself, it is not unreasonable to suggest that it gave the young person an additional skill for the employment market, offset the potential of future criminal convictions for driving without a licence and furthermore, made the possibilities for alternative and broader social participation away from criminality a closer reality for him. James' account draws attention to the relevance of what Griffin and Kelleher (2010: 38) describe as 'participatory probation supervision' whereby officers link 'with the expertise of probationers, who can define both the difficulties they face and the solutions most likely to be effective for them'.

Forming a new identity away from offending behaviour is central to developing and sustaining a non-offending lifestyle and gaining access to meaningful training and education opportunities is therefore an important element for young people in transition to adulthood (Mulvey *et al.* 2004). Such opportunities offer the potential for increased support, structure and direction as well as accreditation and skills (Graham and Bowling 1995; Milbourne 2009). Young people said that involvement in an educational or training programme during the supervision period was actively encouraged by their probation officers. While initially reluctant to attend, or primarily motivated by a perception that participation would 'look good' in the context of future court appearances, many explained how their attitude had changed over time as they came to see the benefit of being involved in education and training programmes. Developing a daily routine, the normality of regular attendance and receiving accreditation provided a sense of achievement and a stimulus to consider possibilities for the future away from a criminal existence, as William described:

> I didn't want to do it at first, I thought 'ah sure it's goin' to be like school'. But it's not an' it's after gettin' me into a routine an' wantin' to do somethin' now, after it, do ye know what I mean? So hopefully I'll continue doin' somethin' after probation. I KNOW I will like, do ye know what I mean? It feels like a job at the end of the day. The difference now is they [probation] give ye options. They'll say well look ye could do this or ye could do that, after this place, do ye know what I mean? … they don't just go 'ah he has six months' probation', get that over with and move on to the next person, it's not like that, it's like what do you want to do next after this, do ye know what I mean? They help you think of the future, they put stuff in front of ye like.
>
> [YP89]

In an example that best highlights the importance of supervisors being persistent in the face of adolescent resistance, Sarah explained that her probation officer's efforts to ensure that she completed her junior school exams (Junior Certificate) two years previously when she had little concern for the future meant that she was now eligible to sit her senior school exams (Leaving Certificate):

> My probation officer actually made me go in and do that Junior Cert. She MADE me, my mam didn't, but my probation officer was like GET IN NOW, she was ringing me GET INTO THE EXAM, she got me out of bed every day for my exams. Before I didn't care, I just didn't want it. Now today I realize what I needed it for but then I didn't, you know what I mean? And she pushed me and pushed me and she got me two tutors, I didn't go to the two tutors, I'd no interest, I went once or twice and I was like 'no I don't want to be with you anymore'. But now I'm actually trying to get tutors because I realize what I need the Leaving Cert for. I don't have the money to pay for it [tutors] and my probation officer knows that, she'll try her hardest she'll try her best to help me.
>
> [YP86]

Although advocating for young people was a pivotal factor in them gaining access to relevant supports, the above examples highlight that ongoing intensive encouragement was an important dimension in sustaining their engagement. Encouragement provided by probation officers is acknowledged as being highly valued by probationers and particularly young probationers (Ditton and Ford 1994; Rex 1999). After being reminded of the consequences of their behaviour, encouragement was the next most common way that young people thought that their probation officer helped them to stay out of trouble. As reflected below in both Anthony's and John's respective accounts, encouragement was broadly categorized as praise for the progress they had already made and also involved signposting to future possibilities:

> Just kind of, she's always tellin' me like what I have to lose like d'you know what I mean, where I've come from an' that, gives me a different perspective on it like. Obviously it's always different like when people are looking in than it is for you looking out like you know what I mean?
>
> [YP75]

> She helps ye, like she'll always look at the good side of things an' all, she'll always say to ye, ye can do this, ye can do that, there's no point in doin' that an' doin' this when ye can do that an' this like. If you're in trouble she'd be like there's no point in gettin' in trouble when ye can move on to do that. She'll always help ye to look at the future an' what have ye an' all that kind of stuff.
>
> [YP84]

McNeill (2006: 134) argues that an important aspect of promoting desistance requires that practitioners develop young people's strengths, suggesting that advocacy should be 'a core task for youth justice staff'. Based on young people's accounts, it appeared that probation officer actions in advocating and accessing services on their clients' behalf had a number of important implications for compliance. It attached a sense of purpose and value to supervision, a factor that is associated with increasing completion rates and overall compliance (Bottoms 2001). Outside of the supervision process, it could be said that the actions of probation officers supported desistance by providing avenues to meaningful social attachments and opportunities to overcome barriers to desistance (see Farrall 2002a). Finally, probation officers' efforts demonstrated their concern and interest in young people's lives and provided them with motivation for attendance and participation at sessions. Indeed, Burnett and McNeill (2005) suggest that building social bonds and capacity with offenders may have a double positive impact in encouraging desistance. In addition to assisting offenders to address barriers to desistance, practitioners' efforts to provide meaningful assistance are important in increasing their clients' willingness to comply:

> there is a synergy between acts of practical assistance and their subjective impact on the working relationship; the worker's actions confirm his or her compassion and trustworthiness, increasing the preparedness of the offender to take steps towards desistance.
>
> (p. 236)

Emotional and personal support

Having someone to talk to and to listen are aspects of the supervisory relationship that are recognized as being valued by probationers and it was no different for the young people in this study (Ditton and Ford 1994; Leibrich 1993; Mair and May, 1997). They described the benefit of being able to talk about day-to-day issues in their lives, as well as their concerns about avoiding offending and future court appearances. As they came to trust their probation officers, talking openly was less challenging and many said that they discussed issues which previously they would have sought to conceal. A contributing factor to the increased openness of the relationship was the commonly reported perception that their probation officers did not judge them for their past behaviours and held respectful attitudes towards them. The nature and circumstances of their young lives meant that personal and family problems were not uncommon and young people, reluctantly at first, turned to their probation officers for advice and assistance. It was the support extended to them in these circumstances, combined with the trust that was built over time, that was most likely to be attributed to changing their opinions about their probation officers and their perceptions of the supervision process. Describing how the relationship changed over time, Dylan outlined a process of gradually realizing the benefit of his probation officer's input, which was consolidated by the support she provided to him following his mother's imprisonment:

> I never listened to my mam and dad like and then she [probation officer] was tellin' me what to do. And especially a woman tellin' me what to do, I'd issues around that big time. And I resisted against it for a year or more, but then I was seein' to know [starting to see] that she was trying to help me. She wasn't against me like, d'you know she was nice like? And then she saved my life like. My mam went to jail, the start of it. And that's when me and [probation officer's] friendship blossomed really 'cause she had me in every day, 'cause she was worried about me, 'cause I'd have mental health problems too, suicide and all that kind of shit. And she helped me through it like. [YP74]

The dynamics created within the supervisory relationship between young people and their probation officers and the support extended to them in the process contributed to changing their perspectives on compliance with the requirements of supervision in a positive direction over time. Through communicating respect, empathy and interest in young people's lives, the supervisory relationship functioned to engage young people emotionally in the process extending their motivation to comply beyond merely a sense of legal obligation (McGuire and Gamble 2006; McCulloch 2010; Ugwudike 2010).

Accepting directive guidance

The extent to which young people interpret intervention in their lives as care or control depends on the nature of the relationship with their supervisor (Triseliotis *et al.* 1998). In this study, the young people's narratives demonstrated that the establishment of positive relationships provided the foundations from which they accepted the legal authority vested in their probation officer to tell them what to do (see Smith *et al.* 2009). Returning for a moment to the case of Dylan, it becomes clear that his interpretation of support from his probation officer was not restricted to opportunities for talking and listening, but extended to quite direct instruction about the pathway he should follow:

> I was destroyed from drugs and she kind of offered me, well she kind of told me I was goin' to [residential drug treatment] and I was like 'no, no I'm not goin' at all' and she told me I'd go to jail. And I went there anyway and my life changed then and that was all thanks to her like 'cause I wouldn't have went. My addiction counsellor was tellin' me go, I just told him to fuck off. But I was on probation and I knew, what she told me I had to do.
>
> [YP74]

Directive guidance is most relevant in light of research which suggests that the use of challenge and openness in the context of a caring professional relationship is more likely to reduce behaviour of an anti-social nature (Triseliotis *et al.* 1998). Indeed, reminders given by their probation officers about the consequences of non-compliance were the factor most often identified by young people as helping them to stay out of trouble. Many described their probation officers as 'straight-talking', which translated into 'no-nonsense' reminders about what would happen if they did not maintain regular contact with the probation service or if they continued to offend:

> My probation officer told me like I know you're a young person under 18 but you have to think, you have to think with your head straight, because if you're going to keep on doing it [offending] like the only place you're going to end up is in a jail, is in prison. And what are you going to do then? You're going to live like that at the mercy of the law.
>
> [YP82]

Overall, participants' perspectives suggest that where they came to trust those with professional social and legal responsibilities towards them, this provided the strongest base from which they accepted directive guidance and instruction. This sense of trust enabled the professional relationship to be sustained even against the background of stark warnings and serious messages about the consequences of ongoing offending. The point is echoed by Chablani and Spinney (2011), who describe the survival of the alliances between young high risk mothers and their youth workers in the aftermath of the latter's actions in filing official child abuse reports against them. Although such actions had the potential to trigger a complete breakdown in the relationship, Chablani and Spinney (2011) explain that the strength of the links previously established with young people enabled relations to be repaired and restored in the longer-term.

Moral appeals and the supervisory relationship

The currency generated from establishing positive relationships provided probation officers with the capacity to make moral appeals to young people. When the young people were asked to speculate about their probation officer's reaction if they were to get into trouble again, most replied that they would feel upset and let down. It was through their descriptions of their probation officers' reactions that young people provided further insight into the type of interactions that took place during the supervision process. Harris (2009: 379) suggests that 'the ways in which officials use shame in the context of formal social control is not easily examined'. Dan provided some insight into the role of shame in explaining how his probation officer would react to his involvement in further offending. His description suggested that the approach embraced the theory and practice of reintegrative shaming whereby disapproval is conveyed in a respectful manner thereby avoiding humiliation and retaining the esteem of the individual (Braithwaite 1989; Makkai and Braithwaite 1994):

> Sometimes I like to think of her [probation officer] as a relative, you know, she's been so good and so nice to me. She would be very disappointed. She wouldn't tell me 'you're stupid', she would just say 'I'm very disappointed, I thought you were better than this, I thought you had your head on your shoulders straight'. She thinks of me as a great person, thinks I'm going to do great in life, thinks I'm going to have exactly what I want and exactly what I ever wanted and dreamed of; so, she wouldn't just leave me out like, she'd always say 'well if you got in trouble maybe you can do something to get out of that trouble', you know, to get out of the problem.
>
> [YP82]

Most young people said that they would feel bad about letting down their probation officer and feelings of disappointment, guilt or shame at their behaviour were linked to their officer's previous efforts to assist them. Following on from Dan's account above, he described his own feelings towards his probation officer's reaction:

> It would make me feel, to be honest, ashamed of myself. It would make me feel very sad in a way because I've disappointed her, because she's done so much for me and if that's the way I pay her back, that's not the way, you know?
>
> [YP82]

Healy (2010) found that the monitoring role of probation had a negative influence on some probationers who continued to offend, while it motivated desisting offenders towards change. In contrast to Joseph's case described earlier in the chapter, young people who had stopped offending and had a positive relationship with their supervisor described the monitoring function of probation as useful in helping them to stay out of trouble. Ben explained that knowing he was being monitored helped him to stay out of trouble:

> If it wasn't for the probation officers I probably would be locked up because I'd know there was no one there to watch me; if I was gettin' into trouble there'd be no one there, but then I knew that they were there if I got caught doin' somethin'.
>
> [YP85]

Monitoring was explained by the young people in terms of their probation officer's authority to contact the police and to request information about their involvement in offending. In this way, monitoring was conceived of in a technological as opposed to a physical sense:

> It's just someone being there being able to look me up, or ring me and say [mock tone of reproachment] 'what's this on the computer?'
>
> [YP86]

Of particular interest were the reasons they gave as to why monitoring by their probation officer helped them to avoid reoffending. They perceived that the prospect of being confronted with new offences by their probation officer, who was known to them, respected by them, and who, in their eyes, 'had done right' by them to be more difficult than confrontation from someone with whom they had no prior connection. Such findings resonate with those which demonstrate that reintegrative shaming is most effective in situations where a relationship of interdependency exists between the regulator and the regulated party (Findlay 1993; Losoncz and Tyson 2007; Makkai and Braithwaite 1994).

Young people's perceptions of power in the supervisory relationship

Crewe (2007) suggests that power exercised in the absence of direct force may be less obvious to its subjects. While power in the context of probation is likely to manifest in subtle forms enmeshed in a complexity of care and control functions, the young people were nonetheless aware of their probation officer's legal powers in responding to non-compliance. Probation officers' use of authority was perceived as fair insofar as young people explained that non-attendance or poor participation at appointments had been discussed with them and they had been given opportunities to improve. At this juncture, it is worth reminding the reader that the discretion afforded to probation officers in the Republic of Ireland in decision making about formal enforcement procedures facilitates a flexible response to episodes of non-compliance and arguably is likely to be a contributory factor in young people's perceptions of fairness (see Chapters 5 and 7).

Probation officers were also seen to exercise authority in a non-confrontational manner, as William explained:

> If ye did stray like not comin' in, she'd give ye a warnin' like. Not 'you better come!' like, but she'll tell ye 'look ye'll have to start comin' in, it's nothin' got to do with me to put ye back where I have to, ye have to go back to court, it's the law', do ye know what I mean?
>
> [YP89]

The execution of power, like the relationship within which it existed, was an interactive and negotiated process that was, according to the young people, contingent on the level of their compliance. Many explained that where they had gained the trust of their probation officer, more flexibility had been afforded to them. Building trust occurred over time and accumulated as a result of them not acquiring further offences or by them addressing offending-related issues such as substance misuse and addiction problems. Being trusted incurred benefits that eased the demands of the supervision process. These were demonstrated most clearly in young people's descriptions of their attendance requirements at appointments. Michael explained the point in outlining his probation officer's response to him now when compared with one year previously when he was taking drugs and continuing to get into trouble. The example demonstrates that overall improvements in young people's behaviour in the community offered more flexibility surrounding the conditions and requirements of supervision:

> If you are trusted you'd get believed; if you're not, it's just no, that's a lot of bull. They [probation officers] know. Before, I could have said all the excuses an' they'd know I was just tryin' to get away with it. But then now, at this stage, I could just ring up an' I could say I have a pain in my head, I can't come in, an' I'd be believed. I'd be let away with that but before if I said look, I'm after breakin' me arm, or I'm in hospital I'm after damagin' meself, it still wouldn't work 'cause they knew what I was doin' like. When you're doin' it for so long like they get used to it after a while. So you build up your trust an' that's the way to do it. You have to build up your trust with your probation officer (snaps fingers) then your probation officer builds up trust with you. An' once you an' your probation officer are workin' together, there's nothin' ever goin' to go wrong.
>
> [YP81]

Despite the flexibility within the process, most of the young people believed that their probation officer would return them to court for not complying with the conditions of supervision. Although no formalized written standards of practice exist for young people on probation in the Republic of Ireland (see Chapter 7), participants spoke of the importance of 'not pushing the boundaries' and 'not crossing the line', suggesting that they understood that doing so would trigger more formal action against them. Persistent random excuses were not perceived to be acceptable and as Claire explained, reasons given for rescheduling appointments had to be reasonable, logical and in line with a broadly compliant script:

> Like you couldn't text her [probation officer] an' say 'ah listen I'm dyin' [hung-over from alcohol], I'm not goin' in' [for a supervision appointment]. If I was sick or if there was someone else ill or if I just literally wasn't able to make it or if I had to mind me brother or somethin', they'd be the only reasons I do make anyway.
>
> [YP80]

Pre-sanction and progress reports authored by probation officers for the courts were identified by young people as the primary mechanism through which power was articulated in practice. They explained that having a poor record of attendance at appointments or failing to fulfil other requirements would be communicated to the judge by their probation officers through the court report:

> If ye have appointments ye go to your probation officer, an' then ye have appointments at such-and-such a place that your probation officer put ye onto, an' then if ye didn't go to them, it's goin' to be your probation officer ringin' up, 'did he go to any of them appointments?', they say 'no', he writes it down on the report, it goes to the court, the next time you're in court the judge reads that an' says 'that fella must not be listenin', he must not be listenin', an' next thing it's lock him up.
>
> [YP83]

> It [non-attendance] gets marked down. It gets said to the judge the next time I'm in court. Fail to attend, Fail to attend. It gets sent back in a report to the judge, doesn't look good in court.
>
> [YP78]

While those who continued to offend took a more critical stance on the court reports written by their supervisors, others referred to the obligation on probation officers to be truthful about their progress when scripting reports. Power in their view emanated within the realms of the criminal justice system and probation officers, as the agents of power, were obliged to act with integrity in executing their role:

> The probation officer has to do it as well. You know, they have to give the report an' that, an' if it's not good like the judge is goin' to lock you up. Well they have to don't they? They can't just like keep writin' you a good report if you're not attendin' them. It's going to have to be bad, she's not going to say well [name] is attendin' me and he's not, you know?
>
> [YP79]

> Like if a judge puts ye on a probation bond an' you're never goin' to meetings, he's goin' to ask the probation officer 'how's yer man doin'?' an' she's goin' to say 'no he hasn't turned up for any meetings or anythin'', like they do have to be truthful.
>
> [YP84]

While formal enforcement proceedings are not commonly initiated against young people on probation in the Republic of Ireland, the use of reports as a mechanism for conveying information about young people's progress was particularly salient for many participants who continued to have criminal cases progressing through the courts. Long delays in processing criminal justice cases involving young people meant that often those who had moved away from offending behaviour continued to make regular appearances in the Children Court while awaiting finalization of their outstanding cases (see Chapter 5). Furthermore, the common judicial practice of deferring sentencing decisions and placing offenders on adjourned supervision means that probation officers are required to submit regular reports on young people's progress to the courts (see Chapter 5 and 6). In these circumstances, it is not difficult to see why the probation officer's role in scripting the content of reports featured strongly in young people's accounts of negotiating compliance while under supervision.

Considerable debate exists in the literature about the influence of pre-sentence reports on judicial decision making (Field and Nelken 2010; Phoenix 2010; Tata *et al.* 2008). Young people perceived their probation officer's report-writing role as a powerful one in that they believed that judges place sizeable value on its contents when deciding their fate. Echoing the views of many of his peers, Dylan's opinion was that 'probation officers make the judges' minds up for them', while Michael described the report as being central to the decision making process in the courts:

> That's number one. That's the main one. The Judge takes the probation officer's views very strongly. On my experiences any way, he's took the probation officer's word on everythin'. What a probation officer thinks an' says, that's it, that's what goes, that's what they put you down on. That's number one, the probation report is number one. Their opinion really makes a difference to the judge, like they're the ones that really decide whether you're goin' to walk out of that courtroom or not.
>
> [YP81]

Young people based their views on previous experiences of receiving stern warnings from judges following 'a bad report' from their probation officer. Contrasting to the negativity associated with court reports in the past, for those who had stopped offending, the court report motivated them to comply insofar as it was seen as an opportunity to have their progress formally acknowledged. This is explained by Dan, who described his motivation for complying with the requirements of supervision:

> That's why I'm so good on probation, like I keep all my appointments so that the judge can have a look at them sheets and say 'well he's keeping all his appointments, he's very good and not getting into trouble, he's doing something in his free time'.
>
> [YP82]

In much the same way as the court report had previously acted as a formal record of their non-compliance, it now represented official endorsement of their progress towards 'a new life' [their words] away from offending. Although no formal process of endorsement exists within the Children Court in the Republic of Ireland, many young people said that they could sense changes in the judge's attitude towards them when they had done well and some reported being applauded for their progress. The relevance of receiving external or public recognition for positive behavioural change has been identified in a study of the Drug Courts in Scotland where offenders 'alluded to the significance of … reviews being conducted in public as a means of demonstrating their progress to other participants, family members and friends' (McIvor 2009: 37). Drawing on the narratives of desisters, Maruna (2001: 157) also highlights the value of formal appraisal, suggesting that although 'the testimony of any conventional other will do, the best certification of reform involves a public or official endorsement from media outlets, community leaders, and members of the social control establishment'.

In contrast to the prison context, research conducted on the role of power in probation supervision has been limited to date. One exception is a US-based study exploring probationers' perspectives of their supervisors' power using French and Raven's (1959) typology of the social bases of power (Smith *et al.* 2009). In summary, French and Raven's typology outlines five dimensions of power: coercive power, which derives from the view that the power-holder has the authority to inflict punishment for non-conformist behaviour; expert power, which is based on recognition of the power-holder's knowledge and expertise; legitimate power, which acknowledges that the power-holder has the right and is in a position to give direction; while referent power is centred on personal feelings of approval towards the power-holder; finally, reward power derives from the perception that those in power can issue incentives for conformist or desirable behaviour (French and Raven 1959; Smith *et al.* 2009). Smith *et al.* (2009) found that probationers were least likely to identify their supervisor's power in relation to reward power. This is not unexpected given criminal justice agency concerns about portraying community disposals as credible responses that do not 'reward' offending behaviour (Worrall and Hoy 2005). Instead, probationers most commonly located power in their supervisor's expertise; in their supervisor's role which permitted them to issue direction; in the fairness and respectfulness demonstrated by supervisors; and in their ability to ensure that punishment is imposed on non-compliant offenders (Smith *et al.* 2009). The evidence presented in this chapter suggests that the extent to which young people are likely to identify the sources and relevance of different forms of power within the supervisory experience will vary according to whether their reasons for compliance are based on moral as well as legal obligation.

Conclusion

This chapter has documented young people's experiences and changing perspectives on compliance while subject to probation supervision, and the reasons underpinning such changes. In most cases, initial resistance to intervention and a reluctance to engage gave way to the establishment of more affirmative attitudes towards probation. The central focus of this chapter concerned the changes that occurred in the dynamics of the relationship between young people and their probation officers over the supervision period. The provision of consistent social and emotional support over time, and probation officers' efforts to advocate and access services on their behalf, contributed to the young people's perception that probation supervision had something valuable to offer them, a factor previously associated with better completion rates and reduced recidivism on community disposals (McCulloch 2010). The establishment of positive relationships provided the foundation from which young people said they more readily accepted 'straight-talking' and directive guidance from their probation officers and served to increase their willingness to comply. The positive nature of the dynamics built through the supervisory relationship enabled probation officers to influence young people's behaviour through reintegrative shaming practices (Braithwaite 1989). For the young people, the shame of being confronted with evidence of further offending by those whom they perceived to have acted with commitment and integrity on their behalf functioned as the main positive deterrent.

Within the supervisory relationship, power was seen to be executed in a non-confrontational and fair manner, no doubt facilitated by the discretion afforded to probation officers in responding to episodes of non-compliance with young people in the Republic of Ireland. Power was identified as responsive to compliance insofar as young people perceived that greater flexibility was extended to them if they demonstrated their commitment to compliance over time. That power was seen to be fairly operated is not insignificant given the growing volume of evidence that links perceptions of procedurally fair and just treatment with greater compliance with the requirements of supervision and an increased sense of obligation towards the law (Jones 1964; Bottoms 2001; Tyler 2006b). It is likely to be especially relevant for young people for whom norms, values and attitudes to the law continue to evolve over adolescence through the process of legal socialization (Fagan and Tyler 2005). Young people recognized the legal powers inherent in their probation officer's authority to require them to attend appointments, to return them to court for non-compliance or to script negative court reports for future appearances. On the basis of their narratives, however, it was clear that legal obligations were strengthened when combined with young people's demonstrated social and psychological attachment and commitment to the supervision process.

As will be outlined in Chapter 9 and mirroring studies of offender desistance (Farrall 2002a; Healy 2010), those who had stopped offending primarily attributed the decision to their own personal motivation. However, most of the young people who had stopped were of the opinion that being on probation helped them to remain out of trouble. For them, probation supervision provided the context from which their efforts to change were nurtured, supported and developed in a way that was more likely to sustain their commitment to non-offending in the longer-term. Although those who continued to offend were less upbeat about the role of probation supervision in their lives, some did identify aspects of the process that had registered with them, but they had not, as yet, translated them into successful efforts to change. Farrall and Calverley's (2006: 48) exploration of the longer-term impact of probation suggest that for some offenders, probation may function 'as a "consciousness-raising" exercise' whereby messages conveyed during supervision do not 'strike a chord' until several years later. Such findings suggest that individual decisions to comply or conform are fluid constructs that change over time. With this in mind, the following chapter explores young people's perspectives on their motivation to stop offending and the influences that contribute to and support the desistance process.

9 Young people's perspectives on transition, change and desistance

Youth crime research is primarily focused on explaining why young people start offending, with considerably less emphasis placed on understanding pathways away from such behaviour. The dearth of focus on exit routes is accounted for, in no small part, by the well-cited adage that most young people grow out of crime. In other words, the weight of criminological attention is not merited for the majority who commit a few minor offences during adolescence and then stop. However, for those with longer and more entrenched involvement in offending behaviour and the criminal justice system, desistance is likely to be a more complex and elongated process. Referred to as 'longer-term legal compliance' in earlier sections of this book, desistance from offending behaviour involves a shift towards conformity by individuals who have previously been non-conformist with the criminal law (Bottoms 2001; Bottoms *et al.* 2004). This chapter focuses on young people's motivations to stop offending and examines their perspectives on the social and psychological processes which facilitate and support desistance and, to a lesser extent, those which stand in their way. Decisions to comply with the criminal law are context specific and are shaped by the exigencies woven into individual criminal justice systems. Turning 18 is a significant milestone in the Irish context, as it marks the point where subsequent offending is dealt with in the adult criminal justice system, and adolescent status becomes considerably less relevant to the outcome of proceedings. It also coincides with a time of change as young people commence the transition to early adulthood and begin to consider the possibility of new and future roles as partners, parents and employees. It is against the background of these particular contexts that this chapter documents young people's changing perspectives on compliance and the journeys away from offending behaviour.

Exploring desistance in late adolescence

Desistance among young people towards late adolescence must be explored against the backdrop of what is commonly known as the 'age–crime curve'. The term refers to 'a characteristic peak found in aggregate crime data when it is plotted against age' (McVie 2009: 39). Notwithstanding differing perspectives on the methodologies used in its construction (McVie 2009; Shapland and

Bottoms 2011), the typical age–crime curve demonstrates a peak in officially recorded and self-reported criminal behaviour in late adolescence followed by a sharp decline throughout early adulthood and a steadier decrease over the life course (Ezell and Cohen, 2005; Piquero, Farrington and Blumstein 2003; Warr 2002). A number of theoretical perspectives provide varying degrees of explanation of the age–crime curve and for the most part, these theories emphasize maturity, and changing social roles in the transition to adulthood, rather than age *per se*. Maturing out of crime is often referenced in relation to Moffitt's (1993) dual taxonomy that differentiates between 'adolescent-limited' and 'persistent life-course' offenders. 'Persistent life-course' offenders, it is suggested, start behaving anti-socially and criminally in childhood and persist with such behaviours into and through adulthood. Arising from experiences of trauma and neglect in their early years, psychological and personality deficits develop which are exacerbated when combined with adverse sociological factors. In contrast, the onset of anti-social and criminal behaviour for 'adolescent-limited' offenders coincides with the teenage years and terminates by early adulthood. Behaviours are explained as situation specific and arising from the strain associated with the 'maturity gap' during the adolescent phase (Moffitt 1993: 687). Moffitt suggests that offending ceases for 'adolescent-limited offenders' when they enter early adulthood as the costs of offending come to outweigh the rewards and individuals acquire status through taking on conventional roles. Exceptions exist which may require more time and effort to exit offending and these include contexts where alternative roles are unavailable or where youth 'fall prey' to 'snares' such as incarceration, drug addiction or teenage pregnancy (ibid.: 691). Some research evidence questions the use of age of onset as the basis for consigning youth to 'adolescent-limited' and 'persistent life-course' groups and challenges the manner in which all offender groups can be feasibly captured within the limitations of a dual taxonomy (Ezell and Cohen 2005). Nevertheless, the basic tenet that most young people mature out of offending behaviour is recognized and supported through empirical research (Rutherford 1992).

Explaining desistance through a developmental lens suggests that movement away from offending is facilitated by the establishment of improved psychosocial competencies and skills in older adolescents when compared with their younger counterparts. Acquiring adequate levels of social and emotional maturity, having greater consideration for future consequences and lower inclinations towards impulsivity and risk-taking behaviour are factors likely to contribute to more mature and responsible decision making (Steinberg and Cauffman 1996; Scott *et al.* 1995). Steinberg *et al.* (2004) suggest that mature individuals are better equipped to cope with the transition to adulthood having obtained the competencies necessary to adapt to the changing duties and functions involved. While differences exist in the relationship between mature decision making and age (see Chapter 4), the evidence also indicates that maturity of judgement exists independent of chronological age (Cauffman and Steinberg 2000a). In other words, maturity is not a guaranteed outcome of the ageing process.

Furthermore, some research suggests that certain aspects of maturity may actually equip individuals with the characteristics required to engage in criminality. For example, Little and Steinberg's (2006) study of drug-dealing and maturity found that youth who report higher levels of involvement in non-marijuana dealing are more resistant to the influence of their peers than other young people. By way of explanation, they suggest that dealing non-marijuana drugs requires initiative and independence and as such, peer resistance is an advantageous quality.

Social bonds theorists posit that as individuals adapt to adult roles and establish relationships and employment ties in the transition from adolescence to adulthood, they develop greater stakes in conformity (Sampson and Laub 1993). Where pro-social ties are established, they often act as sources of informal social control, meaning that new ways of living become less compatible with the risks and endeavours of criminal behaviour. Desistance from offending is seen to mirror the pace at which enhanced social ties are developed over time (Laub and Sampson 2001). A number of studies identify that young women are more likely to desist at an earlier age than young males (Graham and Bowling 1995; Flood-Page *et al.* 2000; McIvor, Murray and Jamieson 2004). Graham and Bowling (1995) report key differences in the social bonds formed by young females in comparison with their male counterparts in the transition to early adulthood. While for young women, desistance was associated with leaving school and home and forming new families and social ties, these factors were less – if at all – relevant in explaining desistance among young males. Transition to adulthood began later for males and was not always complete by their mid-twenties. Furthermore, young men were found to be dependent on their family of origin, less likely to form families of their own or to be responsible for themselves or others (ibid.). Barry (2007) argues that acquiring opportunities to access social capital during the transition to adulthood may positively enhance the likelihood of desistance. In her study, those who had desisted from offending reported greater opportunities for achieving 'social recognition' through capital accumulation and expenditure such as taking on an employment or caring role when compared with those who had not. Young women were found to have greater access to such opportunities arising from expectations on them to care for family members, a factor which is attributed to higher levels of desistance among females than males (ibid.). Finally, Barry (2006) suggests that while early adulthood may broaden horizons for conventional and legitimate opportunities, limited access to them is likely to act as a heavy impediment to change. This argument is supported in earlier research which reports that positive changes in individuals' social circumstances are important factors in motivating desistance (Farrall 2002a).

The complexity associated with the desistance process is highlighted by Warr (2002: 108), who explains that while social ties such as employment and marriage may reduce individuals' contact with their peers, it is equally plausible that the disconnect occurs as a result of 'increasing psychological and emotional autonomy'. Other theorists argue that improved social bonds do not lead to an inevitable shifting away from criminality and suggest that the likelihood of change is enhanced when cognitive shifts occur in the individual's identity and concept of self (Cernkovich and Giordano 2001; Giordano, Cernkovich and Rudolph, 2002). Giordano *et al.* (2002) focus attention on the role of interaction between the individual and the environment in explaining desistance. Based on a follow-up study of male and female adolescent offenders, they outline four types of 'cognitive transformations' as dimensions of the desistance process. The first relates to the individual's openness to change, while the second emphasizes their attitude towards exposure to opportunities or 'hooks for change' such as a new relationship or a job. Here Giordano *et al.* (2002: 1001) highlight that the most salient aspect is that individuals perceive new situations as both positive and 'fundamentally incompatible with continued deviation'. A third type of cognitive transformation happens when individuals begin to structure alternative conventional identities to replace their old deviant selves, while the fourth and final type signals the relative completeness of the desistance process and occurs when past criminal and anti-social behaviours are no longer seen as 'positive, viable, or even personally relevant' (Giordano *et al.* 2002: 1002).

The theoretical applicability of many of the perspectives outlined above extend beyond explaining desistance in the transition to early adulthood and have wider applicability across the life course. Some place greater emphasis on subjective and cognitive perspectives (Giordano *et al.* 2002; Maruna 2001) while others caution against ignoring the role of social factors with a reminder that 'agency is always exercised within the context of social structures' (Farrall, Bottoms and Shapland 2010: 547). Nevertheless, over the last decade or so, theorists have drawn on a fusion of cognitive, psychological and social structural influences to explain the processes involved in making and sustaining the decision to stop offending (see Laub and Sampson 2003). This is summed up by McNeill (2003), who describes that:

> desistance resides somewhere in the interfaces between developing personal maturity, changing social bonds associated with certain life transitions, and the individual subjective narrative constructions which offenders build around these key events and changes.
>
> (p. 151).

Defining what constitutes desistance

Opinion differs on how desistance is defined, measured and conceptualized in practice, leading Laub and Sampson (2001: 11), among others, to suggest that it is useful to make a distinction between desistance as a 'causal process that supports the termination of offending' from 'termination of criminal activity as an event' (ibid.: p.3). Increasingly, desistance is less commonly envisaged as a termination event and more frequently understood as a gradual process that unfolds over time (Farrall 2002a; Leibrich 1993; Maruna 2001). Operationalizing desistance in this way encapsulates the complexities involved in the process of cutting ties with offending behaviour and, according to Farrall and Calverley (2006):

> better captures the true nature of desisting from offending – in which 'lulls' in offending, temporary resumption of offending and the like are common – and provides a schema in which *reductions* in offence severity or the frequency with which offences were admitted to could be interpreted as indications of the *emergence* of desistance.
>
> (p. 18).

Distinguishing between pauses in individual criminal careers and maintaining 'the continued state of non-offending' (Maruna, Immarigeon and LeBel 2004: 18) is another challenge faced by criminologists and contributes to the argument that 'the problem with operationalizing desistance ... is one of permanence' (Piquero 2004: 104). Maruna *et al.* (2004: 19) propose that a distinction is made between primary and secondary desistance, with the former referring to 'any lull or crime-free gap in the course of a criminal career' and the latter as 'the movement from the behaviour of non-offending to the assumption of the role or identity of a "changed person"'. They argue that secondary desistance should be the focus of desistance research. Determining at what point individuals should be ascribed the status of desister has been the subject of considerable debate and cut-off points vary considerably between studies (Farrall and Calverley 2006; Healy 2010; Maruna 2001). Identifying desistance through a reliance on self-report data can be distorted by the extent to which respondents accurately and truthfully recall information; official data may be equally problematic given the differences between actual and reported levels of crime (Graham and Bowling 1995; Leibrich 1993). Nonetheless, both self-report and official criminal record data provide baseline indicators of the temporal distance offenders have travelled on the desistance route.

In this study, the young people were identified as desisters if they had not reoffended for six months or more based on self-report data and official criminal record data provided by their probation officers. In total, 14 young people were categorized as desisters and the remaining six – five of whom had reoffended within the last month and another who had done so within the last three months – as offenders. This threshold is lower than that used in other studies of youth and young adult offenders where the limit is a minimum period of one year (Graham and Bowling, 1995; Jamieson, McIvor and Murray 1999). Labelling young people as desisters and others as offenders on the basis of difference in the number of months since last reoffending, is, on the surface, an exercise of splitting hairs given the propensity for relapse, especially among adolescent populations. The research therefore sought to cross-reference offending data with participants' accounts and perspectives on compliance. Narratives were categorized according to the reasons that young people said would motivate them to stop offending. Drawing on the work of Bottoms (2001) and Tyler (2006a), the sample was divided into those who described their principal motivation to avoid offending in normative terms, and those who based their decisions first and foremost on instrumental reasons. In other words, the analysis sought to distinguish between participants who primarily complied due to internal factors such as personal commitments to self and attachments to others, and those who did so in response to external motivating factors such as the incentives and disincentives built into the system such as avoiding prison, for example. The rationale for choosing to categorize cases in this way was based on existing research which suggests that normative reasons are likely to be more compatible with sustaining desistance in the longer-term (Jones 1964; Tyler 1990). Making such a distinction is in no way to suggest that participants were motivated only by internal or by external reasons. Indeed, Bottoms (2001) reminds us that decisions to comply are likely to be based on complex interactions between normative and instrumental mechanisms as well as influences linked to habit, routine and constraint (see Chapter 3). What emerged from the exercise was that those who described normative reasons as the dominant influence underpinning their motivation were also the participants that had been identified as desisters on the basis of the self-report and official data. Their accounts suggested that they perceived themselves to be socially and psychologically distanced from offending behaviour. In contrast, the primary motivation outlined by the offender group related to instrumental reasons. Most of these young people expressed a desire to stop offending, but as yet had been unable to do so, affirming Bottoms and Shapland's (2011: 63) conclusion that 'for potential desisters, changing a pattern of behaviour is more difficult than forming the wish to change behaviour'. It is important to note that while categorizing participants according to their motivations to comply is useful to capture the essence of their current perspectives on compliance, compliance is more accurately envisioned as a fluid construct that alters over time as change occurs in individuals' cognitive and psychological perspectives, social circumstances and interactions with others (Tyler, 1990; Tyler and Huo, 2002). Those who continued to offend had an average of three previous convictions (SD = 1.63) while the average for desisters was 2.7 (SD = 1.44). The small size of the offender group, however, cautions against drawing substantive conclusions.

The qualitative evidence provides a clearer indication in this regard and suggests that despite ongoing involvement in criminality and difficulties in perceiving pathways out of it, offenders were not committed to the idea of a criminal lifestyle for the future. Instead, like participants in Bottoms and Shapland's (2011) study, offenders shared similar conventional future aspirations – a job, a house and family of their own – with their desisting counterparts, albeit with less clearer focus on how they would achieve them. In this way, it is suggested that differences between the two groups were indicative of where they were located on the spectrum between offending and desistance (Barry 2007; Farrall and Calverley 2006) and the extent to which they had contemplated or taken action towards change (Prochaska *et al.* 1992).

The social and legal context of change in late adolescence

Before exploring the standpoints of the desister and offender groups in this study, it is worth turning for a moment to examine the common social and legal context that acted as a backdrop for all participants' perspectives on compliance. Most young people explained that being involved in criminality when they were younger was exciting, gave them something to do and often brought status through the acquisition of material goods, as explained here by Dan:

> When I was young at that age like and I used to do all them things I used to feel good, because I didn't worry about not having a nice jacket on me, or not having a nice phone, I just used to walk in and back out and I had it in my pocket. I was seeing things as if I'd never need a job in my life, you know, robbing is the best thing in the world, keep on doing it, you know? It was the desire of having everything and not paying for anything.
>
> [YP82]

Now, as they stood on the cusp of early adulthood, the earlier appeal of criminality gave way to a sense of weariness for those who continued to offend, and a relief to have escaped for those who had stopped offending. Barry (2010: 133) suggests that at the onset stage, offending behaviour is a form of 'social integration' through which adolescents acquire material goods, status and sociability; the benefits that accrue are largely perceived as positive in that they provide a sense of identity and belonging. However, the attractiveness of offending declines over time and the motivation to continue is more likely to be driven by perceived need, addiction or financial expectation (Barry 2006). Its diminishing appeal is compounded where responsibilities to family and to children begin to emerge. MacDonald *et al.* (2011: 145) argue that continued involvement in criminality acts as 'a moratorium on the achievement of normal youth transitions to adulthood' insofar as criminal behaviour, drug use, and imprisonment are unlikely to make individuals appealing as 'employees, partners and fathers'. Weariness with offending was matched with fatigue arising from continued involvement in the criminal justice system, which was described by young people as moving circuitously between criminal justice organizations, going 'up and down' and 'over and back' and 'in and out' of police stations, courts, probation offices and sometimes prison. Fatigue structured the experiences of all participants given that most continued to have cases waiting to be finalized through the courts; however, the extent to which it propelled individuals to stop offending varied between cases. As mentioned in the introduction, turning 18 years was the entry point for young people into the adult criminal justice system, a prospect which many spoke about with trepidation. Both desisters and offenders with serious charges pending in the courts, or subject to suspended sentences, and even those who were not, were mindful that the risk of imprisonment was increasingly likely and a factor that framed, if not influenced, motivation to comply. Concern about the seriousness of future sanctions meted out by the criminal justice system further contributed to the allure of a crime-free existence.

Personal motivation to change

Echoing findings from previous research, the most common explanation provided by young people who had stopped offending was that they had grown up and matured (Barry 2006; Jamieson *et al.* 1999). Many of the young people said that becoming more mature provided them with a clearer perspective on their involvement in criminal behaviour and caused them to reflect on the future direction of their lives. They also linked maturity to a heightened awareness of the consequences of their behaviour for themselves and others, becoming more independent-minded, as well as listening to those who sought to help them. While they explained maturity as something that had happened to them, they portrayed their actual decision to change as something they consciously chose to do. In other words, like the young adult desisters in Barry's (2006) and Shapland and Bottoms' study (2011), change was not a passive process, but rather an active, hard-fought commitment to pursue a better way. Steinberg *et al.* (2004: 24) suggest that the development of psychosocial capacities represents a form of human capital for adolescents and young adults. They put forward the idea that 'psychosocial capital' offers young people the resources to create and avail of 'positive life experiences'. 'Wanting a better life' and 'wanting more out of life' were commonly used expressions in young people's explanations of factors that motivated their decisions to desist from offending behaviour. Stopping or drastically reducing their use of alcohol or drugs was a central element in 10 of the 14 desisters' stories of change. Three had completed residential alcohol or drug treatment, four had stopped taking drugs by confining themselves to a bedroom in their family home while going through the withdrawal process and three others said that they had stopped drinking alcohol because it invariably led them into trouble. Although change was tough, most of them rejected the idea that change was a struggle and this was mostly because it was something that they wanted for themselves. The essence of their perspectives was captured in Dan's words, who said of change: 'it was my own free-will'. Participants also described a sense of being ready to break from past behaviour. Anthony's account of the difference in his attitude towards residential drug treatment when he was 18 years old compared to his earlier years echoes the importance of offender readiness for change highlighted in previous research (Giordano *et al.* 2002):

> I was only 15 the first time going to treatment, just going on 16 actually the first time I was in treatment. I was only getting in there to get off the streets like, that's all I was doing, to keep people happy like.
> *MS: What was different this time do you think?*
> It was for me, definitely, it was for no one else like you know what I mean? I wanted to do it for me like. You are not going to do it for anyone else, you

> might be able to do it for a couple of weeks or a couple of months like but eventually you are not, things are going to fall apart. You grow up a lot as well like d'you know what I mean? I did, it took me a long time to do, you know for that four years, like maturity it took a long time. It really only happened in the last six or seven months you know, that's just being honest like.
>
> [YP75]

Many who had stopped or reduced their consumption of alcohol or drugs said that no longer having the shadow of daily use hanging over them, nor being continually preoccupied with acquiring money, gave way to a clearer view on what they wanted from their lives. It seemed that the psychological shifts that occurred through the maturation process and which prompted their motivation to stop using substances were further strengthened by sober and drug-free mindsets. Peter, who had recently completed residential alcohol treatment, explained the impact of sobriety on his worldview:

> It's just like I can kind of see what I want to do with my life really, and d'you know I'm thinking more clear like. Usually I was just thinking there's nothing to do around here and that all I can do is get cans [beer] or whatever, but once you actually I suppose do try and give it up like, you see more things to do really like d'you know? You look for things to do and you find more things so it just makes it a lot better like.
>
> [YP73]

The process of change

Shapland and Bottoms (2011) suggest that late adolescence and early adulthood are periods when those with heavily involved criminal pasts contemplate the future and reflect upon whether they wish to continue offending into adulthood. Young people described their motivation to stop offending as being driven by an increased awareness of the profound personal and social consequences for themselves and others. Some, such as Catherine, related increased consciousness to bringing about an immediate change in the direction of their lives:

> I turned 18 an' I just kind of turned around an' I said 'oh shit I can't do this much longer' d'ya know? My body was wrecked anyway. I was wrecked. Weight was fallin' off me. My face was sinking in. I was all cut up, you know from doing shit to myself like an' I just stopped. I came back here [family home]. You can only do what I did for a certain amount of years 'cause if you keep doin' it like you'll end up fuckin' very sad an' lonely or else dead, it never ends good like, drugs can't end good. You know they can't like.
>
> [YP76]

Claire is more typical of other desisters in her account of how the consequences of ongoing offending behaviour gradually came to be realized over time based on a series of events and experiences. She identified weariness related to repeated committals to the Children Detention School system and a slow realization of the consequences associated with her chaotic lifestyle as the starting point in her contemplating change:

> I done loads of times in there [Children Detention School], like so, I just got bored of it. If I wasn't in me house I'd be in there, and if I wasn't in [Children Detention School] I'd be doin' a rough, like stayin' out an' not goin' home, [staying in] different people's houses, in town, goin' missin' an' all. I needed to start coppin' on like because it was either gonna be me dead or someone else dead, if things had of got any worse than they were. I was on drugs, [smoking] heroin, I was involved with much older people than me, like in their late twenties an' all an' just hangin' out.
>
> [YP80]

Thinking about change did not, however, translate into taking action towards it. Although Claire stopped smoking heroin, she went on to develop a serious alcohol problem. She recalled that her lifestyle remained the same and eventually culminated in her assaulting and causing serious harm to another person while under the influence of alcohol. Change did not occur immediately after this incident but over the months that followed and in the process of going through the courts, Claire said that she gradually came to realize that alcohol was a problem for her.[1] This was a view that was confirmed in her mind by the opinions of others and by reading newspaper coverage of her case. In the final instance, it appeared that addressing her alcohol problem, the prospect of a custodial sentence, a desire for a better life and a shift in her perception of her identity as a female and its compatibility with ongoing offending were the factors that came together to propel her towards change:

> I realized what I actually done like, what the drink caused me to do or the effect it had on me I knew I had a problem with the drink. I knew, if I didn't stop now, it was never going to stop 'cause I had the time to think it, that I needed to stop. I had like thought that I needed to stop, told meself like an' then other people was tellin' me, an' I was in the paper an' everybody seen like, it [newspaper] said '[surname] had drink issues', so I knew I had an issue. I'm lookin' at a [custodial] sentence now. I'm after coppin' on and I just want to, it's not nice for a girl to be involved with all that an' I want to go places with me life. Prison it's not a life for me, definitely not for me.
>
> [YP80]

Farrall and Calverley's (2006) exploration of the emotional trajectories of desistance reports that individuals at the early stages tend to express a narrower range of emotions than those at a later stage of desistance. Feeling 'happier' and 'better in myself' were the most commonly expressed emotions among early desisters (ibid: 108). Overwhelmingly, young people in this study expressed that they were more content with their lives as a result of not offending. They attributed this to no longer having a sense of apprehension and uncertainty about the police calling to their homes, receiving new summonses, or being arrested. Having achieved a semblance of normality in their lives, they came to enjoy the relative stability brought about by desistance and were motivated not to return down old roads again. Catherine, who had moved back to her family home following a number of placements in residential care interspersed with periods when she was smoking heroin and staying with older peers, described the emotional benefits of change:

> I don't ever want to go back down that road. I'm a far happier person now than I was, d'ya know? And at least I know what's goin' on around me now. I'm not so out of it that I can't even, d'ya know, I didn't even know where I was before. Now I know who my real friends are, an' I know how things work.
>
> [YP76]

Ben, whose previous offending was associated with a severe alcohol problem, encapsulated the perspectives of other participants in his description of having a 'new life' as a result of the changes he had made in his behaviour. Like the desisters in Barry's (2006) study, change brought practical, social and relational benefits:

> It's like a new life or something an' I'm not in trouble now or anything like. It's way better like, I'm less stressed and there's no hassle with the Gardaí [police]. I'm trusted at home. It's a definite change from this time last year. It's way different like. I don't really hang around with my friends anymore like, just the odd time. I'm drivin' now as well. I like drivin' an' I can go places with my girlfriend now. If I didn't have the car now I'd be either out in her house or my house 'cause I don't want to go out with everyone 'cause they'll be all drinkin'. I'm finished with the court now, it got finalized on Thursday. My curfew was taken off me an' all my bail restrictions are gone.
>
> [YP85]

Mulvey *et al.* (2004: 218) suggests that 'any long-term reorientation away from antisocial activity toward more socially acceptable behaviors requires an enduring shift in how one sees oneself'. While frequently referring to the length of time since they last offended as evidence of change, it was in their descriptions of themselves as transformed individuals that young people most clearly conveyed their changed sense of self. Sarah, who had been a persistent shoplifter since childhood, described her changed perspective:

> The way I was before you wouldn't trust me around your schoolbag never mind your handbag. And the way I am now I'm just like somebody that

> you'd never think was a robber, you'd never ever think that I would do anything like what I used to do, never. It's completely in the past. Me being the way I am now, I just go into a shop and I'm not getting a second thought of taking something. You know, just go in and look at it and don't think I'm going to rob that like, just go in, if you want to get it, buy it next week, buy it the week after, buy it when you have money like. That's the way I put it.
>
> [YP86]

Many young people expressed a strong sense of achievement in their efforts to change, suggesting that desistance, certainly at the early stages, requires conscious effort (Maruna and Farrall 2004). Anthony took considerable pride in describing his current status following a number of years of involvement in the criminal justice system:

> First time in six years I've a clean slate, nearly seven years. It's weird. Jus' different like you know what I mean, not having any Guards or anything like it's grand like. I enjoy it like. A clean slate like, there's nothin' better than a clean slate.
>
> [YP75]

Hope has been previously identified as characterizing the experiences of young adult and adult desisters (Barry 2006; Farrall and Calverley 2006; MacDonald *et al.* 2011) and it was the same for desisters in this study. Hope is an important emotion in light of the evidence which suggests that a positive outlook is more likely to result in successful outcomes. Nevertheless, despite only one young person having full-time employment, few desisters raised the issue of poor employment prospects at a time when the economy in Ireland was in the midst of the most crippling recession of recent decades. Bottoms *et al.* (2004: 375) caution against an overemphasis on agency without consideration for structural factors and suggest that while individual agency may be genuine 'it is also constrained … by lack of self-awareness and lack of full contextual awareness'. To suggest that participants in this study were unaware of the broader social context would be presumptuous without further exploration. It may well be that the 'relative lack of *sociological* understanding of their lives' (MacDonald *et al.* 2011: 150) was characteristic of their young age and lack of experience about the financial realities of maintaining themselves on a daily basis. That half of the desisters were attending educational or training programmes (often through links established with community-based organisations and the Probation Service) may also have influenced their perceptions in a positive direction. This explanation is in keeping with Griffin and Kelleher's (2010: 39) study of marginalized men aged 18–33 years that reports greater optimism among younger men involved in training initiatives than in men over 23 years who they described as having 'all but lost hope'. Alternatively, their failure to mention the economic context could signal a quieter acceptance of the relatively poor employment prospects they faced as young people with criminal histories and limited, if any, educational or vocational qualifications.

Desistance and social relationships: the role of family, partners and children

Police searches, attacks on the home, constant arguments and parental anxiety were just some of the features of family life that young people described when they had been involved in offending. They attributed growing up to gaining greater insight into the effects of their behaviour on family members and they came to appreciate that their family had remained loyal to them despite their past behaviour. Peter explained that his mother and grandmother's unfailing belief that he would eventually change was an important aspect of his decision to stop offending and he described why they continued to be the most important people in his life:

> When I was getting myself in trouble my mother and nana never really I suppose lost faith, they never thought 'oh he's a waste of space' and he's never going to amount to anything d'you know they always gave me support or whatever like.
>
> [YP73]

New relationships with family are associated with generating positive emotions among desisters (Farrall and Calverley 2006). In this study, young people explained that the decision to stop offending brought closer relationships with family members and these relationships in turn were credited as a motivating factor in supporting desistance:

> I've better relationships an' all at home, nice friends, totally different friends. I've good relationships, like I've too much now to lose, like I want to go to college an' all now. Now that I'm off the drink, I'm after gainin' so much with me family and new friends an' I'm after comin' off drugs an' everythin'. I'm after turnin' me life around, I don't want to go back there.
>
> [YP80]

Young people's changed attitudes also triggered an eagerness in many of them to recompense by making a positive contribution to the family. This most commonly manifested in a commitment not to create further anxiety for their parents, to do what was asked of them, to help out with household tasks or to take on a caring role for younger siblings, a parent or a grandparent. Undertaking gestures that make amends for past actions enables the offender to gain respect for self and to demonstrate respect for others (Braithwaite and Mugford 1994). For young people, the chance to be seen in a new and positive light by family members through engaging in purposeful activity was a rewarding experience and one which allowed them to show appreciation for the loyalty shown to them in the past. Wayne expressed his desire to reciprocate the support given to him by assisting his parents through his mother's recent illness:

> My mother is fairly sick at the moment, she had a heart attack, so that's the main priority now at the moment to try and do everything I can for her now to keep her resting … my parents stood by me through a lot of tough times as well so it's just I'll stick by them now as well do you know?
>
> [YP70]

In explaining how he responds to family members now compared to the past, Kevin echoed the changed sentiments of other participants in demonstrating greater empathy towards parents and siblings:

> Every time I was gone like me mother was up, down in the sitting room like walkin' around 'til four or five o'clock in the mornin' thinkin' like 'oh well, he's gonna be found in a ditch' or 'he's gonna be shot', you know? I felt bad on her like. She stuck with me. I don't want me mother worryin' no more like you know, an' me sisters, me sisters worry an awful lot about me. I don't let them down now. I do everything that she asks, well whatever she asks me I will do like, you know?
>
> [YP79]

Shapland and Bottoms (2011) suggest that as offenders make the decision to desist, they seek out the support of parents and partners. Support from family and significant others have been previously identified as important features of the desistance process for young people (Barry 2006). Not all desisters had the benefit of family support, but for those that did, it played an important part in supporting their decision to change. Anthony for example, had been asked to leave the family home because of the impact of his drug dealing. On being informed of his willingness to attend drug treatment, his parents welcomed him back, a gesture that he regarded as directly relevant to supporting his commitment to change, both before and after treatment:

> *MS: How important was it to be invited back to your family home?*
> I wouldn't have got clean otherwise and I had to be clean to go into treatment. So I just did cold turkey for three weeks, didn't go outside the door, inside at home, and went into treatment then, came back out and moved back in home. And then my mam an' dad they give me a bit of advice an' that on what the right way is, to work out things. My mam an' dad actually are very helpful, they'd drop me to me aftercare an' all that. They took me back into the family home. You can't ask for more like, you know what I mean?
>
> [YP75]

Anthony's experience was not unique and the importance of having a secure base to return to was emphasized by all of those who had sought to address alcohol and drug problems. Support from family extended out in a wide variety of ways and included opportunities to talk, being given tasks to occupy their time and reminding young people about probation appointments, among others. Barry (2006) emphasizes the importance of providing opportunities to young people to gain the respect and trust of others. Similarly, in this study taking on roles within the family, demonstrating responsibility and honesty, setting a good example and helping others are just some of the types of activities associated with generating a strong sense of achievement in young people and encouraging desistance. The family functioned to support desistance by providing opportunities for young people to demonstrate that they had changed their ways and could be trusted in a variety of different social situations. One participant, for example, expressed his pride at being allowed to take charge of the family business while his sibling was on holiday, while for others, opportunities came through the routine aspects of daily life such as being permitted to remain in the house without supervision or through their observations that money, jewellery and other valuables were no longer locked away. Opportunities to demonstrate change was an important aspect of young people's narratives and built on their motivation to maintain desistance. So too was the praise and encouragement received from family members. This was evident during interviews when young people frequently drew on the views of close significant others to validate their own perceptions of themselves as changed persons. James described his changed identity in the context of what his wider family network including cousins said about him:

> I'm determined like, I changed everythin' around like, even everyone around here says I've changed a lot like, ye know? They think I'm like a different fella altogether now … family, an' my cousins an' all 'cause the cousins like they'd ask me will I go drinkin' like an' I tell them no, I tell them I want to watch a DVD or somethin'.
>
> [YP87]

Relationship with partner

The creation of conventional bonds is a major component of supporting the desistance process (Shover 1996). Bottoms and Shapland (2011: 62) describe the establishment of a meaningful relationship with a partner as 'a "hook" factor that helped men to take seriously the possibility of attempting to desist'. Among the desisters in this study, 10 of the 14 had a boyfriend or girlfriend and in seven of these cases, they credited their partner's input with assisting them to avoid reoffending. None of their partners had ever been involved in offending and young people were strongly of the opinion that the relationship would break down if they were to reoffend. The five male participants identified support and direction provided by their girlfriends as the aspect of the relationship that helped them to stay out of trouble. This consisted of reminding them about their probation appointments, discussing problems with them, and providing an alternative perspective on their lifestyle and associations. Both Michael's and James' narratives demonstrated the role of informal social control within their respective relationships:

> My girlfriend made me happy, an' just made me open me eyes to a lot of things, made me realise who me friends were, an' what friends really are, because I just thought anybody that'd pick up on me they're me friends, any person who said that they were me friend that was it at one stage. But she just opened me eyes up to a lot of things.
>
> [YP81]

> I met my girlfriend around that time [time of making the decision to stop] and she told me to straighten myself out like d'ye know? She told me like make sure ye attend everythin' like 'cause if ye don't you're goin' back to court an' ye'll get jail an' all this. My life's changed around now an' I can't be actin' the fool an' messin' around. Like she'd just get vexed if I went an' left her here, if I went up around town actin' the fool, d'ye know?
>
> [YP87]

The young females differed from their male counterparts in the way that they explained the role that their partners played in motivating them to desist. What emerged as the primary factor for them was the shame they anticipated from their boyfriends' reactions to further offending. Claire described her mixed feelings when a joking reference was made to her past behaviour:

> Now, I usen't care years ago. I used to think I was mad, 'cause you know I was part of all this, just you know, but now like people look at you totally different. Even me boyfriend like he does be saying, 'oh scumbag', he does call me, just messing like. But I like it in a way it helps me in a way 'cause it keeps me on the straight and narrow like. So I like it, but I don't at the same time.
>
> [YP80]

The motivating influence of children

The importance young people attached to children, including younger siblings and relatives, and their offspring was noteworthy. Following long periods of their adolescence immersed in lifestyles and routines shared with their offending peers, returning home often only to eat, to wash and to sleep, young people were in effect not always known to their younger brothers, sisters, nieces and nephews, some of whom had been born during this period. Changing their behaviour brought them back into the family home and led to the establishment of relationships with the children in their lives, sometimes for the first time. They were motivated to avoid setting a bad example for their younger peers by engaging in any of the behaviours associated with their pasts. After establishing these new-found family attachments and rekindling others, the prospect of a custodial sentence acted as a strong motivation to avoid future offending. Luke captures the essence of the influence that children played in participants' lives in describing his feelings about his young niece, who shared the family home with him:

> She [niece] only went two there in December, I love her to bits. Plus as well she'd be only startin' talkin' an' imagine if I was locked up for about two years or somethin' then that's two years of my life gone without seein' her.
> [YP83]

Having children is an important factor in desistance for some young men and young women (Barry 2006; McIvor *et al.* 2004). Three desisters – Michael, Sarah and William – had become parents in the previous 12 months. William lived apart from his girlfriend and baby and although expressing a desire to be there for his child, it was in the cases of Michael and Sarah – who lived with their children – where the relevance of the parenting role to desistance was most evident. Both of these young people shared similarities in that they had not had a consistent father figure in their lives and their mothers had also been unavailable to them at various periods during their childhood. Michael's mother was a drug addict and his father had died at a young age. Sarah explained that her mother was a shoplifter for as long as she could remember and had been to prison on a number of occasions; she had never known her father. Perhaps unsurprisingly, the sense of loss associated with the absence of a consistent parent in their lives was woven into their respective accounts and both were strongly motivated to avoid offending so that they could be present for their children in a way that neither had experienced themselves. Michael identified his child, alongside his partner, as the main reason for going straight. Asked specifically about the motivation his child provided, he outlined that not having his father around when he was growing up, and the presence of a number of anti-social 'father figures' in his life, was not something he wanted for his daughter:

> I grew up without a father, I don't want my child to do that. I know how hard it is like. It's not the hardest thing in the world obviously, a lot of people do, but it's not as easy when you haven't got that father figure in your life, an' discipline, I had no discipline all me life, I could do what I wanted when I wanted, an' there was nothin' anybody could do or say. Like for a long while there, me little brother's father, I've always classed him as my father 'cause my da's dead since I'm 3 years of age, an' he reared me but he wasn't a great example either, in an' out of prison all his life, an' me uncles are all in an' out of prison all their lives, an' still now they're still goin' in an' out of prison like, but I just chose that I didn't want to be like me little brother's da an' me uncles an' so on. I'd lose everythin' now at this stage. Even if I was to mess around once I'd lose everythin'. I can't afford that. It's after takin' me this hard to build all this up, I'm after comin' through drink, drugs an' a lot of other shit as well on top of that an' I'm just pullin' meself out the opposite side.
> [YP81]

Like Michael, Sarah's perspective was contextualized within her past experiences, but also projected towards the future in providing a better life for her son:

> I grew up like in a way where my mam was always going to prison. So I grew up that kind of way where I was looking at my mam, she was going away for days on end and I was hopin' for her to come home this day and that day, you know? If I didn't have [the baby] I don't think I'd be the way I am now. I probably would have changed in bits and ways but I wouldn't be in getting my Leaving Cert [Final State School Examinations], put it that way. I wouldn't be getting a better life for him and me.
>
> [YP86]

A sense of shame arising from the stigma of involvement in the criminal justice system weighs heavier on female offenders as legal responses are likely to be influenced by societal expectations of what constitutes proper female behaviour (Covington 2008; Gelsthorpe and Sharpe 2006). An additional aspect of Sarah's account, and where it diverges from Michael's, lies in the way in which shame associated with continued offending was perceived in light of her parenting responsibilities:

> After [the baby] came along, it was really [the baby], I didn't want to be going into court and everyone knowing that I've a child at home and I'm putting myself lower to be in a courthouse, do you know, it's not nice. It's not worth it. And that's the way I look at it now. If I see a girl on the street going around like a junkie, I'd be thinkin' if I didn't have the baby would that be me? You know? Now I'd be thinking it but I'd never judge, but for ME and what I think of me before, that thought would be in my head. But I'm looking at some of my friends and they're still going to court today, a few of them have kids today and they didn't change, so I can't explain it. It happened to me, I was lucky, I took the escape door, you know?
>
> [YP86]

For both these young people, parenting was incompatible with continued offending by virtue of their desire to be there for their child and to provide better direction and opportunities for them. Their perspectives echoed those outlined by Hughes (1998: 146), who identified 'respect and concern for children' as one of the key turning points for desistance among a sample of young African-American and Latino-American males. Love for their own children, a desire to be there for them as they grow up and the capacity for children to trigger feelings of self-worth were factors relevant to encouraging change. Both Michael's and Sarah's accounts also demonstrate that the extent to which becoming a parent promotes desistance is likely to vary according to the individual's involvement in the parenting role, past experiences and current orientations towards behavioural change. Graham and Bowling (1995: 76) argue that becoming a parent influences an individual's identity, and fosters a sense of responsibility, leading to greater recognition of the needs of others. These developments, which they suggest occur 'gradually among men and more immediately among women', are associated with changes in thinking that are congruent with reduced offending and desistance (ibid.).

Distancing oneself from criminal peers

Breaking ties with criminal peers is an integral part of maintaining efforts to stop offending (Graham and Bowling 1995; Jamieson *et al.* 1999; Shapland and Bottoms 2011) and was the most commonly reported feature of change among desisters in this study. MacDonald *et al.* (2011) suggest that the social networks of young persistent offenders narrow over time as their associations with criminal and drug-involved peers lead to increasing exclusion and stigmatization by others. Cutting loose from criminal peers offers the potential for young people to develop broader social networks, but detaching is not an easy process. The covert and surreptitious nature of criminal involvement means that suspicion is often cast on those who seek to quit, and social and psychological pressure is applied to maintain the *status quo*. Not giving in to pressure from peers requires a strong sense of personal agency as well as the necessary psychosocial competencies to adequately manage and cope with the emotional demands of the situation (Zimring 2000). The challenge of moving away from offending peers is confounded when the elements of an offending lifestyle continue to be easily accessible. Many desisters lived in environments where getting their hands on any range of illegal substances was a straightforward process requiring nothing more than knowing the contact details of the local suppliers. Claire, who had a history of alcohol and drug problems, described the effortlessness involved in gaining access to alcohol and drugs:

> Drugs are everywhere. They're outside me door like, well not literally outside the door. Because it's so easy just to go back on the drink and drugs, it's only a phone call like for anythin', then it's only like a few minutes walk to someone. It's there on a plate. It's there on a plate for you.
>
> [YP80]

Knowing what they wanted, becoming independent, and being able to say no, were the types of changes that young people described as making it easier to resist the lure of anti-social peers than in their younger days. Kevin, who had cut all ties with his criminal peers at the time of interview, outlined how his capacity to resist the influence of anti-social peers changed over time:

> When I was 16 like I was hangin' around with 22 year olds, 23 year olds you know? And like I was the fool for them, they'd make me do everything like you know? I wouldn't be made do it now. I just wouldn't let them do it now to me. I was afraid back then because they were twenty two and twenty three year olds you know?
>
> [YP79]

In another example, Michael described the steps he took to avoid getting into trouble again by not relenting to the pressure put on him by friends:

> It's very hard. Because them people [old friends] would do anythin' for you at one stage, an' then the next stage you're tellin' them 'no, look I can't'. An' they're ringin' to ask you to do somethin' for them an' you're sayin' 'listen, I can't'. There's a very good friend of mine that's in prison now an' I had to tell him 'look, I'm not bein' funny, I'm gettin' a new [telephone] number just 'cause of you'. He was ringin' me askin' me to go up to the prison an' throw things [drugs] over, an' I said to him 'look, when you get out, when you have everythin' sorted an' you get out, come an' look for me then, but just don't … not while you're in there'. It got rid of him, he hasn't rang me since, so I was delighted, I really am.
>
> [YP81]

For young people, maturity brought a greater awareness of the need to distance themselves from old criminal peers and it raised their consciousness about how the most routine activities such as spontaneously meeting old friends on the street could potentially lead to trouble. While maturity had brought greater insight and improved skills to manage situations, it was clear that participants' level of commitment to change acted as the driving force in putting these changes into practice in their everyday lives. Anthony was similar to other desisters in recognizing the ease at which he could get back into trouble again if he was to resume contact with offending peers:

> I broke away from all my old friends about the last six or seven months like. Just too much trouble, just had to be done like. If I wanted to do anything with myself, I had to get away from them like you know? Just can't be around them, that's it 'cause I'd just pick up drugs again like. There'd always be somethin' bad would come out of it like. There's nothin' good goin' to come out of it even if it's only a game of ball chances are you're going to go back maybe a week or two down the line an' you'd have another game of ball an' sure then after a game of ball you'll end up drinkin' an' you'll end up takin' drugs an' gettin' arrested. It's just a chain like, just can't do it like.
>
> [YP75]

Shapland and Bottoms (2011: 274) draw on Kennett's (2001) concept of 'diachronic self-control' to explain the types of strategies adopted by desisters in maintaining their non-offending status. Diachronic self-control refers to the process of managing routine activities in a way that minimizes exposure to temptation. Desisters recounted deliberate efforts to detach from offending peers, in order to avoid the potential of future temptation. For some, it involved staying away from areas such as the city centre where they would have previously engaged in criminal activity. However, the reality for many was that they lived in close proximity to their peers which meant that contact could not be avoided completely. In these contexts, it seemed that desisters had adapted strategies to minimize contact, which included spending substantially less time with them, avoiding certain areas, remaining indoors often for long periods of time, keeping themselves busy and establishing new routines and activities. For these young people, it could be said that desistance from offending and the lifestyle associated with it involved a process of identifying potentially risky situations in advance and developing strategies to overcome them. In so doing, it required young people to consciously side-step, dodge and avoid the litany of illicit enticements and opportunities that were readily available to them.

Offenders' perspectives

For those who disclosed recent offending, their accounts conveyed a strong sense of perceiving themselves to be unable to change their behaviour. Although a small group of six cases, the differences that existed between them highlight the importance of avoiding a tendency to ring-fence non-conformers as a homogenous category. Three participants attributed excessive consumption of alcohol as the main obstacle to desistance and described their inability to stop drinking as the trigger factor for getting into trouble. Losing their temper, getting into fights, becoming involved in public order incidents and assaults were frequent outcomes of their drinking experiences. Although demonstrating insight into their behaviour and attempting on occasions to stop, they described returning repeatedly to the same patterns. Henry's experience was similar to others in his explanation of how getting drunk often culminated in being arrested for further offending:

> I was actually going well for a while like and I got arrested last month. It's hard like, like when you're drinking and you're saying 'oh I'm not going to get in trouble now'. When you get drunk then it's a different story like you know? I don't think about it then, the morning after I'd go 'fuck sake, what did I do?' If I got angry I just wouldn't care like I'd just do stuff and fuck it I don't care about prison like. Then when you calm down again you're like 'ah fuck sake'. That's how easy it is like.
>
> [YP72]

Despite their awareness, none of the three participants anticipated that they would change their drinking habits in the near future. When asked about what would motivate them to stop offending, avoiding prison was a key factor cited. It was especially pertinent for two of the young people who had cases involving serious offences pending in the courts. In this context, they were concerned not to increase the potential risk of a custodial sentence by getting arrested again before their cases were finalized. Lesser significance was attached to the social relationships in their lives than the desister group, but family members were nevertheless cited as a reason for wanting to avoid custody. One young person had become a father in recent months and another, who was living in supported lodgings after periods in residential care, had re-established a relationship with his younger siblings. In both cases, children were identified as important influences on them. For example, when asked to recall an occasion when he was tempted to offend but chose not to, Jason explained that the reason was due to the birth of his child:

> I was goin' to get in a [stolen] car, just said 'fuck it, it's not worth it' 'cause the kid was there, the kid was born so it's not worth it anymore. The kid was born at the time so I says 'it's not worth it any more'.
>
> [YP78]

Two other participants, Joseph and Robert were the most pessimistic about the prospect of change. They explained their offending behaviour as being entirely attributed to external factors and their accounts were characterized by a complete absence of any sense of personal agency about their situation. In Joseph's case, blame for his offending was apportioned to police harassment while Robert gave the need for money, stress related to his home life and the nature of his community as reasons for continued offending. Questions about motivation to stop offending elicited responses that suggested their focus was centred on not getting caught, as described here by Joseph:

> As you're getting older like and you are going in and out of courts like, you realize then the closer you are, the more charges you get, the closer you are to getting to prison like. So the more you realize like, you'd be thinking like if you're caught the probation officer would find out about it and he'd send you back to court like.
>
> [YP71]

When asked, they made no reference to significant social relationships in their lives. They shared similar experiences to young people in the desister group whose parents were involved in the criminal justice system or who were unavailable to them due to addiction and other issues, but they differed in not having any alternative sources of support in their lives. Their attitudes towards offending and to their future involvement in the criminal justice system reflected their broader sense of fatalism towards life in general. This is best captured in the discussion that followed from asking Robert about his motivation to comply:

> My main motivation is just to stay out of them courts. That's really all, just gettin' out of them courts. It's horrible it is. I just don't want to go back to prison. Ye start feelin' depressed an' all that after a while, 'cause yer trapped in yer cell. I don't want to go back to prison – it's not worth it.
> *MS: You've said that quite a bit — it's not worth it – what do you mean by that?*
> It's just not worth goin' down that track 'cause when you get locked up, yer just goin' to keep goin' back an' back an' back, d'ye know like that? Because, they say in prison, wherever ye write your name, you're always

goin' to come back to that. An' one of me mates were in there, has his name all over one of them prison walls, an' ever since he put that there he's always been back to that cell, since he writ his name he's been goin' back to them an' all, so they always say, wherever ye write yer name ye'll always come back.
MS: Who says that?
Me mates that were in there.
MS: And do you believe that?
I do. I've scribbled out all me names, I scribbled all me names out, just in case.

[YP88]

Sam, the final of the six offender cases, stood apart from his peers in that he experienced greater difficulty in articulating his perspective. Questions that required him to reflect on the past or to project to the future yielded limited insights beyond expressing a desire to avoid prison. These limitations were confirmed by his probation officer, who explained that his level of immaturity, ADHD and mild learning disability were factors that resulted in this young person's restricted ability to comprehend rules and to cope in mainstream social situations. The case of Sam was important in demonstrating that chronological age is not always the most effective indicator in decision making about individual maturity and points to the need for flexibility when responding to young people in the criminal justice system. Overall, when examined together, what differed between those who continued to offend and their desisting counterparts was the extent to which the former group perceived themselves to lack control over their lives and offending behaviour. Although disillusioned and frustrated with their continuing involvement in offending, leaving it behind posed a more difficult challenge (Haigh 2009; Maruna 2001).

Conclusion

This chapter explored desistance against the background of late adolescence where young people were commencing the transition to early adulthood. Decisions to comply are mediated by psychological and social factors (Bottoms 2001; Cauffman and Steinberg 2000a) and in this study a key driver was the changes that came about through the process of maturity. Maturity as described by young people was attributed to shifting their subjective perspectives about the utility of offending behaviour and its impact on their family and their future lives. It was also associated with providing the skills and insight to better manage and resist criminal influences. While maturity was perceived as acquiring the tools to stop offending, those who had desisted explained that change was something that they had chosen for themselves. It was an active process that necessitated conscious effort to avoid situations that would place them at risk of reoffending. Maturity also equipped them to address the problems associated with their offending behaviour, which for many involved problematic alcohol and drug use.

For most young people, the process of change unfolded over time and emerged gradually as they came to realize the consequences of their offending behaviour for themselves and others. Feelings of happiness and hope among participants are characteristic of emotions expressed by desisters (Farrall and Calverely 2006). Many participants described themselves as 'a new person' or having a 'new life'. They were positive and upbeat about the future. Yet, they were not detached from the challenges they faced, especially the risk of relapse when living in environments where illicit commodities were easily accessible. Such concerns are warranted given the evidence which suggests that the likelihood of relapse is high for individuals seeking to break free from drug and offending-related lifestyles. Maintaining the decision to stop offending therefore involved ongoing conscious efforts to minimize or avoid individuals and influences that could, if allowed, sabotage their efforts.

In tandem with psychological and cognitive changes as described above, change occurred in young people's social relationships as they developed or rebuilt ties with family, significant others and new non-offending peers and networks. The relationships in their lives were identified as a major factor in motivating and supporting desistance. Family members supported the desistance process by offering practical assistance and encouragement. In cases where young people perceived that their families had stood by them throughout their past involvement in the criminal justice system, they were keen to repay their support by engaging in activities, such as doing what they were asked or taking care of a family member. These activities served to imbue participants with a sense of purpose and gave them opportunities to demonstrate that they had changed; in doing so, they provided additional motivation for young people to continue desisting. Male and female participants differed in their perspectives on the influence of their partners in helping them to avoid future trouble. While young males alluded to the usefulness of the directive guidance and informal social control roles adapted by their female partners in the relationship, the small number of young females described the shame associated with their boyfriends' reactions as a positive deterrent to future offending. Children including younger siblings, relatives and their children emerged as one of the strongest motivating influences associated with desistance. Enjoying time with younger children, wanting to show a good example, and providing a better life for their own children propelled some young people to continue on compliant pathways. Development and change in social bonds such as interpersonal relationships and employment that are associated with the transition to early adulthood weave their way into and through young people's lives in unique ways. As Graham and Bowling (1995) warn, they do not act as a panacea in explaining why desistance occurs. Indeed, as demonstrated in this chapter, individuals' past experiences, current psychological and cognitive orientation and future aspirations are likely to influence the extent to which social changes are perceived as opportunities and motivators to change (Giordano *et al.* 2002).

In the six cases of young people who continued to offend, change was something that they desired, but had not yet achieved. Some demonstrated insight into the obstacles that hindered desistance but felt unable to maintain the changes that they had previously sought to make. Although identifying imprisonment as the main reason for compliance, motivation to comply was partly linked to their wish not to be parted from family members. In other cases, participants believed that factors external to themselves were responsible for their offending behaviour. This in turn affirmed their view that they had a complete absence of control over their situation and ability to change their behaviour. Their perspectives towards compliance and change were reflective of the pessimism and sense of fatalism identified in previous studies of individuals who pursue criminal pathways (Maruna 2001). For them, the threat of losing their freedom through periods of imprisonment was the only motivational influence on their efforts to comply.

Young people's accounts suggested that desistance is a challenging process that requires strong personal agency as well as the input and support of significant others. In line with previous criminal justice research, their narratives demonstrate the important role played by informal social networks – primarily the family – in supporting young people's efforts to change their behaviour (Haines 1990). Their stories further point to the need for the focus of supervision to be firmly grounded in supporting young people's decisions to stop offending and assisting them in maintaining 'longer-term legal compliance' (Bottoms 2001: 89).

10 Conclusion

Despite being centrally relevant to effective supervision practice, encouraging offenders to comply with the requirements of community supervision has been the subject of limited empirical investigation (Ugwudike, 2010; McCulloch, 2010). This book has sought to address part of this gap by examining the processes that underpin compliance against the background of the unique challenges of supervising young offenders in the community. Central among these challenges is that practitioners seek to effect change in young people who by virtue of their age, maturity level, social circumstances and involvement in offending behaviour have limited stakes in conformity. Encouraging compliance through deterrent-based strategies that are underpinned by the threat of future punishment – such as breach proceedings or a custodial sentence – is likely to have less impact on adolescents who are less future-orientated than their adult counterparts (Cauffman and Steinberg 2000a; Scott *et al.* 1995). Indeed, high reconviction rates following custody demonstrates its ineffectiveness in activating compliance in young people (Standing Committee for Youth Justice 2010). Moreover, it points to the need for an alternative strategy to address non-compliance that shifts the emphasis away from reactive measures, to an approach based on preventing or minimizing non-compliance in the first instance. Drawing on a synthesis of the main themes that emerged in this book, the key components of a strategy that seeks to promote compliance with young people beyond a narrow reliance on enforcement-based mechanisms are now mapped out.

Communicating compliance

Promoting compliance through a process of ongoing communication with young people was a central tenet of the approach adopted by practitioners in this study. Communication was facilitated over time through the establishment of positive relationships; however, connecting with young people in the first instance tended to commence from a low baseline given that many of them had been involved in offending behaviour for considerable periods of time, were reluctant to change, and were frequently distrustful of those in authority, including supervisory staff. The relevance of exploring the client's understanding of the community disposal, communicating supervision expectations and the consequences of non-compliance have been highlighted in previous research (Ditton and Ford 1994; Trotter 1999). Practitioners were similarly of the view that where substantial efforts were made prior to, or at the beginning of the supervision period, to ensure that young people fully grasped what compliance entailed, the likelihood of non-compliance declined considerably. This approach, termed 'front-end compliance', was distinguished by practitioners from responses located at the 'back-end' of the process that rely on enforcement proceedings to address non-compliance. Front-end compliance is based on procedural justice principles, in that young people are made aware from the onset about the potential outcomes for failing to comply thereby increasing individual perceptions of fair treatment (Tyler 1990; Fagan and Tyler 2005). That young people were developmentally programmed to think, and act, in the short-term meant that communicating reminders about expectations and the consequences of non-compliance was an ongoing task for supervisors and one that involved relaying the same information in different ways and on different occasions. It appeared to be a successful strategy in that young people attributed these reminders as the most critical factor in helping them remain out of trouble. Findings from Rex's (1999) study pointing to encouragement as a prominent factor in probationers' explanations of what helped them to stop offending also resonated in the experiences of young people in this study. The communicative approach to promoting compliance was a collaborative effort that gave young people a sense of ownership in the process, by negotiating the timing of appointments to facilitate attendance for example, and thereby involving them directly in resolving barriers to non-compliance. Where non-compliance occurred, it was not always the case that formal sanctions followed; however, practitioners were unified in their view that the unacceptable nature of the behaviour had to be consistently communicated and addressed with young people to convey the seriousness of the situation and to foster offenders' perceptions of procedural justice (see Chapter 7). Promoting compliance through ongoing communication was a challenging strategy when working with young people who were not always disposed to taking direction and who tended to have a shorter or less focused attention span than their adult counterparts. Active and participatory modes of communication, such as engaging young people in dialogue and demonstrating compliance through role play and pro-social modelling, were strategies employed to capture and sustain young people's attention over time (see also Trotter 1999). Communicating with young people through medias that they were familiar with increased their responsiveness to their supervisors' expectations. In this regard, sending text messages to remind young people about appointments was a widely adopted strategy to encourage compliance among practitioners.

The offender–supervisor relationship

The centrality of the supervisory relationship as a platform to motivate change in offenders' attitudes towards compliance with the requirements of supervision emerged as a central theme in this book. Practitioners perceived the relationship, not as an end in itself, but as the vehicle to effect change and as a legitimizing influence in the supervision process. The value and legitimacy vested in the relationship was credited by young people to the practical and emotional support provided by their supervisor (see also Rex 1999). Supervisors' willingness to advocate and access services on young people's behalf and the provision of emotional support in resolving individual and family problems was highly valued and strongly contributed to participants' perceptions of the benefit of the supervision process. A further source of legitimacy was located in young people's acknowledgement that their supervisor had continued to work with them, despite periods in the past when they had been unwilling or reluctant to comply. Young people's accounts resonated strongly with research, demonstrating that individuals are more likely to view the law as legitimate and to comply when they perceive that the authorities tasked with implementing it have acted in a procedurally fair manner (Fagan and Tyler 2005; Tyler 1990; Tyler and Huo 2002). The establishment of a positive supervisory relationship formed the basis from which initial ambivalence or hostility towards supervision gave way to a willingness to actively participate at sessions. In essence, it shifted young people's level of involvement over time, from partaking at the minimum level required to avoid sanction (formal compliance) to a situation where they engaged more fully in the process (substantive compliance) (Robinson and McNeill 2010). Furthermore, participants who held positive perceptions of their supervisor were open to directive guidance and welcomed the monitoring aspect of community supervision. Positive perceptions also activated a strong sense of moral obligation to comply in that young people were reluctant to let down their supervisors by reoffending and were also keen to avoid the shame of being confronted with new offences (Makkai and Braithwaite 1994). These findings point to the importance of the supervisory relationship in providing the conditions from which normative mechanisms of compliance are activated (Bottoms 2001). Their relevance is grounded in the evidence which suggests that compliance underpinned by normative motivations is more likely to be sustained in the longer-term (Tyler 1990).

Building personal and social capacity

The social and psychological changes that occurred in young people's lives as they approached early adulthood had direct relevance in explaining their changing perspectives on compliance. In line with previous studies (Barry 2006; Jamieson *et al.* 1999), increased maturity was the most common explanation for behavioural change among young people who had stopped offending. Maturity was attributed to providing a heightened awareness of the consequences of ongoing offending for themselves and others and with enhancing their ability to better manage and resist potential triggers to offending. These findings, coupled with those in the broader desistance literature (Giordano *et al.* 2002; Healy 2010), suggest that there is potential within the supervisory context to enhance compliance by working with young people to support and expedite the development of maturity. Cognitive-behavioural techniques have a long-established history in offender supervision programmes; however, the relevance of psychosocial maturity to young people's decision making as outlined in Chapter 4 suggests that the maturation process might also be enhanced by focusing on psychosocial maturity. The process of developmental maturity may be best facilitated where supervisors can demonstrate compliant behaviour through role play or pro-social modelling as well as through fostering and developing pro-social ties by linking young people to mentoring programmes or education and training opportunities. While maturity may be improved through one-to-one work at supervision appointments, it could be said that opportunities to develop the psychosocial skills required to negotiate a successful transition to adulthood will have greatest impact when applied to real-life contexts in the community.

While maturity was a factor that supported desistance, young people ascribed the decision to stop offending as something that they had consciously chosen for themselves. Nevertheless, like desisters in previous studies (Barry 2006; Shapland and Bottoms 2011), the decision to go straight was challenging and required substantial support and ongoing encouragement from supervisors, family members and significant others. A number of commentators emphasize the importance of social structural factors and opportunities in supporting the desistance process (Bottoms *et al.* 2004; Farrall 2002b; McNeill 2006). The capacity of supervisors to access relevant supports and services that capitalize on their clients' desire to address barriers to desistance offer much promise in any strategy to promote compliance. Peter's experience – outlined in Chapter 8 – of his probation officer's willingness to access alcohol treatment for him after he had made the decision to stop drinking, demonstrates the type of practical assistance that is central to supporting change. This level of responsiveness requires that supervision is individualized to the needs of each offender and that supervisors work in partnership with their clients to identify the issues that both support and act as barriers to desistance. The merit of providing access to opportunities to build social capacity as part of a strategy to promote compliance is borne out in the accounts of many young people who described how their initial reluctance to attend training or education placements changed over time as they came to value the structure it provided to their daily routine, and the sense of achievement that emanated from continued participation and accreditation.

Similar to previous research on offending populations (Haines 1990), both young people and practitioners explained how members of the immediate or extended family provided for young people's needs in ways that supported the desistance process. The case of Anthony – an ex-drug user, who explained that he would not have been able to detox prior to attending drug rehabilitation had his parents not allowed him to return to the family home – highlights the role of the family in supporting compliance (see Chapter 9). The family also played a vital role in supporting desistance through the routine activities of daily life in the home. Being asked to take care of younger siblings or to run errands were the types of activities described by young people as giving them a sense of purpose and a chance to make amends for their previous behaviour. In addition, measures such as being trusted to remain unsupervised in the family home, or noticing that valuable items were no longer locked away, were indicators to young people that their efforts to change were recognized. In subtle ways, these small gestures provided the type of acknowledgement that has previously been identified as important to offenders in assisting their efforts to change (McIvor 2009; Maruna 2001). The role of the family in supporting young people as they moved away from offending behaviour reiterates the critical relevance of supporting families as a strategy to encourage 'longer-term legal compliance' (Bottoms 2001: 89). Furthermore, it points to the need to establish a strong relationship with the family from the start of supervision, so as to be best placed to strengthen their capacity to support the desistance process in the longer-term.

Interpreting compliance in practice

While legal, policy and organizational directives may impose the formal parameters of what defines non-compliance, as front-line decision makers, practitioners and their managers play an important role in interpreting young people's behaviour and determining what constitutes non-compliance. Where behaviour is interpreted as non-compliance, it potentially places young people at increased risk of being further processed through the criminal justice system. While non-compliance is most commonly conceived of in legal and policy terms as non-attendance at scheduled appointments, the evidence presented in this book indicates that practitioners' assessments of young people's compliance extended beyond an expectation to attend appointments and included judgement about their willingness to participate at supervisory sessions. Furthermore, it incorporated perceptions about young people's behaviour at home, at school and in the community (see Chapter 6). Practitioners' accounts suggest that a narrative script of compliance is constructed, based on the client's attitude and behaviour within and outside of appointments, which in turn forms the basis of decision making when incidents of non-compliance occur. The point is best demonstrated by Michael – in Chapter 8 – who explained that since he had given up drugs and stopped offending, he was no longer admonished for cancelling appointments in the way that he would have been in the past. If we are to draw implications from Michael's observation, it might be that how compliance is conceptualized by practitioners is likely to be shaped and influenced by changes in young people's social and psychological orientation towards compliance over time. It also suggests that compliance is constructed on an ongoing basis throughout the supervision period through the interactions that take place between young people and their supervisors.

One of the main challenges identified by practitioners in interpreting young people's behaviour as non-compliant was the difficulty of distinguishing between behaviour that was indicative of an outright unwillingness to contemplate change, from that which was related to such factors as immaturity, poor communication skills, cognitive difficulties or trauma-related attachment issues. The relevance of making such distinctions is particularly pertinent given the prevalence of emotional, psychological, learning and behavioural difficulties in the profile population of young people in the criminal justice system (Hayes and O'Reilly

2007; Tolan and Titus 2009). The case identified by two practitioners in Chapter 7 who described working with a young person for more than two months before he gradually opened up to them, suggests that caution must be exercised to ensure that adolescent immaturity or cognitive or emotional problems are not mistaken for non-compliance. It was in these more complex cases where practitioners described the need to rely on their training, professional discretion, and consultation with line managers to unpack the underpinning narrative of compliance. The complexity and uniqueness of young people's circumstances highlights the pivotal nature of professional discretion in the provision of fair and equitable outcomes for young people (see also Eadie and Canton 2002). It also demonstrates the importance of having trained youth justice specialists, backed up by a supportive management structure, involved in the assessment and supervision of young people's cases. Emphasizing the role of practitioners in determining what constitutes non-compliance is not to downplay the influence of organizational policy in deciding how compliance is defined in practice. Nor is to neglect the broader youth justice context within which practitioners operate. Indeed, as outlined in Chapter 2, the ethos and value-base of the youth justice system in each jurisdiction are likely to exert the strongest influence in determining how young people deemed to be non-compliant will be defined, categorized and processed through the criminal justice system. Rather, the intention is to highlight the subjective and interactive processes involved in constructing compliance and to signal the dangers involved where stringent limitations are imposed on practitioner and managerial discretion.

Although its significance in the supervision of young offenders varies considerably between jurisdictions (Bateman 2011; Batchelor and Burman 2010; Maxwell and Morris (2006), enforcement as a strategy to encourage compliance continues to retain prominence in the context of community disposals. That said, emerging policy developments, theory and research point to a gradual shift towards exploring the potential of adopting policy and practice approaches that promote compliance beyond a reliance on enforcement procedures (PBNI 2011; Robinson and McNeill 2010; Ugwudike 2010). The advancement of practice in this direction offers much promise given that the mechanisms that underpin compliant behaviour are likely to differ between individual offenders and to vary over time (Bottoms 2001; Robinson and McNeill 2010). As argued in this book, compliance-based practice is especially important for young people, who are least likely to be psychologically programmed or adequately socially located to be deterred by stringent enforcement action.

Notes

1 Introduction

1 Five focus groups were facilitated in total. Two each were held with YPP and YJA staff respectively and one was completed with PBNI staff. In lieu of a second PBNI focus group, interviews were held with five individual probation officers. This was due to the logistical challenges of bringing together staff that were geographically dispersed throughout the region for a focus group in one location. Measures were put in place to ensure that these data were not over-represented in the study and to this end, data were analysed collectively using a similar approach to the focus group data analysis.

2 The care of horses is seen as an important social role for Traveller men and is perceived as a full-time occupation (Irish Traveller Movement n.d.).

2 Responding to non-compliance with the requirements of community disposals

1 The Ministry of Justice (2011a: 48) defines breach of a statutory order as follows: 'Breach of statutory order or of conditional discharge is an offence of failing without reasonable excuse to comply with the requirements of an existing statutory order or the conditions of a discharge. The offence is only counted where the failure is proved to the satisfaction of the court and the original order is revoked and/or an additional order or other disposal is imposed'.

2 Technical violations are described as violations of probation, parole, or valid court orders; acts that disobey or go against the conditions of probation or parole. Committed youth/juveniles placed in a facility as part of a court-ordered disposal have been adjudicated and disposed in juvenile court or convicted and sentenced in criminal court – see Glossary http://www.ojjdp.gov/ojstatbb/ezacjrp/ (accessed 31 January 2012).

3 Charges were aggregated on the first date of appearance in youth court in 2001–02. In all, 38 per cent of failure to comply cases related to a single failure to comply, 17.5 per cent involved multiple failures to comply while just over one-third (37 per cent) contained criminal offences alongside a failure to comply charge(s). The remainder were accounted for by administrative or criminal code charges.

4 Although minority youth are overrepresented in the custodial system, Hart (2011) reports that in England and Wales, white youth are more likely to be in custody for breach-related offences. US data suggest that technical violations were the most serious offence for 18 per cent of Hispanic youth, compared with 13 per cent of white, American Indian and Asian youth and 12 per cent of black youth in 2010. Taken as a whole, national data are likely to mask state-wide differences and further investigation is required to explain the processes involved (Sickmund *et al.* 2011).

5 Hart (2011: 27) notes that not all individuals on YOT interventions are eligible for the breach meeting process 'due to overriding risk assessments and risk management plans'.

3 Compliance theory, research and practice

1 Prochaska *et al.* (1992) 'stages of change' model offers a framework for understanding variations in individuals' readiness for change. The model suggests that offenders require different types of support based on their position within the change process as they pass through the cyclical phases of pre-contemplation (not thinking of changing one's behaviour), contemplation (seriously considering changing one's behaviour in the near future), preparation (making plans and intending to change one's behaviour in the very near future, may have started to make minor changes), action (engaged in changing one's behaviour) and maintenance (working to consolidate gains from one's changed behaviour and prevent relapse). Individuals may move back and forth between stages as part of the process of change.
2 EURO-JUSTIS is a research project with nine partners in seven EU member states. According to Hough *et al.* (2011: 251) the aim of the project is to 'develop tools to enable evidence-based assessment of public trust in justice and feelings of security across Europe'.
3 The scheme, originally launched in 1995, incentivizes prisoners to conform by linking rewards to conduct and performance. Overall, the scheme seeks to promote responsible behaviour in prisoners and encourages participation in work, sentence planning, activities designed to reduce reoffending and other constructive action.
4 Moral reasons included that 'offending was no longer what they wanted to do. It was not who they wanted to be. It would interfere with what they wanted to achieve in life. It would upset those they cared about' (Shapland and Bottoms, 2011: 272–3).

4 The context of community supervision: adolescent development and social circumstances

1 The sample consisted of 40 per cent African American, 23 per cent Hispanic, 35 per cent non-Hispanic white, 1 per cent Asian and 1 per cent other ethnic identities. Males made up 56.8 per cent of the community sample and 66.3 per cent of the detained sample. On average, three-quarters of all participants were categorized in the two lowest socio-economic classes (Grisso *et al.* 2003).
2 The wording of the warning is as follows: You have the right to remain silent. Anything you say can and will be used against you in a court of law. You have the right to speak to an attorney, and to have an attorney present during any questioning. If you cannot afford a lawyer, one will be provided for you at government expense (Miranda vs. Arizona).
3 Wikström and Butterworth (2006) drew on the work of Grasmick *et al.* (1993) in developing a scale to measure self-control.
4 An anecdotal example is where young offenders opt for a short period of detention rather than agreeing to complete a longer programme of rehabilitation in the community which would require them to address offending-related issues as well as their social and personal problems.
5 Here, exposure to severe violence was significantly related to violent crime and relationship violence in early adulthood.
6 In 44 of the 149 cases young people had completed the minimum amount of education required under statute, i.e. to remain in school until 16 years or to complete three years of post-primary education. However, it is not clear if some of these cases were accounted for within the 21 cases who were still at school.

5 The social and criminal justice context of supervising young offenders

1 These data only represent incidents that were reported to the police. Anecdotal evidence suggests that the actual number of incidents is likely to be considerably higher.
2 Recent criticism has been levelled at governmental progress in implementing the Strategy by a team of external experts tasked with reviewing the youth justice system in Northern Ireland. They argued that fresh impetus and commitment was needed in order for the Strategy to have a real impact on children's lives (see DOJ 2011).
3 Offences which are not automatically eligible for youth conferencing include: 'offences with a penalty of life imprisonment, offences which are triable, in the case of an adult, on indictment only and scheduled offences which fall under the Terrorism Act (2000)' (O'Mahony and Campbell, 2006: 102).
4 A review of the youth justice system in Northern Ireland published in late 2011 recommended that the age of criminal responsibility be raised to 12 years with immediate effect (DOJ 2011).
5 The Indeterminate Custodial Sentence (ICS) is intended for the most serious violent and sexual offences. The court sets the minimum custodial period (not less than two years) before an individual can be considered for release and remission does not apply. If released, lifetime supervision under licence may be a requirement. The Extended Custodial Sentence (ECS) is the second sentence and applies to violent and sexual offences where the maximum penalty does not exceed 10 years. Sentences are determinate and require a stipulated period of custody and supervision under licence. Eligibility to be considered for release occurs when half of the custodial period is served and periods of supervision may extend up to five years for violent offenders and eight years for sexual offenders.
6 In practice, electronic monitoring is used mainly as a condition of bail for young people in Northern Ireland.
7 Referrals are recorded by primary offence on each occasion.
8 A reduction in the numbers of young people held within the prison service estate in Northern Ireland has been reported and attributed to combined input from the NIPS, the PBNI and the YJA to reduce the number of juveniles held on remand in Hydebank Wood in Belfast. In a further development, the Minister for Justice in Northern Ireland announced in June 2012 that in all but the most exceptional circumstances, young offenders under 18 years would no longer be detained at Hydebank Wood from 1 November 2012.
9 Interview with Key Informant, 11 February 2011.
10 Section 52(2), Children Act 2001 (as substituted under section 129, Criminal Justice Act 2006). Furthermore, in the case of a child up to 14 years charged with a criminal offence, no further proceedings can be taken (other than remand on bail or in custody) except by, or with the consent of, the Director of Public Prosecution (DPP). Section 52(4), Children Act 2001 (as substituted under section 129, Criminal Justice Act 2006).
11 There are exceptions to this rule where a child is charged with an offence, such as if it is considered in the public interest, to avoid an injustice to the child or if the child is unlawfully at large. Reporting restrictions also apply to children subject to Behaviour Orders but they can be lifted to ensure the order is complied with.
12 Other referrals included a very small number of statutory orders such as attendance centre orders (48 cases), community responsibility orders (49 cases) and reparation orders (two cases) (Tate and Lyness 2011).
13 Figures provided by the PBNI Research and Statistics Unit 14 January 2011.
14 Outside of these areas, young people are supervised as part of a generic youth–adult caseload.

15 Data are based on the caseload as of December 2011. Age was calculated based on the court date when the referal was made to the Probation Service (Probation Service 2012).

6 Constructing compliance on offender supervision

1 In October 2011, PBNI introduced a new Best Practice Framework which incorporated a revised version of the Northern Ireland Standards as well as detailed Best Practice Guidance to support professional judgement in the application of standards. A key change is that Standards and Best Practice Guidance are now applied at three different levels: lower, standard and higher, and have direct implications across all aspects of probation work including the level of contact maintained with offenders. The level of application is based on professional judgement, criteria relating to the level of application, and with a view to minimizing risks to the community and to others (see PBNI 2011).

7 Promoting compliance and responding to non-compliance as part of the supervision process

1 Findings from a study of an Intensive Probation Programme for young offenders conducted in Northern Ireland had the benefit of criminal record data that provided the date of offence as well as date of reconviction. It was therefore possible to identify that half of those who were reconvicted within two years had first reoffended within five weeks of being first placed on the programme (Seymour 2003).

2 For instance, teenage female clients from the Roma community were often married and parents were not involved in their cases, while in some communities practitioners described a relatively high prevalence of grandparents with direct responsibility for young people whose parents were often deceased. A main factor of this phenomenon was attributed to the impact on mortality rates arising from the heroin epidemic in Dublin in the 1980s and early 1990s.

8 Young people's perspectives on the supervision process

1 In the small number of cases where this occurred, young people and their probation officers reported that they had been given another opportunity from the courts to engage in probation supervision.

2 Probation officers were asked about their expectations of compliance within the supervisory context. They were asked to describe each young person's compliance in terms of attendance at sessions, participation at sessions, reoffending and overall level of compliance over time.

9 Young people's perspectives on transition, change and desistance

1 Her probation officer corroborated this view and outlined that it was six to nine months or more after the assault before YP80 'began to turn her life around', returned to school and availed of the extensive support provided through the school and by addiction services.

Bibliography

Altschuler, D. and Armstrong, T. (2001) 'Reintegrating high-risk juvenile offenders into communities: experiences and prospects', *Corrections Management Quarterly*, 5(3): 72–88.

Altschuler, D. and Brash, R. (2004) 'Adolescent and teenage offenders confronting the challenges and opportunities of reentry', *Youth Violence and Juvenile Justice*, 2(1): 72–87.

An Garda Síochána (2011) *Annual Report of the Committee Appointed to Monitor the Effectiveness of the Diversion Programme 2010*. Dublin: An Garda Síochána.

Arthur, R. (2005) 'Punishing parents for the crimes of their children', *Howard Journal of Criminal Justice*, 44(3): 233–53.

Audit Commission (2004) *Youth Justice: A Review of the Reformed Youth Justice System*. London: Audit Commission.

Auld, J., Gormally, B., McEvoy, K., and Ritchie, M. (1997) *Designing a System of Restorative Community Justice in Northern Ireland: A Discussion Document*. Belfast: The Authors.

Ayres, I. and Braithwaite, J. (1992) *Responsive Regulation: Transcending the Deregulation Debate*. New York: Oxford University Press.

Bamford Review of Mental Health and Learning Disability (N. Ireland) (2006) *A Vision of a Comprehensive Child and Adolescent Mental Health Service*. Online. Available at: <http://www.dhsspsni.gov.uk/camh-vision-comprehensive-service.pdf> (accessed 31 January 2012).

Barry, M. (2006) *Youth Offending in Transition: The Search for Social Recognition*. Abingdon: Routledge.

Barry, M. (2007) 'Youth offending and youth transitions: the power of capital in influencing change', *Critical Criminology*, 15(2): 185–98.

Barry, M. (2010) 'Youth transitions: from offending to desistance', *Journal of Youth Studies*, 13(1): 121–36.

Barry, M. (2011) 'Explaining youth custody in Scotland: the new crisis of containment and convergence', *Howard Journal of Criminal Justice*, 50(2): 153–70.

Batchelor, S. and Burman, M. (2010) 'The children's hearing system', in J. Johnstone and M. Burman (eds) *Youth Justice Series: Policy and Practice in Health and Social Care (9)*. Edinburgh: Dunedin Academic Press.

Bateman, T. (2011) '"We now breach more kids in a week than we used to in a whole year": the punitive turn, enforcement and custody', *Youth Justice*, 11(2): 115–33.

Bazeley, P. (2009) 'Analysing qualitative data: more than "identifying themes"', *Malaysian Journal of Qualitative Research*, 2(2): 6–22.

Bazemore, G. and Schiff, M. (1996) 'Community justice/restorative justice: prospects for a new social ecology for community corrections', *International Journal of Comparative and Applied Criminal Justice*, 20(2): 311–35.

Bazemore, G. and Schiff, M. (2005) *Juvenile Justice Reform and Restorative Justice: Building Theory and Policy from Practice*. Cullompton: Willan Publishing.

Beetham, D. (1991) *The Legitimation of Power*. London: Macmillan Education Ltd.

Belfast Telegraph (2010) 'Call to tackle Northern Ireland segregation with mixed housing estates', 28 May 2010.

Berman, A. (2005) 'Throw out the bathwater but keep the baby! The role of the supervisory relationship in "what works" initiatives among Swedish male probationers', *British Journal of Community Justice*, 3(3): 15–30.

Berridge, D., Brodie, I., Pitts, J., Porteous, D., and Tarling, R. (2001) *The Independent Effects of Permanent Exclusion from School on the Offending Careers of Young People Home Office Occasional Paper No. 71*. London: Home Office.

Bishop, D., Leiber, M., and Johnson, J. (2010) 'Contexts of decision making in the juvenile justice system: an organizational approach to understanding minority over-representation', *Youth Violence and Juvenile Justice*, 8(3): 213–33.

Bonnie, R. and Grisso, T. (2000) 'Adjudicative competence and youthful offenders', in T. Grisso and R. Scwartz (eds) *Youth on Trial: A Developmental Perspective on Juvenile Justice*. Chicago: University of Chicago Press.

Boswell, G. (1996) 'The essential skills of probation work', in T. May and A. Vass (eds) *Working with Offenders: Issues Contexts and Outcomes*. London: Sage Publications.

Bosworth, M. and Carrabine, E. (2001) 'Reassessing resistance: race, gender and sexuality in prison', *Punishment and Society*, 3(4): 501–15.

Bottoms, A. (2001) 'Compliance and community penalties', in A. Bottoms, L. Gelsthorpe and S. Rex (eds) *Community Penalties: Change and Challenges*. Cullompton: Willan Publishing.

Bottoms, A. and Shapland, J. (2011) 'Steps towards desistance among male young adult recidivists', in S. Farrall, M. Hough, S. Maruna, and R. Sparks (eds) *Escape Routes: Contemporary Perspectives on Life After Punishment*. Abingdon: Routledge.

Bottoms, A., Gelsthorpe, L., and Rex, S. (2001) 'Concluding reflections', in A. Bottoms, L. Gelsthorpe and S. Rex (eds) *Community Penalties: Change and Challenges*. Cullompton: Willan Publishing.

Bottoms, A., Shapland, J., Costello, A., Holmes, D. and Muir, G. (2004) 'Towards desistance: theoretical underpinnings for an empirical study', *Howard Journal of Criminal Justice*, 43(4): 368–89.

Boyle, J. (2008) *Evaluation of Intensive Support and Monitoring Services (ISMS) within the Children's Hearings System*. Edinburgh: Scottish Government. Online. Available at: <http://www.scotland.gov.uk/Resource/Doc/234329/0064165.pdf> (accessed 31 January 2012).

Braithwaite, J. (1989) *Crime, Shame and Reintegration*. Cambridge: Cambridge University Press.

Braithwaite, J. and Mugford, S. (1994) 'Conditions of successful reintegration ceremonies dealing with juvenile offenders', *British Journal of Criminology*, 34(2): 139–71.

Braithwaite, V. (2003) 'Dancing with tax authorities: motivational postures and non-compliant actions', in V. Braithwaite (ed.) *Taxing Democracy: Understanding Tax Avoidance and Evasion*. Aldershot: Ashgate.

Brown, S. (1995) 'Crime and safety in whose "community"? Age, everyday life, and problems for youth policy', *Youth and Policy: The Journal of Critical Analysis*, 48: 27–48.

Brown, S. (1998) *Understanding Youth and Crime: Listening to Youth*? Buckingham: Open University Press.

Bryan-Hancock, C. and Casey, S. (2010) 'Psychological maturity of at-risk juveniles, young adults and adults: implications for the justice system', *Psychiatry, Psychology and Law*, 17(1):57–69.

Bryan-Hancock, C. and Casey, S. (2011) 'Young people and the justice system: consideration of maturity in criminal responsibility', *Psychiatry, Psychology and Law*, 18(1): 69–78.

Burke, H., Carney, C., and Cook, G. (1981) *Youth and Justice: Young Offenders in Ireland*. Dublin: Turoe Press.

Burnett, D., Noblin, C., and Prosser, V. (2004) 'Adjudicative competency in a juvenile population', *Criminal Justice and Behavior*, 31(4): 438–62.

Burnett, R. and McNeill, F. (2005) 'The place of the officer-offender relationship in assisting offenders to desist from crime', *Probation Journal*, 52(3): 221–42.

Burnett, R. and Maruna, S. (2006) 'The kindness of prisoners: strengths-based resettlement in theory and in action', *Criminology and Criminal Justice*, 6(1): 83–106.

Byrne, B., McCoy, S., and Watson, D. (2008) *School Leavers' Survey Report 2007*. Dublin: The Economic and Social Research Institute and Department of Education and Science.

Byrne, D. and Smyth, E. (2010) *No Way Back? The Dynamics of Early School Leaving*. Dublin: Liffey Press.

Campbell, C., Devlin, R., O'Mahony, D., Doak, J., Jackson, J., Corrigan T., and McEvoy, K. (2005) *Evaluation of the Northern Ireland Youth Conference Service, NIO Research and Statistical Series: Report No. 12*. Belfast: Northern Ireland Office, Research and Statistics Branch.

Campbell, L. (2010) 'Responding to gun crime in Ireland', *British Journal of Criminology*, 50(3): 414–34.

Canton, R. and Eadie, T. (2008) *Accountability, Legitimacy, and Discretion: Applying Criminology in Professional Practice*, in B. Stout, J. Yates and B. Williams (eds) *Applied Criminology*. London: Sage Publications.

Cardenas, S. (2007) *Conflict and Compliance State Responses to International Human Rights Pressure*. Philadelphia: University of Pennsylvania Press.

Carr, N. (2008) 'Minorities and youth justice: an Irish concern?', in ACJRD (ed.) *Minorities, Crime and Justice, ACJRD 11th Annual Conference 2008*. Dublin: Association for Criminal Justice Research and Development.

Carroll, J. and Meehan, E. (2007) *The Children Court: A National Study*. Dublin: Association for Criminal Justice Research and Development.

Case, S. (2006) 'Young people "at risk" of what? Challenging risk-focused early intervention as crime prevention', *Youth Justice*, 6(3): 171–9.

Case, S. (2007) 'Questioning the "evidence" of risk that underpins evidence-led youth justice interventions', *Youth Justice*, 7(2): 91–105.

Case, S. and Haines, K. (2009) *Understanding Youth Offending: Risk Factor Research, Policy and Practice*. Cullompton: Willan Publishing.

Cauffman, E. and Steinberg, L. (2000a) '(Im)maturity of judgment in adolescence: why adolescents may be less culpable than adults', *Behavioral Sciences and the Law*, 18(6): 741–60.

Cauffman, E. and Steinberg, L. (2000b) 'Researching adolescents' judgment and culpability', in T. Grisso and R. Schwartz (eds) *Youth on Trial: A Developmental Perspective on Juvenile Justice*. Chicago: University of Chicago Press.

Central Statistics Office (2011a) *Census of Population 2011 Preliminary Results*. Dublin: Central Statistics Office.

Central Statistics Office (2011b) *Quarterly National Household Survey Quarter 3 2011 (December 2011)*. Dublin: Central Statistics Office.

Cernkovich, S. and Giordano, P. (2001) 'Stability and change in antisocial behavior: the transition from adolescence to early adulthood', *Criminology* 39(2): 371–410.

Cesaroni, C. and Alvi, S. (2010) 'Masculinity and resistance in adolescent carceral settings', *Canadian Journal of Criminology and Criminal Justice*, 52(3): 303–20.

Chablani, A. and Spinney, E. (2011) 'Engaging high-risk young mothers into effective programming: the importance of relationships and relentlessness', *Journal of Family Social Work*, 14(4): 369–83.

Chapman, T. (2000) *Time to Grow: A Comprehensive Programme for People Working with Young Offenders and Young People at Risk*. Lyme Regis, Dorset: Russell House Publishing.

Chapman, T. and Hough, M. (1998) *Evidence Based Practice: A Guide to Effective Practice*. London: Her Majesty's Inspectorate of Probation.

Charmaz, K. (2006) *Constructing Grounded Theory: A Practical Guide Through Qualitative Analysis*. London: Sage Publications.

Children and Young Persons Review Group (1979) *Report of the Children and Young Persons Review Group (The Black Report)*. Belfast: The Stationery Office.

Chitsabesan, P., Bailey, S., Williams, R., Kroll, L., Kenning, C., and Talbot, L. (2007) 'Learning disabilities and educational needs of juvenile offenders', *Journal of Children's Services*, 2(4): 4–17.

Clear, T. and Latessa, E. (1993) 'Probation officers' roles in intensive supervision: surveillance vs. treatment', *Justice Quarterly*, 10(3): 441–62.

Clear, T., Rose, D., and Ryder, J. (2001) 'Incarceration and the community: the problem of removing and returning offenders', *Crime and Delinquency*, 47(3): 335–51.

Cloward, R. (1959) 'Illegitimate means, anomie, and deviant behaviour', *American Sociological Review*, 24(2): 164–76.

Colwell, L., Cruise, K., Guy, L., McCoy, W., Fernandez, K., and Ross, H. (2005) 'The influence of psychosocial maturity on male juvenile offenders' comprehension and understanding of the *Miranda* warning', *The Journal of the American Academy of Psychiatry and the Law*, 33(4): 444–54.

Combat Poverty Agency (2004) *Annual Report 2004*. Dublin: Combat Poverty Agency.

Commission to Inquire into Child Abuse (2009) *Final Report of the Commission to Inquire into Child Abuse*. Online. Available at: <http://www.childabusecommission.com/rpt/pdfs/> (accessed 31 January 2012).

Committee of Inquiry into the Penal System (1985) *Report of the Committee of Inquiry into the Penal System (The Whitaker Report)*. Dublin: The Stationery Office.

Committee on Reformatory and Industrial Schools Systems (1970) *Reformatory and Industrial Schools Systems Report (Kennedy Report)*. Dublin: The Stationery Office.

Convery, U., Haydon, D., Moore, L., and Scraton, P. (2008) 'Children, rights and justice in Northern Ireland: community and custody', *Youth Justice*, 8(3): 245–63.

Corcoran, M., Gray, J., and Peillon, M. (2007) 'Ties that bind? The social fabric of daily life in new suburbs', in T. Fahey, H. Russell, and C. Whelan (eds) *Best of times? The Social Impact of the Celtic Tiger*. Dublin: Institute of Public Administration.

Council of Europe (2008) *Recommendation CM/Rec (2008) 11 of the Committee of Ministers to Member States on the European Rules for Juvenile Offenders Subject to Sanctions or Measures*. Strasbourg: Council of Europe.

Court Service (2011) *Annual Report of the Court Service 2010*. Dublin: The Stationery Office.

Covington, S. (2008) 'The relational theory of women's psychological development: implications for the criminal justice system', in R. Zaplin (ed.) *Female Offenders: Critical Perspectives and Effective Interventions,* 2nd edn. London: Jones and Bartlett Publishers.

Crawford, A. (2009) 'Criminalizing sociability through anti-social behaviour legislation: dispersal powers, young people and the police', *Youth Justice*, 9(1): 5–26.

Crawford, A. and Newburn, T. (2003) *Youth Offending and Restorative Justice: Implementing Reform in Youth Justice*. Cullompton: Willan Publishing.

Crewe, B. (2007) 'Power, adaptation and resistance in a late-modern men's prison', *British Journal of Criminology*, 47(2): 256–75.

Criminal Justice Inspection NI (2008) *Youth Conference Service: Inspection of the Youth Conference Service in Northern Ireland*. Belfast: Criminal Justice Inspection Northern Ireland.

Criminal Justice Inspection (NI) (2011) *An Inspection of Prisoner Resettlement by the Northern Ireland Prison Service*. Belfast: Criminal Justice Inspection Northern Ireland.

Criminal Justice Review Group (2000) *Review of the Criminal Justice System in Northern Ireland*. Belfast: The Stationery Office.

Cruise, K., Fernandez, K., McCoy, W., Guy, L., Colwell, L., and Douglas, T. (2008) 'The influence of psychosocial maturity on adolescent offenders' delinquent behavior', *Youth Violence and Juvenile Justice* 6(2): 178–94.

Dáil Éireann Select Committee on Crime (1992) *Juvenile Crime - Its Causes and its Remedies*. Dublin: The Stationery Office.

Dawson, H., Dunn, S., and Morgan, V. (2007) *Evaluation of the Attendance Centre Order Final Report*. Belfast: Northern Ireland Office. Online. Available at <http://www.youthjusticeagencyni.gov.uk/publications_library/> (accessed 31 January 2012).

Dawson, H., Dunn, S., Morgan, V., and Hayes, A. (2004) *Evaluation of Youth Justice Agency Community Services, NIO Research and Statistical Series: Report No.11*. Belfast: Northern Ireland Office, Statistics and Research Branch.

Denov, M. (2004) 'Children's rights or rhetoric? Assessing Canada's youth criminal justice act and its compliance with the UN Convention on the Rights of the Child', *International Journal of Children's Rights* 12(1): 1–20.

Department of Education Northern Ireland (2011) *Enrolments at Schools and in Funded Pre-School Education in Northern Ireland 2010/11 (Revised)*. Belfast: Department of Education. Online. Available at: <http://www.deni.gov.uk/enrolments_at_schools_and_in_funded_preschool_education_2010_11__revised_.pdf> (accessed 31 January 2012).

Department of Justice (DOJ) (2011) *A Review of the Youth Justice System in Northern Ireland*. Belfast: Department of Justice.

Department of Justice, Equality and Law Reform (2006) *Report on the Youth Justice Review*. Dublin: The Stationery Office.

de Winter, M. and Noom, M. (2003) 'Someone who treats you as an ordinary human being ... homeless youth examine the quality of professional care', *British Journal of Social Work*, 33(3): 325–37.

Ditton, J. and Ford, R. (1994) *The Reality of Probation*. Aldershot: Avebury.

Donnellan, M. and McCaughey, B. (2010) 'The public protection advisory group: a model for structured co-operation', *Irish Probation Journal*, 7: 6–14.

Doran, P. and Cooper, L. (2008) 'Social work: The core qualification of probation officers in Northern Ireland', *Irish Probation Journal*, 5: 23–35.

Doran, P., Duncan, L., Gault, L., and Hewitt, R. (2010) 'Probation Board for Northern Ireland service users survey', *Irish Probation Journal*, 7: 133–9.

Dowden, C. and Andrews, D. (2004) 'The importance of staff practice in delivering effective correctional treatment: a meta-analytic review of core correctional practice', *International Journal of Offender Therapy and Comparative Criminology*, 48(2): 203–14.

Drakeford, M. (2010) 'Devolution and youth justice in Wales', *Criminology and Criminal Justice* 10(2): 137–54.

Eadie, T. (2000) 'From befriending to punishing: changing boundaries in the probation service', in N. Malin (ed.) *Professionalism, Boundaries and the Workplace.* London: Routledge.

Eadie, T. and Canton, R. (2002) 'Practising in a context of ambivalence: the challenge for youth justice workers', *Youth Justice*, 2(1): 14–26.

Ellis, T., Heddermann, C., and Mortimer, E. (1996) *Enforcing Community Sentences: Supervisors' Perspectives on Ensuring Compliance and Dealing with Breach, Home Office Research Study No.158*. London: Home Office.

Eriksson, A. (2009) *Justice in Transition: Community Restorative Justice in Northern Ireland*. Cullompton: Willan Publishing.

Etzioni, A. (1961) *A Comparative Analysis of Complex Organizations*. New York: Free Press.

European Committee for the Prevention of Torture and Inhuman or Degrading Treatment or Punishment (CPT) (2007) *Report to the Government of Ireland on the Visit to Ireland Carried out by the European Committee for the Prevention of Torture and Inhuman or Degrading Treatment or Punishment CPT/Inf (2007) 40*. Strasbourg: Council of Europe.

Expert Group on the Probation and Welfare Service (1999) *Final Report*. Dublin: Stationery Office.

Ezell, M. and Cohen, L. (2005) *Desisting from Crime: Continuity and Change in Long-Term Crime Patterns of Serious Chronic Offenders*. Oxford: Oxford University Press.

Fagan, J. (2000) 'Contexts of choice by adolescents in criminal events', in T. Grisso and R. Schwartz (eds) *Youth on Trial: A Developmental Perspective on Juvenile Justice*. Chicago: University of Chicago Press.

Fagan, J. and Tyler, T. (2005) 'Legal socialization of children and adolescents', *Social Justice Research*, 18(3): 217–42.

Farrall, S. (2002a) *Rethinking What Works with Offenders: Probation, Social Context and Desistance from Crime*. Cullompton: Willan Publishing.

Farrall, S. (2002b) 'Long-term absences from probation: officers' and probationers' accounts', *Howard Journal of Criminal Justice*, 41(3): 263–78.

Farrall, S. and Calverley, A. (2006) *Understanding Desistance from Crime: Theoretical Directions in Resettlement and Rehabilitation*. Maidenhead: Open University Press.

Farrall, S., Bottoms, A., and Shapland, J. (2010) 'Social structures and desistance from crime', *European Journal of Criminology*, 7(6): 546–70.

Fawcett, M. (2000) 'The changing family in Northern Ireland: young people and divorce', *Youth and Society*, 32(1): 81–106.

Fay, M., Morrissey, M., and Smyth, M. (1998) *Mapping Troubles-Related Deaths and Deprivation in Northern Ireland*. Belfast: INCORE/CTS.

Field, S. (2007) 'Practice cultures and the "new" youth justice in (England and) Wales', *British Journal of Criminology*, 47(2): 311–30.

Field, S. and Nelken, D. (2010) 'Reading and writing youth justice in Italy and (England and) Wales', *Punishment and Society*, 12(3): 287–308.

Findlay, M. (1993) 'Police authority, respect and shaming', *Current Issues in Criminal Justice*, 5(1): 29–41.

Fitzgibbon, W., Hamilton, C., and Richardson, M. (2010) 'A risky business: an examination of Irish probation officers' attitudes towards risk assessment', *Probation Journal*, 57(2): 163–74.

Fitzpatrick, A. (2011) 'A review of the role of anti-social behaviour orders in the context of youth justice in Ireland', unpublished thesis, Dublin Institute of Technology.

Flood-Page, C., Campbell, S., Harrington, V., and Miller, J. (2000) *Youth Crime: Findings from the 1998/1999 Youth Lifestyles Survey. Home Office Research Study No. 209.* London: Home Office.

Ford, M., Wentzel, K., Wood, D., Stevens, E., and Siesfeld, G. (1989) 'Processes associated with integrative social competence: emotional and contextual influences on adolescent social responsibility', *Journal of Adolescent Research*, 4(4): 405–25.

Freeman, S. and Seymour, M. (2010) '"Just waiting": The nature and effect of uncertainty on young people in remand custody in Ireland', *Youth Justice*, 10(2): 126–42.

French, J. and Raven, B. (1959) 'The bases of social power', in D. Cartwright (ed.) *Studies in Social Power.* Ann Arbor: Institute for Social Research, University of Michigan Press.

Fried, C. and Reppucci, N. (2001) 'Criminal decision making: the development of adolescent judgment, criminal responsibility and culpability', *Law and Human Behavior*, 25(1): 45–61.

Fulton, B. (2008) 'Northern Ireland', in A. van Kalmthout and I. Durnescu (eds) *Probation in Europe.* Nijmegen: Wolf Legal Publishers.

Fulton, B., Latessa, E., Stichman, A., Travis, L. Corbett, R., and Harris, M. (1997) 'A review of research for practitioners', *Federal Probation*, 61(4): 65–75.

Galaway, B. (1988) 'Crime victim and offender mediation as a social work strategy', *Social Service Review*, 62(4): 668–83.

Garda Press Office (2010) 'Behaviour orders'. E-mail (01 November 2010).

Gelsthorpe, L. and Sharpe, G. (2006) 'Gender, youth crime and justice', in B. Goldson and J. Muncie (eds) *Youth Crime and Justice.* London: Sage Publications.

Gillen, J. (2006) 'The age of criminal responsibility: "the frontier between care and justice"', *Child Care in Practice*, 12(2): 129–39.

Giordano, P., Cernkovich, S., and Rudolph, J. (2002) 'Gender, crime and desistance: toward a theory of cognitive transformation', *American Journal of Sociology*, 107(4): 990–1064.

Goldson, B. (2010) 'The sleep of (criminological) reason: knowledge-policy rupture and New Labour's youth justice legacy', *Criminology and Criminal Justice*, 10(2): 155–78.

Goldson, B. (2011) '"Time for a fresh start", but is this it? A critical assessment of the report of the independent commission on youth crime and antisocial behaviour', *Youth Justice*, 11(1): 3–27.

Goldson, B. and Hughes, G. (2010) 'Sociological criminology and youth justice: comparative policy analysis and academic intervention', *Criminology and Criminal Justice*, 10(2): 211–30.

Gottfredson, M. and Hirschi, T. (1990) *A General Theory of Crime.* Stanford, CA: Stanford University Press.

Graham, J. and Bowling, B. (1995) *Young People and Crime, Home Office Research Study No.145*. London: Home Office.

Grasmick, H., Tittle, C., Bursik Jr, R., and Arneklev, B. (1993) 'Testing the core implications of Gottfredson and Hirschi's general theory of crime', *Journal of Research in Crime and Delinquency*, 30(1): 5–29.

Griffin, M. and Kelleher, P. (2010) 'Uncertain futures: men on the margins in Limerick City', *Irish Probation Journal*, 7: 24–45.

Griffin, K., Botvin, G., Scheier, L. Diaz, T., and Miller, N. (2000) 'Parenting practices as predictors of substance use, delinquency, and aggression among urban minority youth: moderating effects of family structure and gender', *Psychology of Addictive Behaviors*, 14(2): 174–84.

Grisso, T. (2000) 'What we know about youths' capacities as trial defendants', in T. Grisso and R. Schwartz (eds) *Youth on Trial: A Developmental Perspective on Juvenile Justice*. Chicago: Chicago University Press.

Grisso, T., Steinberg, L., Woolard, J., Cauffman, E., Scott, E., Graham, S., Lexcen, F., Reppucci, N., and Schwartz, R. (2003) 'Juveniles' competence to stand trial: a comparison of adolescents' and adults' capacities as trial defendants', *Law and Human Behavior*, 27(4): 333–63.

Gyateng, T., McSweeney, T., and Hough, M. (2010) *Key Predictors of Compliance with Community Supervision in London*. London: The Institute for Criminal Policy Research, King's College London.

Haigh, Y. (2009) 'Desistance from crime: reflections on the transitional experiences of young people with a history of offending', *Journal of Youth Studies*, 12(3): 307–22.

Haines, K. (1990) *After-care Services for Released Prisoners: A Review of the Literature*. A Report commissioned and funded by the Home Office Research and Planning Unit. Cambridge: Institute of Criminology, University of Cambridge.

Haines, K., (2009) 'The dragonisation of youth justice', in W. Taylor, R. Earle, and R. Hester (eds) *Youth Justice Handbook: Theory, Policy and Practice*. Cullompton: Willan Publishing.

Halpern-Felsher, B. and Cauffman, E. (2001) 'Costs and benefits of a decision: decision-making competence in adolescents and adults', *Journal of Applied Developmental Psychology*, 22(3): 257–73.

Hammarberg, T. (2008) 'A juvenile justice approach built on human rights principles', *Youth Justice*, 8(3): 193–6.

Hammersley, R., Marsland, L., and Reid, M. (2003) *Substance Use by Young Offenders: The Impact of the Normalisation of Drug Use in the Early Years of the 21st Century, Home Office Research Study No. 261*. London: Home Office.

Hargie, O., O'Donnell, A., and McMullan, C. (2011) 'Constructions of social exclusion among young people from interface areas of Northern Ireland', *Youth and Society*, 43(3): 873–99.

Harris, A. (2009) 'The role of power in shaming interactions: how social control is performed in a juvenile court', *Contemporary Justice Review*, 12(4): 379–99.

Hart, D. (2011) *Into the Breach: The Enforcement of Statutory Orders in the Youth Justice System*. London: Penal Reform Trust.

Haydon, D. (2009) *Developing a Manifesto for Youth Justice in Northern Ireland: Background Paper*. Belfast: Include Youth.

Haydon, D. and Scraton, P. (2000) '"Condemn a little more, understand a little less": The political context and rights implications of the domestic and European rulings in the Venables-Thompson case', *Journal of Law and Society*, 27(3): 416–48.

Hayes, J. and O'Reilly, G. (2007) *Emotional Intelligence, Mental Health and Juvenile Delinquency*. Cork: Juvenile Mental Health Matters.

Haynie, D., Petts, R., Maimon, D., and Piquero, A. (2009) 'Exposure to violence in adolescence and precocious role exits', *Journal of Youth and Adolescence*, 38(3): 269–86.

Healy, D. (2010) *The Dynamics of Desistance: Charting Pathways Through Change*. Cullompton: Willan Publishing.

Healy, D. and O'Donnell, I. (2005) 'Probation in the Republic of Ireland: context and challenges', *Probation Journal*, 52(1): 56–68.

Healy, D. and O'Donnell, I. (2010) 'Crime, consequences and court reports', *Irish Criminal Law Journal*, 20(1): 2–7.

Hearnden, I. and Millie, A. (2004) 'Does tougher enforcement lead to lower reconviction?', *Probation Journal*, 51(1): 48–58.

Hedderman, C. (2003) 'Enforcing supervision and encouraging compliance', in W. H. Chui and M. Nellis (eds) *Moving Probation Forward Evidence, Arguments and Practice*. Harlow: Pearson Education Ltd.

Hedderman, C. and Hough, M. (2004) 'Getting tough or being effective: what matters?', in G. Mair (ed.) *What Matters in Probation*. Cullompton: Willan Publishing.

Herrera, V. and McCloskey, L. (2001) 'Gender differences in the risk for delinquency among youths exposed to family violence', *Child Abuse and Neglect*, 25(8): 1037–51.

Hillian, D. and Reitsma-Street, M. (2003) 'Parents and youth justice', *Canadian Journal of Criminology and Criminal Justice*, 45(1): 19–41.

Hillyard, P., Rolston, B., and Tomlinson, M. (2005) *Poverty and Conflict in Ireland: An International Perspective*. Dublin: Institute of Public Administration and the Combat Poverty Agency.

Hoeve, M., Smeenk, W., Loeber, R., Stouthamer-Loeber, M., van der Laan, P., Gerris, J., and Semon Dubas, J. (2007) 'Long-term effects of parenting and family characteristics on delinquency of male young adults', *European Journal of Criminology*, 4(2): 161–94.

Hoffman, S. and Macdonald, S. (2011) 'Tackling youth anti-social behaviour in devolving Wales: a study of the tiered approach in Swansea', *Youth Justice*, 11(2): 150–67.

Hollin, C. (1996) 'Young offenders', in C. Hollin (ed.) *Working with Offenders: Psychological Practice in Offender Rehabilitation*. Chichester: Wiley.

Home Office (1992) *National Standards for the Supervision of Offenders in the Community 1992*. London: Home Office.

Home Office (1995) *National Standards for the Supervision of Offenders in the Community 1995*. London: Home Office.

Hopkinson, J. and Rex, S. (2003) 'Essential skills in working with offenders', in W. H. Chui and M. Nellis (eds) *Moving Probation Forward: Evidence, Arguments and Practice*. Harlow: Pearson Education Ltd.

Horgan, G. (2011) 'The making of an outsider: growing up in poverty in Northern Ireland', *Youth and Society*, 43(2): 453–67.

Horgan, G., Gray, A., and Conlon, C. (2010) *Young People not in Education, Employment or Training Policy Brief*. ARK Northern Ireland: Economic and Social Research Council, University of Ulster, Queen's University Belfast. Online. Available at: <http://www.ark.ac.uk/pdfs/policybriefs/policybrief3.pdf> (accessed 21 January 2012).

Hough, M., Ruuskanen, E., and Jokinen, A. (2011) 'Trust in justice and the procedural justice perspective: editors' introduction', *European Journal of Criminology*, 8(4): 249–53.

Hourigan, N. (2011) 'Lessons from Limerick: policing, children protection and regeneration', in N. Hourigan (ed.) *Understanding Limerick: Social Exclusion and Change.* Cork: Cork University Press.

Hucklesby, A. (2009) 'Understanding offenders' compliance: a case study of electronically monitored curfew orders', *Journal of Law and Society*, 36(2): 248–71.

Hughes, G., McGinnity, F., O'Connell, P., and Quinn, E. (2007) 'The impact of immigration', in T. Fahey, H. Russell and C. Whelan (eds) *Best of Times? The Social Impact of the Celtic Tiger.* Dublin: Institute of Public Administration.

Hughes, M. (1998) 'Turning points in the lives of young inner-city men forgoing destructive criminal behaviors: a qualitative study', *Social Work Research*, 22(3): 143–51.

Include Youth (2008) *A Manifesto for Youth Justice in Northern Ireland*. Belfast: Include Youth.

Independent Commission on Youth Crime and Antisocial Behaviour (2010) *Time for a Fresh Start: The Report of the Independent Commission on Youth Crime and Antisocial Behaviour*. London: The Police Foundation.

Independent Research Solutions (2008) *Effective Practice Lessons from Research: A Report of the Evaluation of the Attendance Centre Order*. Belfast: Youth Justice Agency.

Ireland, T. and Smith, C. (2009) 'Living in partner-violent families: developmental links to anti social behavior and relationship violence', *Journal of Youth and Adolescence*, 38(3): 323–39.

Irish Examiner (2011) 'Boy had almost 40,000 worth of cannabis in schoolbag', 14 October 2011.

Irish Prison Service (2010) *Annual Report of the Irish Prison Service 2009*. Dublin: The Stationery Office.

Irish Traveller Movement (n.d.) *Report on the Socio-Economic Consequences of the Control of Horses Act 1996 on the Traveller Community*. Online. Available at: <http://www.itmtrav.ie/uploads/EndofTheRoad.pdf> (31 January 2012).

Irish Youth Justice Service (2008) *National Youth Justice Strategy 2008-10*. Dublin: The Stationery Office.

Irish Youth Justice Service (2010) *Annual Report of the Irish Youth Justice Service 2009*. Dublin: The Stationery Office.

Iselin, A., DeCoster, J., and Salekin, R. (2009) 'Maturity in adolescent and young adult offenders: the role of cognitive control', *Law and Human Behavior*, 33(6): 455–69.

Jamieson, J., McIvor, G., and Murray, C. (1999) *Understanding Offending Among Young People*. Edinburgh: The Stationery Office.

Jarman, N. (2003) 'Victims and perpetrators, racism and young people in Northern Ireland', *Child Care in Practice*, 9(2): 129–39.

Jarman, N. (2004) 'From war to peace? Changing patterns of violence in Northern Ireland, 1990–2003', *Terrorism and Political Violence*, 16(3): 420–38.

Jarman, N. and Monaghan, R. (2003) *Racist Harassment in Northern Ireland*. Belfast: Office of the First Minister and Deputy First Minister.

Jones, J. (1964) 'The nature of compliance in correctional institutions for juvenile offenders', *Journal of Research in Crime and Delinquency*, 1(2): 83–95.

Kazdin, A. (2000) 'Adolescent development, mental disorders, and decision making of delinquent youth', in T. Grisso and R. Schwartz (eds) *Youth on Trial: A Developmental Perspective on Juvenile Justice*. Chicago: University of Chicago Press.

Kelly, K., Comello, M., and Hunn, L. (2002) 'Parent-child communication, perceived sanctions against drug use, and youth drug involvement', *Adolescence*, 37(148): 775–87.

Kemshall, H. (2008) 'Risks, rights and justice: understanding and responding to youth risk', *Youth Justice*, 8(1): 21–37.

Kemshall, H. and Wood, J. (2008) 'Risk and public protection: responding to involuntary and "taboo" risk', *Social Policy and Administration*, 42(6): 611–29.

Kennett, J. (2001) *Agency and Responsibility: A Common-Sense Moral Psychology*. Oxford: Oxford University Press.

Kerig, P., Ward, R., Vanderzee, K., and Arnzen Moeddel, M. (2009) 'Posttraumatic stress as a mediator of the relationship between trauma and mental health problems among juvenile delinquents', *Journal of Youth and Adolescence*, 38(9): 1214–25.

Kierkus, C. and Baer, D. (2003) 'Does the relationship between family structure and delinquency vary according to circumstances? An investigation of interaction effects', *Canadian Journal of Criminology and Criminal Justice*, 45(4): 405–29.

Kilcommins, S., O'Donnell, I., O'Sullivan, E., and Vaughan, B. (2004) *Crime, Punishment and the Search for Order in Ireland*. Dublin: Institute of Public Administration.

Kilkelly, U. (2005) *The Children's Court: A Children's Rights Audit*. Cork: University College Cork.

Kilkelly, U. (2006) *Youth Justice in Ireland: Tough Lives, Rough Justice*. Dublin: Irish Academic Press.

Krisberg, B., (2006) 'Rediscovering the juvenile justice ideal in the United States', in J. Muncie and B. Goldson (eds) *Comparative Youth Justice*. London: Sage Publications.

Laird, R., Pettit, G., Bates, J., and Dodge, K. (2003) 'Parents' monitoring-relevant knowledge and adolescents' delinquent behavior: evidence of correlated developmental changes and reciprocal influences', *Child Development*, 74(3): 752–68.

Lasley, J. (2003) 'The effect of intensive bail supervision on repeat domestic violence offenders', *Policy Studies Journal*, 31(2): 187–207.

Laub, J. and Sampson, R. (2001) 'Understanding desistance from crime', in M. Tonry (ed.) *Crime and Justice: A Review of Research Vol. 28*: 1–69. Chicago: University of Chicago Press.

Laub, J. and Sampson, R. (2003) *Shared Beginnings, Divergent lives: Delinquent Boys to Age 70*. Cambridge, MA: Harvard University Press.

Leibrich, J. (1993) *Straight to the Point: Angles on Giving up Crime*. Dunedin: University of Otago Press.

Little, M. and Steinberg, L. (2006) 'Psychosocial correlates of adolescent drug dealing in the inner city: potential roles of opportunity, conventional commitments, and maturity', *Journal of Research in Crime and Delinquency*, 43(4): 357–86.

Loeber, R. (1990) 'Development and risk factors of juvenile antisocial behavior and delinquency', *Clinical Psychology Review*, 10(1): 1–41.

Loeber, R. and Stouthamer-Loeber, M. (1986) 'Family factors as correlates and predictors of juvenile conduct problems and delinquency', in M. Tonry and N. Norris (eds) *Crime and Justice: An Annual Review of Research, Vol. 7*: 29–149. Chicago: University of Chicago Press.

Losoncz, I. and Tyson, G. (2007) 'Parental shaming and adolescent delinquency: a partial test of reintegrative shaming theory', *Australian and New Zealand Journal of Criminology*, 40(2): 161–78.

Lowe, N., Dawson-Edwards, C., Minor, K., and Wells, J. (2008) 'Understanding the decision to pursue revocation of intensive supervision: a descriptive survey of juvenile probation and aftercare officers', *Journal of Offender Rehabilitation*, 46(3/4): 137–69.

MacDonald, R., Webster, C., Shildrick, T., and Simpson, M. (2011) 'Paths of exclusion, inclusion and desistance', in S. Farrall, M. Hough, S. Maruna, and R. Sparks (eds) *Escape Routes: Contemporary Perspectives on Life After Punishment.* Abingdon: Routledge.

McAlister, S., Scraton, P., and Haydon, D. (2009) *Childhood in Transition: Experiencing Marginalisation and Conflict in Northern Ireland.* Belfast: School of Law, Queen's University Belfast.

McAra, L. and McVie, S. (2005) 'The usual suspects? Street-life, young people and the police', *Criminology and Criminal Justice*, 5(1): 5–36.

McAra, L. and McVie, S. (2010) 'Youth crime and justice: key messages from the Edinburgh study of youth transitions and crime', *Criminology and Criminal Justice*, 10(2): 179–209.

McAra, L. and McVie, S. (2011) 'Youth justice? The impact of system contact on patterns of desistance', in S. Farrall, S. Maruna, and R. Sparks (eds) *Escape Routes: Contemporary Perspectives on Life After Punishment.* Abingdon: Routledge.

McCluskey, J., Mastrofski, S., and Parks, R. (1999) 'To acquiesce or rebel: predicting citizen compliance with police requests', *Police Quarterly*, 2(4): 389–416.

McCrystal, P., Percy, A., and Higgins, K. (2007) 'School exclusion drug use and antisocial behaviour at 15/16 years: implications for youth transitions', *Vulnerable Children and Youth Studies*, 2(3): 181–90.

McCullagh, C. (2011) 'Getting a fix on crime in Limerick', in N. Hourigan (ed.) *Understanding Limerick: Social Exclusion and Change.* Cork: Cork University Press.

McCulloch, T. (2005) 'Probation, social context and desistance: retracing the relationship', *Probation Journal*, 52(1): 8–22.

McCulloch, T. (2010) 'Exploring community service, understanding compliance', in F. McNeill, P. Raynor, and C. Trotter, (eds) *Offender Supervision: New Directions in Theory, Research and Practice.* Abingdon: Willan Publishing.

McEvoy, K. and Mika, H. (2001) 'Punishment, politics and praxis: restorative justice and non-violent alternatives to paramilitary punishments in Northern Ireland', *Policing and Society*, 11(3-4): 359–82.

McGagh, M., Gunn, E., and Lillis, R. (2009) 'Strengthening families programme: an inter-agency approach to working with families', *Irish Probation Journal*, 6: 113–23.

McGee, H., Garavan, R., de Barra, M., Byrne, J., and Conroy, R. (2002) *The SAVI Report: Sexual Abuse and Violence in Ireland.* Dublin: Liffey Press.

McGuire, J. and Gamble, W. (2006) 'Community service for youth: the value of psychological engagement over number of hours spent', *Journal of Adolescence*, 29(2): 289–98.

McGuire, J. and Priestly, P. (1995) 'Reviewing what works: past, present and future, in J. McGuire (ed.) *What Works: Reducing Reoffending: Guidelines from Research and Practice.* Chichester: Wiley.

McIvor, G. (1992) *Sentenced to Serve: The Operation and Impact of Community Service by Offenders.* Aldershot: Avebury.

McIvor, G. (2002) *What Works in Community Service?* CJSW Briefing Paper 6. Edinburgh: Criminal Justice Social Work Development Centre for Scotland, University of Edinburgh.

McIvor, G. (2009) 'Therapeutic jurisprudence and procedural justice in Scottish drug courts', *Criminology and Criminal Justice*, 9(1): 29–49.

McIvor, G., Murray, C., and Jamieson, J. (2004) 'Desistance from crime: is it different for women and girls?', in S. Maruna and R. Immarigeon (eds) *After Crime and Punishment: Pathways to Offender Reintegration.* Cullompton: Willan Publishing.

McNeill, F. (2003) 'Desistance-focused probation practice', in W. H. Chui and M. Nellis (eds) *Moving Probation Forward: Evidence, Arguments and Practice.* Harlow: Pearson Education Ltd.

McNeill, F. (2006) 'Community supervision: context and relationships matter', in B. Goldson and J. Muncie (eds) *Youth Crime and Justice.* London: Sage Publications.

McNeill, F. (2009) 'Supervising young offenders: what works and what's right?', in M. Barry and B. Goldson (eds) *Youth Offending and Youth Justice, Research Highlights 52.* London: Jessica Kingsley Publishers.

McNeill, F. (2010) 'Youth justice: policy, research and evidence', in J. Johnstone and M. Burman (eds) *Youth Justice.* Edinburgh: Dunedin Academic Press.

McNeill, F. (2011) 'Probation, credibility and justice' *Probation Journal*, 58(1): 9–22.

McVerry, P. (1998) 'Government report to the U.N. Committee on the rights of the child', *Working Notes, 'Do Poor Children Deserve Perfect Teeth?' Issue* 31. Online. Available at: <http://workingnotes.ie/index.php/item/government-report-to-the-un-committee-on-the-rights-of-the-child> (accessed 31 January 2012).

McVie, S. (2009) 'Criminal careers and young people', in M. Barry and F. McNeill (eds) *Youth Offending and Youth Justice Research Highlights 52.* London: Jessica Kingsley Publishers.

McVie, S. (2011) 'Alternative models of youth justice: lessons from Scotland and Northern Ireland', *Journal of Children's Services*, 6(2): 106–14.

Magill, C. and Hamber, B. (2011) 'If they don't start listening to us, the future is going to look the same as the past: young people and reconciliation in Northern Ireland and Bosnia Herzegovina', *Youth and Society*, 43(2): 509–27.

Mair, G. and May, C. (1997) *Offenders on Probation, Home Office Research Study No.167.* London: Home Office.

Makkai, T. and Braithwaite, J. (1994) 'Reintegrative shaming and compliance with regulatory standards', *Criminology*, 32(3): 361–85.

Marsh, S. and Evans, W. (2009) 'Youth perspectives on their relationships with staff in juvenile correction settings and perceived likelihood of success on release', *Youth Violence and Juvenile Justice*, 7(1): 46–67.

Marshall, T. (1996) 'The evolution of restorative justice in Britain', *European Journal of Criminal Policy and Research*, 4(4): 21–43.

Maruna, S. (2001) *Making Good: How Ex-Convicts Reform and Rebuild Their Lives.* Washington, DC: American Psychological Association.

Maruna, S. and Farrall, S. (2004) 'Desistance from crime: a theoretical reformulation', *Kölner Zeitschrift für Soziologie und Sozialpsychologie*, 43: 171–94.

Maruna, S., Immarigeon, R., and LeBel, T. (2004) 'Ex-offender reintegration: theory and practice', in S. Maruna and R. Immarigeon (eds) *After Crime and Punishment: Pathways to Offender Reintegration.* Cullompton: Willan Publishing.

Maruna, S., Wright, S., Brown, J., van Marle, F., Devlin, R., and Liddle, M. (2007) *Youth Conferencing as Shame Management: Results of a Long-Term Follow-Up Study.* Online. Available at: <http://youthjusticeagencyni.gov.uk/document_uploads/SHAD_MARUNA_STUDY.pdf> (accessed 31 January 2012).

Matthews, B. and Hubbard, D. (2007) 'The helping alliance in juvenile probation: the missing element in the "what works" literature', *Journal of Offender Rehabilitation*, 45(1-2): 105–22.

Maxwell, G. and Morris, A. (2006) 'Youth justice in New Zealand: restorative justice in practice?', *Journal of Social Issues*, 62(2): 239–58.

May, C. and Wadwell, J. (2001) *Enforcing Community Penalties: The Relationship Between Enforcement and Reconviction, Findings 155*. London: Home Office.

Mayock, P. and O'Sullivan, E. (2007) *Lives in Crisis: Homeless Young People in Dublin*. Dublin: Liffey Press.

Mayock, P. and Vekić, K. (2006) *Homelessness in Dublin City: Key findings from the First Phase of a Longitudinal Cohort Study, the National Children's Strategy Research Series*. Dublin: The Stationery Office.

Milbourne, L. (2009) 'Valuing difference or securing compliance? Working to involve young people in community settings', *Children and Society*, 23(5): 347–63.

Milligan, S. (2010) 'Youth court statistics 2008/2009, statistics Canada catalogue No. 85-002-x', *Juristat*, 30(2): 1–37. Online. Available at: http://www.statcan.gc.ca/pub/85-002-x/2010002/article/11294-eng.pdf (accessed 31 January 2012).

Ministry of Justice (2011a) *Youth Justice Statistics 2009/10 England and Wales*. London: Ministry of Justice. Online. Available at: <http://www.justice.gov.uk/publications/docs/yjb-annual-workload-data-0910.pdf> (accessed 31 January 2012).

Ministry of Justice (2011b) *National Standards for the Management of Offenders in England and Wales*. London: Ministry of Justice.

Modecki, K. (2008) 'Addressing gaps in the maturity of judgment literature: age differences and delinquency', *Law and Human Behavior*, 32(1):78–91.

Modecki, K. (2009) '"It's a rush": Psychosocial content of antisocial decision making', *Law and Human Behavior*, 33(3):183–93.

Moffitt, T. (1993) 'Adolescence-limited and life-course-persistent antisocial behavior: a developmental taxonomy', *Psychological Review*, 100(4): 674–701.

Monteith, M., Lloyd, K., and McKee, P. (2008) *Persistent Child Poverty in Northern Ireland*. Belfast: Queen's University Belfast and Save the Children.

Moore, R. (2004) 'Intensive supervision and surveillance programmes for young offenders: the evidence base so far', in R. Burnett and C. Roberts (eds) *What Works in Probation and Youth Justice: Developing Evidence-Based Practice*. Cullompton: Willan Publishing.

Moore, R., Gray, E., Roberts, C., Taylor, E., and Merrington, S. (2006) *Managing Persistent and Serious Offenders in the Community: Intensive Community Programmes in Theory and Practice*. Cullompton: Willan Publishing.

Morgan, K. (1995) 'Variables associated with successful probation completion', *Journal of Offender Rehabilitation*, 22(3/4): 141–53.

Mulvey, E., Steinberg, L., Fagan, J., Cauffman, E., Piquero, A. Chassin, L., Knight, G., Brame, R., Schubert, C., Hecker, T., and Losoya, S. (2004) 'Theory and research on desistance from antisocial activity among serious adolescent offenders', *Youth Violence and Juvenile Justice*, 2(3): 213–36.

Muncie, J. (2005) 'The globalization of crime control – the case of youth and juvenile justice: neo-liberalism, policy convergence and international convention', *Theoretical Criminology*, 9(1): 35–64.

Muncie, J. (2009) *Youth and Crime,* 3rd edn. London: Sage Publications.

Muncie, J. (2011) 'Illusions of difference: comparative youth justice in the devolved United Kingdom', *British Journal of Criminology*, 51(1): 40–57.

Muncie, J. and Goldson, B. (2006) 'England and Wales: the new correctionalism', in J. Muncie and B. Goldson (eds) *Comparative Youth Justice*. London: Sage Publications.

Murray, C. (2010) 'Conceptualizing young people's strategies of resistance to offending as "active resilience"', *British Journal of Social Work*, 40(1): 115–32.

Nagin, D. (1998) 'Criminal deterrence research at the outset of the twenty-first century', in M. Tonry (ed.) *Crime and Justice: A Review of Research,* Volume 23: 1–42. Chicago: University of Chicago Press.

National Children's Strategy (2000) *The National Children's Strategy: Our Children-Their Lives*. Dublin: The Stationery Office.

NCISH National Confidential Inquiry into Suicide and Homicide by People with Mental Illness (2011) *Suicide and Homicide in Northern Ireland*. Manchester: University of Manchester. Online. Available at: <http://www.manchester.ac.uk/nci> (accessed 31 January 2012).

Nixon, E. and Halpenny, A. (2010) *Children's Perspectives on Parenting Styles and Discipline: A Developmental Approach, The National Children's Strategy Research Series*. Dublin: The Stationery Office.

Nolan, B. and Maître, B. (2007) 'Economic growth and income inequality: setting the context', in T. Fahey, H. Russell, and C. Whelan (eds) *Best of Times? The Social Impact of the Celtic Tiger*. Dublin: Institute of Public Administration.

Northern Ireland Courts and Tribunal Service (2011) *Judicial Statistics 2010*. Belfast: Northern Ireland Courts and Tribunal Service.

O'Donnell, I. (2007a) 'Crime and its consequences', in T. Fahey, H. Russell, and C. Whelan (eds) *Best of Times? The Social Impact of the Celtic Tiger*. Dublin: Institute of Public Administration.

O'Donnell, I. (2007b) 'A society on a knife edge', *Sunday Business Post*, 1 July 2007.

O'Dwyer, K. (2005) 'Victim-offender mediation with juvenile offenders in Ireland', in A. Mestitz and S. Ghetti (eds) *Victim-Offender Mediation with Young Offenders in Europe: An Overview and Comparison of 15 Countries*. Dordrecht: Springer Publications.

Office of the First Minister and Deputy First Minister (2006) *Our Children and Young People – Our Pledge: A Ten Year Strategy for Children and Young People in Northern Ireland 2006-2016*. Belfast: Office of the First Minister and Deputy First Minister.

Office of the Minister for Children and Youth Affairs (OMCYA) (2010) *State of the Nation's Children: Ireland 2010*. Dublin: The Stationery Office.

O'Leary, P. and Halton, C. (2009) 'Young persons' probation in the Republic of Ireland: an evaluation of risk assessment', *Irish Probation Journal*, 6: 97–112.

O'Mahony, D. and Campbell, C. (2006) 'Mainstreaming restorative justice for young offenders through youth conferencing: the experience of Northern Ireland', in J. Junger-Tas and S.H. Decker (eds) *International Handbook of Juvenile Justice*. Dordrecht: Springer.

O'Mahony, D. and Chapman, T. (2007) 'Probation, the state and community - delivering probation services in Northern Ireland', in L. Gelsthorpe and R. Morgan (eds) *Handbook of Probation*. Cullompton: Willan Publishing.

O'Mahony, D. and Doak, J. (2006) 'The enigma of community and the exigency of engagement: restorative youth conferencing in Northern Ireland', *British Journal of Community Justice*, 4(3): 9–24.

O'Mahony, D. and Seymour, M. (2001) 'The evaluation of the Watershed programme final report', unpublished report, School of Law, Queen's University Belfast.

Ombudsman for Children's Office (2011) *Young People in St. Patrick's Institution: A Report by the Ombudsman for Children's Office*. Dublin: Ombudsman for Children's Office.

Pardini, D., Loeber, R., and Stouthamer-Loeber, M. (2005) 'Developmental shifts in parent and peer infuences on boys' beliefs about delinquent behavior', *Journal of Research on Adolescence*, 15(3): 299–323.

Parsai, M., Marsiglia, F., and Kulis, S. (2010) 'Parental monitoring, religious involvement and drug use among Latino and non-Latino youth in the Southwestern United States', *British Journal of Social Work*, 40(1): 100–14.

Paternoster, R., Brame, R., Bachman, R., and Sherman, L. (1997) 'Do fair procedures matter? The effect of procedural justice on spouse assault', *Law and Society Review*, 31(1): 163–204.

Peterson-Badali, M., Abramovitch, R., Koegl, C., and Ruck, M. (1999) 'Young people's experience of the Canadian youth justice system: interacting with police and legal counsel', *Behavioral Sciences and the Law*, 17(4): 455–65.

Phoenix, J. (2010) 'Pre-sentence reports, magisterial discourse and agency in the youth courts in England and Wales', *Punishment and Society*, 12(3): 348–66.

Piquero, A. (2004) 'Somewhere between persistence and desistance: the intermittency of criminal careers', in S. Maruna and R. Immarigeon (eds) *After Crime and Punishment: Pathways to Offender Reintegration*. Cullompton: Willan Publishing.

Piquero, A., Farrington, D., and Blumstein, A. (2003) 'The criminal career paradigm', in M. Tonry (ed.) *Crime and Justice: A Review of Research, Vol. 30*: 359–506. Chicago: University of Chicago Press.

Piquero, A., Fagan, J., Mulvey, E., Steinberg, L., and Odgers, C. (2005) 'Developmental trajectories of legal socialization among serious adolescent offenders', *Journal of Criminal Law and Criminology*, 96(1): 267–98.

Police Service for Northern Ireland (PSNI) (2011a) *Annual Report of the Chief Constable and Accounts 2010-11*. Online. Available at: <http://www.psni.police.uk/chief_constables_annual_report_2010_to_2011.pdf.> (accessed 31 January 2012).

Police Service for Northern Ireland (PSNI) (2011b) *Paramilitary Style Incidents: Freedom of Information Request*. Online. Available at: http://www.psni.police.uk/para_style_incidents.pdf (accessed 31 January 2012).

Police Service for Northern Ireland (PSNI) (2011c) 'Query'. E-mail (16 December 2011).

Prior, D. and Mason, P. (2010) 'A different kind of evidence? Looking for "what works" in engaging young offenders', *Youth Justice*, 10(3): 211–26.

Prison Review Team (2011) *Review of the Northern Ireland Prison Service: Conditions, Management and Oversight of all Prisons Final Report*. Belfast: Department of Justice. Online. Available at: <http://www.dojni.gov.uk/index/publications/publication-categories/pubs-northern-ireland-prison-service/owers-review-of-the-northern-ireland-prison-service.pdf> (accessed 31 January 2012).

Probation Board for Northern Ireland (PBNI) (2011) *Best Practice Framework Incorporating Northern Ireland Standards*. Online. Available at: <http://www.pbni.org.uk/archive/Guide%20to%20Information/What%20are%20our%20priorities/ServiceStandards/PBNIstandardsmanual_v1%20MASTER%2029.09.11.pdf> (accessed 31 January 2012).

Probation Service (2008) *The Probation Service Strategy Statement 2008-10*. Dublin: The Stationery Office.

Probation Service (2011a) *Annual Report of the Probation Service 2010*. Dublin: The Stationery Office.

Probation Service (2011b) 'Probation statistics'. E-mail (24 October 2011).

Probation Service (2012) 'Statistics and information clarification'. E-mail (12 January 2012).

Prochaska, J., DiClemente, C., and Norcross, J. (1992) 'In search of how people change: applications to addictive behaviors', *American Psychologist*, 47(9): 1102–14.

Raby, R. (2005) 'What is resistance?', *Journal of Youth Studies*, 8(2): 151–71.

Raftery, M. and O'Sullivan, E. (1999) *Suffer the Little Children: The Inside Story of Ireland's Industrial Schools*. Dublin: New Island.

Raynor, P. and Vanstone, M. (1997) *Straight Thinking on Probation (STOP): The Mid-Glamorgan Experiment, Probation Studies Unit Report No. 4*. Oxford: Centre for Criminological Research, University of Oxford.

Raynor, P., Ugwudike, P. and Vanstone, M. (2010) 'Skills and strategies in probation supervision: the Jersey study', in F. McNeill, P. Raynor, and C. Trotter (eds) *Offender Supervision: New Directions in Theory, Research and Practice.* Abingdon: Willan Publishing.

Rex, S. (1999) 'Desistance from offending: experiences of probation', *Howard Journal of Criminal Justice*, 38(4): 366–383.

Roberts, C. (2004) 'Offending behaviour programmes: emerging evidence and implications for practice', in R. Burnett and C. Roberts (eds) *What Works in Probation and Youth Justice: Developing Evidence-Based Practice.* Cullompton: Willan Publishing.

Robinson, A. (2011) *Foundations for Offender Management: Theory, Law and Policy for Contemporary Practice*. Bristol: Policy Press.

Robinson, G. and McNeill, F. (2010) 'The dynamics of compliance with offender supervision', in F. McNeill, P. Raynor, and C. Trotter (eds) *Offender Supervision: New Directions in Theory, Research and Practice.* Abingdon: Willan Publishing.

Rodham, K., Brewer, H., Mistral, W., and Stallard, P. (2006) 'Adolescents' perception of risk and challenge: a qualitative study', *Journal of Adolescence*, 29(2): 261–72.

Rutherford, A. (1992) *Growing out of Crime: The New Era*, 2nd edn. Winchester: Waterside Press.

Salmi, V. and Kivivuori, J. (2006) 'The association between social capital and juvenile crime: the role of individual and structural factors', *European Journal of Criminology*, 3(2): 123–48.

Sampson, R. and Bartusch, D. (1998) 'Legal cynicism and (subcultural?) tolerance of deviance: the neighborhood context of racial differences', *Law and Society Review*, 32(4): 777–804.

Sampson, R. and Laub, J. (1993) *Crime in the Making: Pathways and Turning Points Through Life*. Cambridge, MA: Harvard University Press.

Sampson, R. and Laub, J. (2001) 'A life course theory of cumulative disadvantage and the stability of delinquency', in A. Piquero and P. Mazerolle (eds) *Life-course Criminology: Contemporary and Classic Readings*. Toronto: Wadsworth.

Schwalbe, C. and Maschi, T. (2010) 'Patterns of contact and cooperation between juvenile probation officers and parents of youthful offenders', *Journal of Offender Rehabilitation*, 49(6): 398–416.

Scott, E. (2000) 'Criminal responsibility in adolescence: lessons from developmental psychology', in T. Grisso and R. Schwartz (eds) *Youth on Trial: A Developmental Perspective on Juvenile Justice.* Chicago: University of Chicago Press.

Scott, E. and Steinberg, L. (2008) 'Adolescent development and the regulation of youth crime', *The Future of Children*, 18(2): 15–33.

Scott, E., Reppucci, N., and Woolard, J. (1995) 'Evaluating adolescent decision making in legal contexts', *Law and Human Behavior*, 19(3): 221–44.

Scottish Government (2011a) *National Outcomes and Standards for Social Work Services in the Criminal Justice System: Community Payback Orders Practice Guidance 2010.* Edinburgh: The Scottish Government.

Scottish Government (2011b) *Assisting Young People Aged 16 and 17 in Court: A Toolkit for Local Authorities, the Judiciary, Court Staff, Police, Crown Office and Procurator Fiscal Service.* Edinburgh: The Scottish Government.

Seymour, M. (2003) 'The community reintegration of young offenders on intensive probation supervision', unpublished thesis, Queen's University Belfast.

Seymour, M. (2006) *Alternatives to Custody.* Dublin: Business in the Community Ireland.

Seymour, M. (2012) 'The Youth Justice System', in C. Hamilton (ed.) *Irish Social Work and Social Care Law.* Dublin: Gill and MacMillan.

Seymour, M. and Butler, M. (2008) *Young People on Remand. The National Children's Strategy Research Series.* Dublin: The Stationery Office.

Seymour, M. and Costello, L. (2005) *A Study of the Number, Profile and Progression Routes of Homeless Persons Before the Court and in Custody.* Dublin: The Stationery Office.

Seymour, M. and Mayock, P. (2009) 'Ireland', in P. Hadfield (ed.) *Nightlife and Crime: Social Order and Governance in International Perspective.* New York: Oxford University Press.

Shapiro, C. and diZerega, M. (2010) 'It's relational: integrating family into community corrections', in F. McNeill, P. Raynor, and C. Trotter (eds) *Offender Supervision: New Directions in Theory, Research and Practice.* Abingdon: Willan Publishing.

Shapland, J. and Bottoms, A. (2011) 'Reflections on social values, offending and desistance among young adult recidivists', *Punishment and Society*, 13(3): 256–82.

Sharp, D. and Atherton, S. (2007) 'To serve and protect? The experiences of policing in the community of young people from black and other ethnic minority groups', *British Journal of Criminology*, 47(5): 746–63.

Sheppard, M. (2002) 'Depressed mothers' experience of partnership in child and family care', *British Journal of Social Work*, 32(1): 93–112.

Sherman, L. (1992) *Policing Domestic Violence: Experiments and Dilemmas.* New York: Free Press.

Shover, N. (1996) *Great Pretenders: Pursuits and Careers of Persistent Thieves.* Oxford: Westview Press.

Sickmund, M., Sladky, T., Kang, W., and Puzzanchera, C. (2011) *Easy Access to the Census of Juveniles in Residential Placement.* Online. Available at: <http://www.ojjdp.gov/ojstatbb/ezacjrp/> (accessed 31 January 2012).

Smandych, R. (2006) 'Canada: repenalization and young offenders' rights', in J. Muncie and B. Goldson (eds) *Comparative Youth Justice.* London: Sage Publications.

Smith, D. and Stewart, J. (1997) 'Probation and social exclusion', *Social Policy and Administration*, 31(5): 96–115.

Smith, H., Applegate, B., Sitren, A., and Springer, N. (2009) 'The limits of individual control? Perceived officer power and probationer compliance', *Journal of Criminal Justice*, 37(3): 241–7.

Smyth, M. (1998) *Half the Battle: Understanding the Impact of the Troubles on Children and Young People.* Derry: INCORE.

Solomon, E. and Allen, R. (2009) *Reducing Child Imprisonment in England and Wales - Lessons From Abroad.* London: Prison Reform Trust.

Springer, N., Applegate, B., Smith, H., and Sitren, A. (2009) 'Exploring the determinants of probationers' perceptions of their supervising officers', *Journal of Offender Rehabilitation*, 48(3): 210–27.

Sprott, J. (2004) *Understanding Cases of Failure to Comply with a Disposition.* Ottawa: Department of Justice. Online. Available at: <http://www.justice.gc.ca/eng/pi/yj-jj/res-rech/sprott/index.html> (accessed 31 January 2012).

Srole, L. (1956) 'Social integration and certain corollaries: an exploratory study', *American Sociological Review*, 21(6): 709–16.

St. Patrick's Institution Prison Visiting Committee (2009) *St. Patrick's Institution Prison Visiting Committee Annual Report for Year Ending 31 December 2008*. Dublin: Department of Justice, Equality and Law Reform.

Standing Committee for Youth Justice (2010) *Response to the Bradley Report and Healthy Children, Safer Communities*. London: SCYJ.

Steinberg, L. and Cauffman, E. (1996) 'Maturity of judgment in adolescence: Psychosocial factors in adolescent decision making', *Law and Human Behavior*, 20(3): 249–72.

Steinberg, L. and Schwartz, R. (2000) 'Developmental psychology goes to court', in T. Grisso and R. Schwartz (eds) *Youth on Trial: A Developmental Perspective on Juvenile Justice*. Chicago: University of Chicago Press.

Steinberg, L. and Scott, E. (2003) 'Less guilty by reason of adolescence: developmental immaturity, diminished responsibility, and the juvenile death penalty', *American Psychologist*, 58(12): 1009–18.

Steinberg, L., Chung, H., and Little, M. (2004) 'Reentry of young offenders from the justice system: a developmental perspective', *Youth Violence and Juvenile Justice*, 2(1): 21–38.

Stephenson, M., Giller, H., and Brown, S. (2007) *Effective Practice in Youth Justice*. Cullompton: Willan Publishing.

Stout, B. (2007) 'Should Northern Irish Probation learn from NOMS?', *Irish Probation Journal*, 4: 25–31.

Sunshine, J. and Tyler, T. (2003) 'The role of procedural justice and legitimacy in shaping public support for policing', *Law and Society Review*, 37(3): 513–48.

Supple, A. and Small, S. (2006) 'The influence of parental support, knowledge, and authoritative parenting on Hmong and European American adolescent development', *Journal of Family Issues*, 27(9): 1214–32.

Svensson, K. (2010) 'Performing caring power in a Scandinavian welfare state', *Revista de Asistent Social*, IX(3): 49–58.

Tata, C., Burns, N., Halliday, S., Hutton, N., and McNeill, F. (2008) 'Assisting and advising the sentencing decision process: the pursuit of "quality" in pre-sentence reports', *British Journal of Criminology*, 48(6): 835–55.

Tate, S. and Lyness, D. (2011) *Youth Justice Agency Annual Workload Statistics 2010/11 Statistical Bulletin 3/2011*. Belfast: Youth Justice Agency Statistics and Research Branch.

Tolan, P. and Titus, J. (2009) 'Therapeutic jurisprudence in juvenile justice', in B. Bottoms, C. Najdowski, and G. Goodman (eds) *Children as Victims, Witnesses, and Offenders*. New York: The Guildford Press.

Tollett, C. and Benda, B. (1999) 'Predicting "survival" in the community among persistent and serious juvenile offenders: a 12-month follow-up study', *Journal of Offender Rehabilitation*, 28(3/4): 49–76.

Treacy, D. (2009) 'Irish youth work: exploring the potential for social change', in C. Forde, E. Kiely, and R. Meade (eds) *Youth and Community Work in Ireland: Critical Perspectives*. Dublin: Blackhall Publishing.

Triseliotis, J., Boland, M., Hill, M., and Lambert, L. (1998) 'Social work supervision of young people', *Child and Family Social Work*, 3(1): 27–35.

Trotter, C. (1996) 'The impact of different supervision practices in community corrections: cause for optimism', *Australian and New Zealand Journal of Criminology*, 29(1): 29–46.

Trotter, C. (1999) *Working with Involuntary Clients: A Guide to Practice*. London: Sage Publications.

Trotter, C. (2010) 'Working with families in criminal justice', in F. McNeill, P. Raynor, and C. Trotter (eds) *Offender Supervision: New Directions in Theory, Research and Practice.* Abingdon: Willan Publishing.

Trotter, C. and Evans, P. (2010) 'Supervision skills in juvenile justice', in F. McNeill, P. Raynor, and C. Trotter (eds) *Offender Supervision: New Directions in Theory, Research and Practice.* Abingdon: Willan Publishing.

Tyler, T. (1990) *Why People Obey the Law*. New Haven, CT: Yale University Press.

Tyler, T. (2006a) *Why People Obey the Law*. Princeton: Princeton University Press.

Tyler, T. (2006b) 'Restorative justice and procedural justice: dealing with rule breaking', *Journal of Social Issues*, 62(2): 307–26.

Tyler, T. and Huo, Y. (2002) *Trust in the Law: Encouraging Public Co-operation with the Police and Courts.* New York: Russell Sage Foundation.

Ugwudike, P. (2010) 'Compliance with community penalties: the importance of interactional dynamics', in F. McNeill, P. Raynor, and C. Trotter (eds) *Offender Supervision: New Directions in Theory Research and Practice.* Abingdon: Willan Publishing.

Ugwudike, P. (2011) 'Mapping the interface between contemporary risk-focused policy and frontline enforcement practice', *Criminology and Criminal Justice*, 11(3): 242–58.

United Nations Committee on the Rights of the Child (2007) *General Comment No.10 Children's Rights in Juvenile Justice*. Geneva: United Nations Committee on the Rights of the Child.

United Nations Committee on the Rights of the Child (2008) *Consideration of Reports Submitted by States Parties under Article 44 of the Convention Forty-Ninth Session Concluding Observations: United Kingdom of Great Britain and Northern Ireland crc/c/gbr/co/4*. Geneva: United Nations Committee on the Rights of the Child.

Viljoen, J., Klaver, J., and Roesch, R. (2005) 'Legal decisions of preadolescent and adolescent defendants: predictors of confessions, pleas, communication with attorneys, and appeals', *Law and Human Behavior*, 29(3): 253–77.

Vogelvang, B. and van Alphen, H. (2010) 'Justice for all: family matters in offender supervision', in F. McNeill, P. Raynor, and C. Trotter (eds) *Offender Supervision: New Directions in Theory, Research and Practice.* Abingdon: Willan Publishing.

Warr, M. (2002) *Companion in Crime: The Social Aspects of Criminal Conduct.* Cambridge: Cambridge University Press.

Warr, M. (2005) 'Making delinquent friends: adult supervision and children's affiliations', *Criminology*, 43(1): 77–105.

Weijers, I. (2004) 'Requirements for communication in the courtroom: a comparative perspective on the youth court in England/Wales and the Netherlands', *Youth Justice*, 4(1): 22–31.

Welsh Assembly Government (2004) *All Wales Youth Offending Strategy*. Cardiff: Welsh Assembly Government.

Whyte, B. (2004) 'Responding to youth crime in Scotland', *British Journal of Social Work*, 34(3): 395–411.

Wikström, P. and Butterworth, D. (2006) *Adolescent Crime: Individual Differences and Lifestyles.* Cullompton: Willan Publishing.

Wild, W. (2011) 'Probation officer role orientation, helping alliance, and probationer readiness for change: the impact on juvenile offender recidivism', unpublished dissertation, Psychology Dissertations Paper 197, Philadelphia College of Osteopathic

Medicine. Online. Available at: <http://digitalcommons.pcom.edu/cgi/viewcontent.cgi?article=1196&context=psychology_dissertations&seiredir=1&referer=http%3A%2F%2Fwww.google.ie%2Furl%3Fsa%3Dt%26rct%3Dj%26q%3Dwild%252C%2520w.%2520%2> (accessed 31 January 2012).

Wong, K., Bailey, B., and Kenny, D. (2010) *Bail Me Out: NSW Young People and Bail*. Marrickville, New South Wales: Youth Justice Coalition. Online. Available at: <http://www.yjconline.net/BailMeOut.pdf> (accessed 31 January 2012).

Worrall, A. (1990) *Offending Women: Female Lawbreakers and the Criminal Justice System*. London: Routledge.

Worrall, A. (1997) *Punishment in the Community: The Future of Criminal Justice*. Harlow: Longman.

Worrall, A. and Hoy, C. (2005) *Punishment in the Community: Managing Offenders, Making Choices*. 2nd edn. Cullompton: Willan Publishing.

Youth Conference Rules (Northern Ireland) 2003 *Statutory Rules of Northern Ireland no. 473*. Online. Available at: <http://www.legislation.gov.uk/nisr/2003/473/pdfs/nisr_20030473_en.pdf> (accessed 31 January 2012).

Youth Justice Agency (YJA) (2008) *Annual Report and Accounts: Report of the Work of the Youth Justice Agency of Northern Ireland 2007-08*. London: The Stationery Office.

Youth Justice Board (2004) *National Standards for Youth Justice Services*. London: Youth Justice Board.

Youth Justice Board (2010) *National Standards for Youth Justice Services*. London: Ministry of Justice.

Zehr, H. (1990) *Changing Lenses: A New Focus for Crime and Justice*. Scottsdale, PA: Herald Press.

Zimring, F. (2000) 'Penal proportionality for the young offender: notes on immaturity, capacity, and diminished responsibility', in T. Grisso and R. Schwartz (eds) *Youth on Trial: A Developmental Perspective on Juvenile Justice*. Chicago: University of Chicago Press.

Author index

General index

For Product Safety Concerns and Information please contact our
EU representative GPSR@taylorandfrancis.com Taylor & Francis
Verlag GmbH, Kaufingerstraße 24, 80331 München, Germany